"What a fabulous book—any industry would be fortunate to have such an exceptional writer as an advocate."

—*Uma Outka, editor-in-chief of* Upline Journal

"Wave 4 is a tidal wave, carrying new millennium surfers into rich ports of call. Once again, Richard Poe is laser accurate in predicting the future. Unless you are online and networking, you may be in an unemployment line and not working! Instead of 'location, location, location,' the secret to wealth is 'direct, direct, direct!'"

—*Dr. Denis Waitley,*
author of The Psychology of Winning for the 21st Century

"Many times precious gems come in a rough form and are not recognized for their value. *Wave 4* certainly polishes the gem of network marketing to allow the brilliance of this great industry to be seen by all. Richard Poe once again makes me not only proud of the 28 years that I've been involved in this industry, but excited about the incredible future ahead for network marketing and all those that choose to embrace it."

—*Pat Davis, CEO of Millionaires in Motion, Inc.*

"A gold mine of informational business-building nuggets that every network marketer should seriously study."

—*Kevin D. Grimes, network marketing attorney*

"Richard Poe has done it again! A must-read for anyone who is ready to be unstoppable in creating a network marketing business beyond their wildest dreams!"

—*Cynthia Kersey, author of* Unstoppable

"A must-read. Seven Pillars of Wave 4 Success will definitely drive your business. We wish that we had them when we started over six years ago."

—*Karl and Fern Prazak, network marketing professionals,*
Gig Harbor, Washington

"I couldn't put the book down. Each lesson is clear, to the point, and right on. Richard Poe is legendary in his ability to explain the present and predict the future of network marketing. How fortunate that he would share his knowledge with such compassion and style. This book should become mandatory for all network marketers."

—*Hilton Johnson, founder of MLM University*

"*Wave 4* forced me to expand my belief of what is possible. Richard so vividly portrays the sheer magnitude of the opportunity in front of all of us. This is not a wave to be watched from the safe distance of the beach. Jump on. This wave could be the ride of our lives."

—*Gary Morgan, network marketing professional*

"As Faith Popcorn is to general marketing, Richard Poe is to network marketing. As with *Wave 3,* Poe continues to keep his finger on the pulse of network marketing in *Wave 4.* If you're serious about controlling your future, master the contents of this book and take it to the bank!"

—*Becky Lam, network marketing professional*

"An interesting blend of predictions, anecdotes, and insights relating to network marketing. A good read for novices and seasoned network marketers."

—*Larry Chonko, Holloway Professor of Marketing*

WAVE 4

Richard Poe

WAVE 4

Network

Marketing

in the

21st Century

PRIMA PUBLISHING

Library of Congress Cataloging-in-Publication Data
Poe, Richard
    Wave 4 : network marketing in the 21st century / Richard Poe.
        p.   cm.
    Includes index.
    ISBN 0-7615-1752-9 (hardback 0-7615-2478-9)
        1. Multilevel marketing—Forecasting. I. Title. II. Title: Wave 4.
    III. Title: Network marketing in the 21st century. IV. Title: Network
    marketing in the twenty-first century.
HF5415.126.P633   1999
658.8'4—dc21   99-37125
                                                                           CIP

99 00 01 02 HH 10 9 8 7 6 5 4 3 2 1
Printed in the United States of America

To my wife, Marie

CONTENTS

Books by Richard Poe:

Wave 3
The Wave 3 Way
The Einstein Factor
Black Spark, White Fire

For more information on *Wave 4*, see these Web sites:

www.richardpoe.com
www.buywave4.com

FOREWORD

John Milton Fogg, the co-founder of *Network Marketing Lifestyles* magazine, once told me that the entire decade of the 1990s, in terms of publishing in the field of network marketing, would one day be defined by the achievements of one man—Richard Poe.

It sounds like hyperbole. But I am inclined to accept John's assessment. It happens that I was Richard's boss at *Success* magazine in May of 1990, when he launched the decade with the first of his bombshells—a magazine column entitled, "Network Marketing: The Most Powerful Way to Reach Consumers in the '90s." John Fogg has called that article "the single most copied and widely distributed essay in the history of magazine publishing."

More hyperbole? I don't think so. The claim strikes me as feasible, considering the millions of individuals in the United States and abroad who are involved with network marketing. I remember the endless flow of people telling me they had read Richard's article. I recall the non-stop telephone calls to the magazine offices of *Success* from people wanting reprints, and I recall nearly a decade of hearing people reciting its headline and quoting phrases from the piece. From my own observation, I would go so far as to say that Richard's column may not only have been the most widely distributed feature in history, but also the one that made the deepest and most lasting imprint on readers' minds.

Now at the end of the decade, Richard has produced *Wave 4,* a book of such power that it dwarfs his previous achievements. Reading it is an exciting—I would say a thrilling—experience.

Like Richard's previous books in the *Wave* series, *Wave 4* reports on the staggering impact of network marketing—also known as multilevel marketing or MLM. Richard tells of its influence on the economy, on the world of business, on the lifestyles, wealth, and happiness of independent distributors who chose it as a way of life. But, in *Wave 4,* he also gives a unique glimpse into how this marketing method is positioned to revolutionize business in the age of the Internet.

Richard was the first to write about network marketing in a mainstream business publication, the first to publish books about it through a respected, mainstream publisher. As I write these words at the annual meeting of the Direct Selling Association in San Diego, I am reminded at every turn of the gigantic impression that Richard has made on the industry.

The event is attended by corporate executives from brand name companies like Amway, Avon, Excel Communications, Herbalife, Nu Skin, and Primerica. All during the four-day meeting, one hears the name Richard Poe and the term "Wave 3" again and again. Already, excitement about the prospect of *Wave 4* ripples through the crowd.

None of this comes as a great surprise to me. Early on, I realized that Richard's career was destined to be one sledgehammer blow after another. I first met Richard more than a decade ago, at a time when I was a magazine editor on the prowl for talent. Richard was a hot, 29-year-old writer in the field of entrepreneurship. I assigned him the back-page column previously written by billionaire magazine owner W. Clement Stone. The change was electrifying. Richard was an immediate smash hit, generating thousands of new readers each month.

Through the years, Richard surprised and amazed me with the variety of his interests. His omnivorous craving for knowledge of all kinds dated from childhood. A prodigy from a family of prodigies (Richard's gifted siblings include one brother who started college at age 14), Richard won a National Science Foundation scholarship at 15, entered college at 16 and pursued an eclectic academic career that took him, among other places, to Leningrad State University in the Soviet Union (where he studied Russian), and to the Buddhist-inspired Naropa Institute where he studied writing with the poet Allen Ginsberg.

One of Richard's keenest interests has been in the field of self-help and creativity. At *Success* magazine, he made the commitment to explore first-hand the ideas he was covering, from research into expanding your intelligence to the self-improvement principles of Dale Carnegie, Stephen Covey, and Napoleon Hill. Richard did not just write about goal-setting, self-discipline, and time management; he dove into the subjects with passionate intensity, applying each new idea to his own life in the most heartfelt manner, and for all to see.

Richard's zeal provoked sneers from some fellow staffers who fancied themselves too sophisticated to waste time on self-improvement. These negativists made it their mission to belittle the way Richard wore his heart on his sleeve. I am happy to recall that those envious detractors were left behind to eat Richard's dust; as the quality and quantity of his professional output soared exponentially, his critics were put to shame.

Today Richard occupies a highly envied position—that of the financially independent author. While others carped and gabbed, Richard parlayed his manifold interests into one blockbuster book after another.

His articles on creativity and self-improvement, for instance, gave rise to a stunning book, *The Einstein Factor*, co-written with Dr. Win Wenger. Based on leading-edge brain and mind research, it is one of the most extraordinary of all self-help books. Reader reviews testify to its awesome power to change lives.

With the fall of the Berlin Wall, Richard grabbed the chance to be among the first to write about the blossoming of free enterprise behind the Iron Curtain. Richard had long predicted communism's demise, having witnessed demonstrations and police crackdowns on the streets of Leningrad during his student days in 1978. Now Richard saw his vision come to pass.

Three times, I sent him to Russia to cover the historic changes there. Richard brought the capitalist revolution alive in a series of articles for *Success,* and later in a critically acclaimed book called *How to Profit from the Coming Russian Boom*—a book that correctly foretold the record 1996-1997 surge in the Russian stock market.

At *Success,* Richard's interest in ancient history often manifested itself in articles about the leadership qualities of Roman emperors or the intuitive practices of Greek philosophers. But I never realized how deeply engrossed he was in the ancient world until he wrote *Black Spark, White Fire,* a book that explored the controversial question of whether Egyptian explorers had discovered, colonized, and civilized a barbarous, tribal Europe thousands of years ago.

I found the book impossible to put down and simply canceled all my other activities so I could devote full time to reading its more than 500 pages of rich and flawless prose. It made the past come alive for me like no other book ever had. As a one-time editor-in-chief of *Science Digest,* I recognized the first-rate quality of Richard's scholarship. *Black Spark* was researched and written with mind-boggling perfection, as solid and full of riches as an ancient pyramid.

Of course, Richard's most successful books—and the ones for which he is best known—are his *Wave 3* books on network marketing. People often say that Richard has done more than any writer to promote and support network marketing. It is a well-meant compliment, but one that fails to point out the full measure of his contribution.

The field has always been aswarm with supporters and promoters. What it needed was someone with a powerful intellect, superb writing skills, and total integrity—someone willing to devote a massive effort to researching and reporting the perils, pitfalls, and remarkable rewards of this fast-changing, revolutionary field. Richard's unique talents, experience, temperament, and knowledge base made him the perfect candidate for the job.

Before Richard began writing about network marketing, a person outside the field was hard-pressed to know just what the business was all about. Everything was murky. Who could grasp what was going on or whether the practices made any business sense? Did the friend who fervently told you about the promises of MLM have any understanding himself? There was simply no way to tell.

Network marketing was indeed performing economic miracles but, from a communications standpoint, the field was in the Dark Ages. Myth and rumor swirled. Truth and falsehood were dancing partners. Countless transient publications sprouted up and died, living just long enough to blare headlines that might be true or might be lies—but who could tell the difference?

The field had thousands of self-annointed prophets, but their voices amounted to a din—undistinguishable, cacophonous, competing—a carnival full of seers and sages on soapboxes shouting out their revelations. No voice rose above the clamor and confusion. No vision had more than a splinter of the truth, a piece of reality, a fraction of the whole.

Richard alone saw the big picture, as he has in each field he has mastered. With Richard came reporting that was well organized and based on hundreds of hours of painstaking and professional research, analysis, and thought. Year after year, article after article, book after book, Richard has been on the leading edge—observing and chronicling one world-changing revolution after another. Through his writings on

MLM, he has created his own revolution by making network marketing a legitimate topic for the business press.

Unquestionably, *Wave 4* is the best of the series. It lays out, in the clearest terms, those little-known business trends that virtually guarantee a network marketing explosion in the twenty-first century. And it explains exactly how you can become part of that revolution.

So let's turn the page and man the barricades. Richard Poe has done it again!

Scott DeGarmo
Co-author, Heart to Heart
Former editor-in-chief and publisher, Success *magazine*

How did we live before 1993? It's hard to remember now. That was the year the National Center for Supercomputing Applications (NCSA) released the Mosaic browser. It enabled ordinary people, for the first time, to navigate the World Wide Web, using easy, point-and-click technology. Before 1993, only computer nerds knew the word *Internet*. Now millions of people buy and sell every day in cyberspace. The Internet has become the fastest-growing sector of the U.S. economy. Online shopping more than doubled, between 1997 and 1998, from $3 to $7 billion. The number of Internet users is expected to hit 510 million worldwide by 2003—177 million in the United States alone.

Future generations will look back upon the 1990s as a decade of extraordinary change. But the Internet was only one innovation among many. Some of the greatest transformations of the decade took place behind the scenes, little noticed by the mainstream media. It was during the 1990s, for instance, that an obscure industry known variously as network marketing, multilevel marketing, or MLM, reached an estimated $80 billion in sales. Roughly 8 million Americans were participating in MLM opportunities by the end of the decade, according to the Direct Selling Association. Like the Internet, network marketing emerged during the 1990s as one of the most powerful new engines driving the twenty-first-century economy.

I confess that I offer these statistics with a certain sense of relief. Those of us in the business of predicting future trends live in constant dread that one of our forecasts may turn out to be false. In this case, fate has spared me that humiliation. Network marketing not only fulfilled, but exceeded, my most optimistic projections.

The first of my forecasts on the subject hit the newsstands in May 1990, when I was senior editor at *Success* magazine. I had written a column called "Network Marketing: The Most Powerful Way to Reach Consumers in the '90s." The story, quite simply, changed my life. Overnight, I became a mini-celebrity in the MLM world. My column was everywhere. Thousands of photocopies were handed out at opportunity meetings around the country. Letters piled up unread in my office. My phone rang without ceasing. I was besieged by excited readers, thanking me for the article and clamoring for more MLM coverage.

My editor, Scott DeGarmo, soon ordered me and fellow senior editor Duncan Anderson to assemble a cover story on network marketing. We rounded up a crack team of writers, researchers, and industry experts, including *Upline* editor John Fogg, *Marketing Insights* editor Valerie Free, yippie-turned-yuppie-turned-MLM-guru Jerry Rubin, and Dr. Srikumar Rao, chairman of the marketing department of Long Island University, among others. Word of the story leaked to the MLM community weeks before it appeared, and the deluge of advance orders was so tremendous, we had to hire a full-time telemarketer to handle them. We called the story "We Create Millionaires" and ran it in the March 1992 issue. Newsstand sales doubled that month.

What was all the excitement about? It arose from the fact that *Success* was the first national business magazine to write positively about the network marketing industry. Until that point, MLMers could expect nothing but hatchet jobs from mainstream reporters. Journalists painted the industry as a get-rich-quick scheme, a pyramid game for the greedy, the desperate, and the gullible. *Success* had taken a huge risk by daring to call MLM the wave of the future. Happily, our judgment was vindicated within a few short years.

Nowadays, prestigious publications from the *Wall Street Journal* to the *New York Times* have begun covering the industry with a new tone of respect. Fortune 500 corporations, such as IBM and MCI, now market products and services through third-party MLM firms. Citigroup, the largest financial services company in the world, sells mutual funds and life insurance through a network marketing subsidiary called Primerica. For the last five years, the number one offering on the American Stock Exchange, in terms of profit growth, has been Pre-Paid Legal Services—an MLM firm. Sales representatives for the $5.2 billion cosmetics giant Avon Products are now routinely given the option of choosing a multilevel compensation plan.

It is almost hard to remember, nowadays, what it was like in that long-ago era when popular opinion linked multilevel marketing with chain letters and pyramid schemes. So completely has the industry's image been rehabilitated that MLM now counts among its champions such moral leaders as Stephen R. Covey—the world-renowned corporate ethics guru and author of the ten-million-copy bestseller *The 7 Habits of Highly Effective People.* "Network marketing gives people a creative opportunity to set up their own business and improve themselves," Covey opines in a March 1999 cover story in *Network Marketing Lifestyles* magazine.

Then, of course, there are my own writings. The success of *Wave 3* and its sequel, *The Wave 3 Way to Building Your Downline,* has reflected the industry's growth, in microcosm. When *Wave 3* was first published in 1994, its subject matter seemed so obscure that many bookstores refused to stock it— that is, until they were deluged by customer requests. Like MLM itself, the *Wave 3* books spread by word-of-mouth. They have not been advertised. They have not been reviewed in major publications. They have not been discussed on TV talk shows. Nor have I touted them on the lecture or seminar circuits. Yet the publishing world has been forced to take note, through the sheer force of their sales.

The *Wave 3* books erupted into public view in November 1996, when both appeared simultaneously on the *BusinessWeek* bestseller list. That same month, *The Wave 3 Way to Building Your Downline* appeared on the *New York Times* business bestseller list. Both books together have sold nearly half a million copies. It is a rare Barnes and Noble superstore that does not feature the *Wave 3* books prominently in its business section today.

News of my books spread through the same word-of-mouth networks that, every day, move hundreds of millions of dollars worth of skin cream, vitamins, herbal supplements, long-distance phone service, life insurance, and Internet access hookups. Their release was announced in fax, voice mail, and e-mail broadcasts; posted on Usenet message boards; touted in satellite conferences; and noted in the internal newsletters of MLM downlines across the country. The *Wave 3* books completely bypassed conventional marketing channels. I personally know of executives at certain prominent New York publishing houses who, to this day, are still scratching their heads, wondering how it happened.

What fuels the grassroots interest in my books is the same force that propelled network marketing itself into an $80 billion business—the yearning of the masses to attain personal and financial freedom through business ownership. Microtechnology has transformed corporate America. Automation is wiping out blue-collar jobs, while decentralization forces more and more white-collar workers into the open market, to peddle their skills as freelance contractors. Unfortunately, most people are ill-equipped to fend for themselves in the twenty-first-century marketplace. They lack the vision, resourcefulness, or ingenuity to create their own enterprises. So they turn, in ever-increasing numbers, to turnkey business systems such as network marketing.

In *Wave 3,* I introduced the concept of mass-marketed MLM—a new generation of network marketing opportunities that simplified and automated many aspects of the business. Wave 3 networkers came to rely on recruiting videos, fax-on-demand services, satellite conferencing, voice mail broadcasts, online prospecting, drop-shipping programs, and other technological innovations to grow their businesses. Wave 3 methods made network marketing truly accessible to the masses for the first time—triggering the industry's tremendous growth during the 1990s.

Now, as we enter the twenty-first century, my new book, *Wave 4,* explores MLM's final frontier—its conquest of corporate America. As jobs vanish, millions of MLM opportunities arise to replace them. The proliferation of new media dilutes the power of advertising, forcing more and more corporations to turn to MLM for direct, word-of-mouth access to the consumer. Network marketing companies are fast evolving into an alternative Distribution Freeway, through which an ever-growing number of Fortune 500 corporations choose to channel their goods and services.

The universal acceptance of MLM as a legitimate—and even superior—marketing tool by mainstream business has accelerated a phenomenon that futurist Barry Carter calls *mass privatization.* As explained in Carter's book *Infinite Wealth,* mass privatization entails a wholesale transfer of business ownership from centralized, corporate bureaucracies into the hands of millions of self-employed individuals.

"It is an organizing system based upon personal ownership and individual liberty," says Carter. "Each individual owns the specific work that he or she performs and is interconnected and interdependent with other individual partners through the Internet and Information Superhighway. There are no managers, salaries, bosses, hierarchies, employees, or central controls."

Network marketing is only one of the vehicles that Carter identifies as contributing to the mass privatization of our economy. But it is clearly the most successful vehicle that anyone has so far devised. MLM offers the first real opportunity for large numbers of people to break free from the nine-to-five grind. It is the twenty-first-century equivalent of the covered wagon and the homestead on the prairie. At a time when people feel increasingly hemmed in by rising costs, proliferating taxes, and expanding bureaucracies, MLM has brought back the free-roving spirit of the frontier.

In *Wave 4,* I offer a complete primer on network marketing in the twenty-first century. It explains what MLM is, how it works, and why it is fast becoming the most dynamic sector of the retail economy. It also gives soup-to-nuts instructions on how to choose a company, analyze a compensation plan, get your business started, and grow your downline, both in cyberspace and in the real world. Beginners will find a comprehensive introduction to the business. Veterans will find a cornucopia of inspiring stories and success tips from the masters.

As the half-million readers of my *Wave 3* books already know, I am not now, nor have I ever been, personally involved in the network marketing industry, either as a distributor or as a trainer. But I presume to offer instruction in this business for the same reason that a penniless, struggling writer named Napoleon Hill once took it upon himself, more than ninety years ago, to teach people the secret to making millions. Hill gleaned his success principles not from his own experience, but from extensive interviews with the leading businessmen of his day. He spent twenty years questioning such legendary figures as Henry Ford, Thomas Edison, Andrew Carnegie, and F. W. Woolworth, distilling from those conversations the most cherished and closely held secrets of the masters. Their hard-won insights formed the backbone of Hill's self-help classics, such as *Law of Success* and *Think and Grow Rich.*

In like manner, I have devoted much of the last ten years of my life to an exhaustive study of the network marketing phenomenon. Following Hill's lead, I have interviewed many of the men and women who made this industry great. Like Hill, I have offered their secrets to a world ever-hungry for self-help guidance. Though I would not presume to imply any comparison between Hill's mighty achievement and my own rather modest one, I do hope that I have gained, from Hill's example, some small measure of proficiency in offering practical and effective counsel to those ambitious and hard-working souls who aspire to economic liberty on the cyber-frontier.

As you embark, dear reader, upon your journey to financial freedom, I wish you the greatest success. May your enterprise thrive. May your faith never flag. And may you never bow your head to any master, save God Himself.

Richard Poe

ACKNOWLEDGMENTS

As the years go by, and the series of Wave books expands, the number of people to whom I find myself indebted seems to grow exponentially. The names that follow can only be a representative sampling. To those named and unnamed, I extend my heartfelt gratitude for your contribution to making *Wave 4* a success.

As always, I thank my wife Marie first and foremost. Thanks also to Duncan Anderson, Scott DeGarmo, John Fogg, Ben Dominitz, Susan Silva, Colby Olds, Jennifer Basye Sander, Stuart Johnson, Leonard Clements, Rod Cook, Ridgely Goldsborough, Corey Augenstein, Paul Zane Pilzer, Lloyd Jassin, and all the rest.

Grateful acknowledgment is made to *Network Marketing Lifestyles* magazine, which published earlier versions of chapters 11 and 40, as well as various other quotes, anecdotes, and observations interspersed throughout this book.

INTRODUCTION

Calvin Coolidge said it: "Persistence alone is omnipotent."

As a writer and editor in the field of entrepreneurship, I have seen the truth of this statement demonstrated time and again.

My friend and colleague Richard Poe is possibly the most persistent man I know. I met him when he joined the staff of *Success* magazine. One of the first things he did was to propose that we do a story about a business that didn't exist—at least not in the eyes of the mainstream business press. That business was network marketing.

Many of our colleagues opposed the idea with some passion, but Richard made a believer of me. He wrote and I edited a story called, "Network Marketing—the Most Powerful Way to Reach Consumers in the '90s." As soon as that issue went on sale, network marketers responded with a roar. Over the next few years, they made our phone and fax ring off the hook, and gave our mailman several pounds of extra mail to carry every day. Even then, some skeptics on the staff refused to accept the importance of MLM. But Richard kept hammering at the subject month after month, until their objections died away.

Richard went on to write best-selling books about MLM, such as *Wave 3* and *The Wave 3 Way to Building Your Downline*. And as his fortunes soared, so did the industry that he championed.

As a journalist, I used to find this a difficult industry to cover, because finding network marketers to talk to used to be like tracking down members of a secret society. Now I run into them wherever I go, from the copy shop down the road from me in the small town where I live to black-tie dinners at New York's Metropolitan Club.

As Richard's books explain, network marketing took off like a rocket in the 1980s. I would argue that it was no coincidence that it happened during that decade. The 1980s saw the birth of the Age of Entrepreneurship. It was during those years that "entrepreneur" ceased to be a dirty word in the business press.

Entrepreneurship is a very different thing from simply owning a small business. When I grew up in the 1950s and '60s, it was normal enough to own a gas station, a barber shop, or a dry cleaner. There were even self-employed artists, writers, and other assorted crazies. My family was full of them.

But it was understood that owning a business had the same purpose as having a job: to make a living. Only wild-eyed dreamers or real-estate shysters thought of owning a business as a means of changing their lives. That was the stuff of jokes, like the one about your nutty uncle who lost a bundle investing in a jackalope ranch. Trying to be an entrepreneur, to most people, meant you had failed at normal life and were trying to find a way to start the game over again, usually by cheating someone else.

But in the 1980s, there was a revolution of business ideas, powered by innovations in 800 numbers, computers, direct mail, plastics. Ordinary people, on their own or through their pension and mutual funds, were making scads of money in the stock market or by selling houses that had increased five-fold in value. Suddenly, it became almost normal to be an entrepreneur hoping to get a five, ten, or hundred-fold return on your investment.

Network marketing was part of that revolution. In what other business can ordinary people earn $10,000 per month, on an initial investment that consists of little more than an $80 starter kit, $300 a month in phone bills, $10,000 a year in car and travel expenses, $700 in depreciation on a computer, and $2,000 in postage and office supplies?

With the aid of new methods such as network marketing, the Age of Entrepreneurship demonstrated that work really can be life-changing. It taught people that you don't have to make others poorer in order to get richer. It showed that human creativity can bring forth wealth out of nothing, just as the silicon computer chip transformed sand—the most common substance on earth, except for sea water—into a multi-trillion-dollar industrial revolution.

In the 1980s, for the first time in recent memory, the term "entrepreneur" came to denote admiration rather than scorn. Correspondingly, the number of network marketers increased several hundred percent.

Now comes a new trend, which Richard calls Wave 4. As he demonstrates in this book, MLM has become one of the most dynamic forces driving the Information Age economy. Major corporations from IBM to Citigroup are using MLM to gain a competitive edge. More and more of the success stories you read in *The Wall Street Journal* are about companies with names like Amway, Herbalife, Primerica, and Excel.

We still have a long way to go. Even now, the news media lag far behind in recognizing MLM's true impact on the economy. To put it bluntly, to most people in the news business, the idea of ordinary people, many of them without academic degrees, running businesses worth millions of dollars is simply scary. But people today are not so dependent on official news sources as they once were.

More and more, when the mainstream media miss the story, the news gets out some other way. Nowadays, if you want to get the lowdown on Washington scandals or Balkan wars, forget CNN and the *New York Times*. Millions of people per day are getting their news uncensored through Web sites such as WorldNetDaily, NewsMax, Free Republic, and The Drudge Report. In the same spirit of do-it-yourself journalism, Richard Poe has bypassed the mainstream media and brought the good news about network marketing to millions of people.

We have seen striking evidence of the public's interest in MLM at my own publication, *Network Marketing Lifestyles*. Until we went on sale in March of 1999, there was no nationally distributed, glossy magazine for network marketers. The cover of our first issue featured Stephen R. Covey, author of the 10-million-copy bestseller *The 7 Habits of Highly Effective People*. In that interview, Stephen openly endorses network marketing as a business and as a way of life. Why did he say this to us and not to the countless other interviewers he's talked to in the past 15 years? Because no mainstream reporter ever bothered to seek his opinion on the subject.

Launching this magazine has been a bit like walking into a professional ballpark and discovering that the game has begun, but your team is the only one that's showed up. No small amount of the credit for this achievement must go to Richard, who showed us the way many years ago, when he wrote that first column about network marketing.

In *Wave 4*, Richard breaks new ground, showing why network marketing is uniquely positioned to profit in the business era just dawning—when entrepreneurial companies and individuals make the trends. Read on. It's your turn to join the power brokers.

Duncan Maxwell Anderson
editorial director, Network Marketing Lifestyles

PART ONE WAVE 4

The New Frontier

CHAPTER 1

The New Pioneers

Whenen the tears came, they took Lisa Wilber by surprise.
What on earth was she crying about? Until that moment,
Lisa had not realized just how upset she felt.

The day had begun routinely enough. Lisa had waited
two hours for the electric man to arrive. Her payment was
four months late, and the electric company was sending a
man to shut the power off. Lisa had waited for him, staring
out the window with $46 clutched in her hand—just enough
to keep the power on for another month.

She knew she was lucky to have that money. So why the
tears? Maybe it was the disgusted way the electric man had
rolled his eyes at her when she came flying out of the trailer
in her sweatsuit, brandishing the money. As Lisa clambered
through the snow, her boot laces flying and her hair wild,
she was acutely conscious of how shabby she looked. The
trailer park, too, was a mess. All around were snowed-in
driveways, dogs barking, broken refrigerators, and rusty
cars disintegrating on cinder blocks.

"The way he rolled his eyes," Lisa remembers, "it felt to
me like he was looking down his nose at me. To him, I
looked like a trailer-park person, like I'd always been that
way, and always would be."

In fact, Lisa had lived in a trailer only two years. But it
seemed to get harder, all the time, to imagine getting out.
Everything she tried just seemed to go wrong. Months be-

fore, Lisa had been laid off from her secretarial job with a software firm. Work was scarce in rural New Hampshire, especially now, in the grip of recession. Lisa's husband barely managed to scrounge up a few hundred dollars per month with his woodcutting business.

They subsisted on macaroni and cheese. Their rattletrap Yugo broke down several times a week. When they needed to buy gasoline, they would pull out the seat cushions, looking for any spare change they might have dropped. Lisa's world had shrunk to a 12- by 70-foot trailer, with only a wood-burning stove to heat it. In the winter, plastic sheets taped over the windows rattled in the breeze, and talk shows gabbled softly on the television all day long. Sometimes Lisa just wanted to scream. That day, when the electric man came, was surely one of them. She went back to the trailer after he was gone, sat down on the couch, and wept until she had no more tears left to cry.

A LOG-CABIN MENTALITY

If you had told Lisa Wilber, at that moment, what loomed in her future, she would not have believed it. Lisa was destined, in just a few years, to draw a six-figure income from her own multimillion-dollar sales organization. Never again would she worry about being laid off, because Lisa would be her own boss. She would take her place among the chosen few, those entrepreneurs who had had the foresight to plan ahead. She would greet the twenty-first century with confidence, secure in the knowledge that her business was fortified against the winds and storms of the global economy.

In short, Lisa was a pioneer. Her drafty trailer was the Information Age equivalent of a sod house on the prairie or a log cabin in the Rockies. Cut off from all possibility of corporate employment, Lisa was forced to adopt a frontier mindset. She had to banish all thought of weekly paychecks, health benefits, vacations, and pensions. She had to look within for the strength to survive.   •

Paradoxically, it was this new way of thinking—forced on Lisa against her will—that would save her. While others clung desperately to their jobs, fearful of any change, Lisa was forced to let go. She became a modern-day homesteader. Generations of Americans had trod this lonely path before. Like them, Lisa would fend for herself in a rugged and pitiless environment. Like the homesteaders of old, Lisa would battle discouragement every day. But also like them, she would conquer her fears and build a new life for herself and her family.

THE RIGHT TOOLS

The old-time pioneers equipped themselves with tools, such as the Winchester rifle and the Colt .45 "Peacemaker," uniquely crafted to help them conquer the western wilderness. Information Age frontiersmen will also pack special weapons—turnkey business strategies designed to help ordinary people thrive in the cyber-economy.

> What is network marketing? It is a strategy for selling products whereby independent salesmen are permitted to recruit other salesmen and to draw commissions from the sales of their recruits.

In her quest for self-sufficiency, Lisa armed herself with one of the most potent of these weapons. It goes by many names. Some call it network marketing, others multilevel marketing, and some just plain MLM. It is not really new. This powerful business technique was invented over fifty years ago. But in the last ten years, late-breaking technological developments have made its peculiar virtues obvious to the corporate mainstream, in a way they never were before.

What is network marketing? It is a strategy for selling products whereby independent salesmen are permitted to recruit other salesmen and to draw commissions from the sales of their recruits. In an MLM organization, you recruit people, who recruit others, who, in turn, recruit others, and so on down the line. Ordinary sales representatives thus acquire the opportunity to build a money-making organization, many levels deep, that can number in the hundreds or even thousands of people.

AN $80-BILLION BUSINESS

In years past, network marketing was dismissed by many business leaders as a get-rich-quick scheme, analogous to chain letters and pyramid scams. But those days are gone. Today Fortune 500 corporations flock to do business through MLM networks, and Wall Street analysts sing the praises of multilevel sales methods.

Indeed, network marketing has grown into one of the driving forces of the twenty-first-century economy. Reliable statistics for MLM's global growth are difficult to pin down, since many companies do not report their sales or membership figures to any trade organization. Nevertheless, based upon available data from the Direct Selling Association (DSA) in Washington, D.C., as well as other industry sources, *Network Marketing Lifestyles* editorial director Duncan Maxwell Anderson estimates that annual sales through MLM organizations have reached about $20 billion in the United States and $80 billion worldwide. The DSA conservatively estimates that about 8 million people engage in network marketing, in the United States alone.

Why do they do it? Because MLM provides an answer to one of the most nagging questions facing people in the Information Age: How do you make a living in a world where there are no more jobs?

DO IT YOURSELF

Frontiers, in every age, offer boundless opportunity. But one thing they don't offer is jobs. The first homesteaders who arrived on the Great Plains were entirely on their own. They had to build their own houses, dig their own wells, plow their own fields, and raise their own livestock. Otherwise, they would have starved.

Life on the cyber-frontier will work much the same way. As the Information Age dawns, it is clear that jobs, as we know them, are becoming obsolete. Millions of people have been laid off from corporate positions in the last twenty years. Many have looked in vain for other jobs with comparable pay, benefits, or security. In the old days, layoffs were seen as a temporary cost-cutting measure. Companies would slash their payrolls to get through tough times. But as soon as the economy picked up, they would hire their workers back. Not anymore.

> As the traditional workforce shrinks, the contingent workforce—those people working on contract, with flexible or part-time hours—grows at an ever-accelerating pace.

Downsizing today happens for a different reason. Companies lay off workers because their plants have moved out of the country—permanently— or because automation has made human effort unnecessary. "Technology makes companies more and more efficient—with fewer and fewer people," says economist Paul Zane Pilzer, author of *Unlimited Wealth, Other People's Money,* and *God Wants You to Be Rich.* "The most profitable companies are the ones doing the most downsizing. That process will continue to accelerate."

Nowadays, downsizing continues through fat and lean times alike. Most of the jobs being slashed will never come back. Even those people who continue working must often change their status from that of employee to freelance contractor. Corporations prefer freelancers, so they can limit a worker's hours as needed and avoid paying benefits. As the traditional workforce shrinks, the contingent workforce—those people working on contract, with flexible or part-time hours—grows at an ever-accelerating pace.

THE DEATH OF JOBS

In *The Sovereign Individual,* economic forecasters James Dale Davidson and Lord William Rees-Mogg predict that the twenty-first century will see the "death of jobs," as we know them. Only in recent years, they explain, has the word *job* come to imply lifetime employment. Past generations understood the term to mean a one-time task that you were hired to do. A blacksmith, for instance, would get a job shoeing a horse. A seamstress would get a job sewing a dress. But no one expected those jobs to last for life. No one expected health benefits, pensions, or gold watches. "Before the industrial era," they write, "permanent employment was almost unknown."

In the Information Age, Rees-Mogg and Davidson predict, the word *job* will return to its older meaning. It will refer to specific and temporary tasks. "Already, major corporations such as AT&T have eliminated all permanent job categories," they observe. "Positions in that large firm are now contingent."

Former Labor Secretary Robert Reich estimates that 20 percent of the U.S. workforce is already self-employed today. If Rees-Mogg and Davidson are correct, that figure may approach 100 percent in the years ahead.

THE END OF RETIREMENT

On the old frontier, there was only one way to ensure a safe and comfortable retirement: you had to build a business—usually a farm—that would continue earning money till the day you died. Information Age pioneers will be faced with a similar challenge. With neither corporate nor government pensions to lean on, they will need to feather their own nests by building strong and self-sustaining businesses.

Independent contractors are not entitled to receive corporate pensions. In the twenty-first century, they will almost certainly get no government money either. Tax-and-spend retirement schemes, such as Social Security, have already run out of steam. No one can afford the taxes any longer to keep them going. Some place their hopes in a new plan to divert Social Security taxes into personal retirement funds, invested in the stock and bond markets. But markets are subject to booms and busts. One good bust, and you can kiss your retirement good-bye.

Even in the happy event that the government would simply give up, allowing people to keep their own money and put it in the bank, many would still fail to achieve a comfortable retirement. At current rates of inflation and interest, a forty-year-old in the year 2000 would need to sock away at least $3 million in order to enjoy a comfortable, middle-class lifestyle in his golden years. But how many middle-class families do you know that can afford to save $3 million?

THE CYBER-FRONTIER

In the nineteenth century, millions flocked to the frontier in Conestoga wagons. Today, it is the frontier that is coming to us. Everyone alive today must confront the cyber-economy, whether we like it or not. How we fare in the years ahead will depend entirely on how soon we accept the inevitable and how energetically we prepare for self-sufficiency. It is a hard life on the cyber-frontier, a life of bone-crushing labor; of hot competition; of risk, fear, and suspense. But just as the old-time pioneers built fortunes in the West, so we have opportunities before us to thrive and prosper as never before, in ways that we could never have imagined back in the old corporate world.

Experts have long predicted that the twenty-first century would be an age of luxury, the Internet a cornucopia of customized service that would cater to consumers' every whim. And so they will be. But we must earn those luxuries by the sweat of our brow. We must earn them by making smart decisions. Our livelihood, in the years to come, will be largely determined by the choices we make today, by the strategies we select for building our Information Age businesses. Those who choose network marketing will be taking a giant step in the right direction.

CHAPTER 2

The Leverage Principle

"Give me a place to stand on," said Archimedes, "and I will move the earth." The greatest of Greek mathematicians was speaking, of course, about the power of leverage. He meant that if he had a large enough fulcrum, a lever of sufficient length, and a place to set up this apparatus, he would be able to move the earth, much as a farmer levers a stone from his field.

Lever and fulcrum are among the simplest devices known to man. Yet they enable a workman to hoist many times his own weight. In the business world, the Leverage Principle is applied with even more wondrous effect. CEOs gain leverage by borrowing money, enabling them to expand operations, raise their stock price, and increase profits far beyond what they could have managed on their cash flow alone. A manager gains leverage by delegating tasks to employees, thus multiplying his personal efforts many times over. "I would rather have one percent of the efforts of a hundred people," billionaire oil tycoon J. Paul Getty is reputed to have said, "than a hundred percent of my own efforts."

Getty was right. No one person has the time or energy to build a successful business on his own. An entrepreneur's success is tied directly to the amount of leverage he can bring to bear. That's where network marketing comes in. It is a system specifically crafted to give ordinary people access to extraordinary leverage.

IN THE BEGINNING

The first Americans to practice leveraged salesmanship were the Indians. They employed the Leverage Principle to great advantage, both in trading among themselves and in dealing with the white man. Agents of the Hudson's Bay Company in Canada, for instance, discovered that the native people from whom they purchased beaver pelts employed a kind of franchise system. Rather than dealing with the English one-on-one, the Indians would descend on the trading post once a year with a great fleet of canoes. Each fleet was commanded by a trading chief, specially selected for his negotiating skill. The chief would charge the other Indians what amounted to a franchise fee for the privilege of joining his fleet—typically, one beaver pelt per canoe. For this price, Indian merchants gained the advantage of being part of a large trading party, with greater bargaining clout.

> An entrepreneur's success is tied directly to the amount of leverage he can bring to bear.

STRENGTH IN NUMBERS

The power of Indian trading blocs was evident in their ability to get the prices they wanted from the white man. The price of a beaver pelt, for example, plummeted from twenty to ten shillings on the London fur market from 1785 to 1793. Logically, the white traders in North America should have made up for their losses by cutting the price paid to native suppliers for each pelt. But the Indians continued to demand the same price as before.

"If they believed . . . that three beaver skins were worth one ax head, then that was that," says Professor Abraham Rotstein of the University of Toronto. According to Rotstein, the frontier prices for thirty-five different trade goods stayed roughly the same for more than a hundred years. No matter how wildly their value fluctuated on the London markets, the Indians would simply not agree to any price changes. And because they employed the Leverage Principle—bargaining collectively, through trading "franchises"—they had the power to enforce their will.

YANKEE PEDDLERS

Yet white traders also knew how to exploit leverage. Great conglomerates like the Hudson's Bay Company and John Jacob Astor's American Fur Company muscled their way ever deeper into North America, relying on their massive size to gain the best deals. As the white man grew in numbers and strength, he ultimately drove the Indians out of business.

During this time, a new economy emerged, in which colonists purchased supplies from "Yankee peddlers"—itinerant salesmen who traveled the country by foot and cart. The peddlers prospered for many years. But they did not use leverage. Each man looked out for himself. Consequently, the Yankee peddlers had little ability to fight back when wholesalers began to employ their own leverage, using the new railroad and canal systems in the 1840s to ship directly to shopkeepers. The new system bypassed the peddlers entirely, and they nearly vanished as a species from the American landscape.

THE DIRECT-SELLING REVOLUTION

Only by exploiting the Leverage Principle for their own purposes did peddlers manage to fight their way back. A new type of salesman arose in the late nineteenth and early twentieth centuries. Like the old-time peddler, he worked for himself. But unlike the peddler, he sold a well-known product with a national brand name. Avon Products, Fuller Brush Company, and Electrolux were among the legendary firms that arose during this period, selling such wares as perfume, brushes, and vacuum cleaners door to door. They were called "direct selling" companies, because they sold directly to the consumer rather than to shops and department stores.

For the manufacturer, direct selling offered the opportunity to put a product right in the customer's face, rather than letting it sit on a store shelf, lost among hundreds of other items. For the salesman, these networks offered wholesale discounts, protected territories, and the prestige of a major brand name. When an Avon lady or a Fuller Brush man came to visit, customers took for granted that their products were trustworthy.

The direct salesman, like the Indian trader before him, gained leverage by working through a network. This new way of selling caught on like wildfire. "There were at least 200,000 persons selling door-to-door in 1920," writes University of California management professor Nicole Woolsey Biggart, in her book *Charismatic Capitalism,* "double the number in 1900."

THE TIME TRAP

Yet there were limits on the direct salesman's leverage. He was caught in a time trap. One man could only hawk so many Fuller brushes or Electrolux vacuum cleaners in the course of a day. His income was limited by the number of hours he worked. As long as he expended physical effort, knocking on doors and wagging his tongue, he made money. But the moment he stopped working—whether to sleep at night, to spend Sunday with his family, or even to nurse a cold—his earnings evaporated. And woe to the man who suffered crippling injury or failing health. His income would decline in proportion to his incapacity.

In short, the early direct sellers earned *linear income*— money paid in exchange for time. Most people, in fact, earn linear income. It's a perfectly fine way to make a living. Doctors, lawyers, and accountants certainly do well on this sort of income. But there is no leverage to it. No matter how much linear income you receive, you must still report for duty and perform physical work—whether arguing a case, examining a patient, or crunching a spreadsheet—in exchange for every penny you make. You are still tied to a forty-hour work week. Your income will never rise past a certain point, dictated by the number of hours available in your working life.

RESIDUAL INCOME

The only kind of income that provides real leverage is *residual* income. This is money that keeps coming in, long after you have completed the work. It is the kind of money that bestselling authors and hit songwriters earn from their royalties, the kind that investors and business owners draw from their stock dividends. Once you have established a residual income stream, it keeps on flowing, even if you decide to take a year off and lie on the beach.

> Only from residual income do great fortunes arise.

Only from residual income do great fortunes arise. Unfortunately, direct selling was unable to offer this benefit in its early years. Thousands of would-be Horatio Alger heroes beat on doors across America, through the 1920s and '30s. But only those who gave up on direct selling and moved on to start their own businesses actually attained financial freedom. The need was great for a new type of work that would combine the accessibility of direct selling with the residual income of genuine business ownership. That demand would soon be fulfilled in a remarkably innovative way.

CHAPTER 3

The Multilevel Solution

Most experts agree that Carl Rehnborg was the first entre-preneur to successfully employ a network marketing pro-gram. Other companies had only flirted with such methods before. As far back as the 1920s, some direct-selling firms had paid one-time finder's fees to their representatives for each new salesman they recruited. Others had even allowed salesmen to collect a percentage of their recruits' gross sales for a limited period of time, say, for the first sixty days after the recruit had joined. But Rehnborg appears to have been the first to allow salesmen to draw permanent commissions from their recruits, a steady income stream that would keep on flowing through the entire life span of the business.

It all began during the 1920s, when Rehnborg had been an overseas manufacturer's representative in China. Civil war broke out, and Rehnborg was trapped for a year in the for-eign settlement of Shanghai. Forced to live on a starvation diet of rice and water, he supplemented his rations by making soup from plants, grass, and even rusty nails (for iron).

Rehnborg's experience taught him profound lessons about the value of nutrition. Back in the United States, he used his training as a chemist to develop food supplements made from alfalfa, parsley, spinach, watercress, carrots, and various minerals and vitamins. He started a company to sell these products in 1934. Originally called the California Vitamin Company, it was later rechristened Nutrilite Products, Inc.—a name destined to resound in the annals of entrepreneurship.

MULTI-TIERED COMMISSIONS

Operating as a conventional direct-selling firm, Nutrilite prospered for many years. But in 1945, Rehnborg tried something different. He introduced a new plan for compensating Nutrilite salesmen. Some accounts say that the plan was developed by Rehnborg himself. Others hold that it was the brainchild of Nutrilite distributors Lee Mytinger and William Casselberry. Whoever invented it, the plan exhibited most of the features that we commonly associate with network marketing today.

It allowed any Nutrilite distributor with twenty-five regular retail customers to recruit new salesmen and to draw a 3 percent commission from their sales. This was not a one-time finder's fee or a temporary reward, but a permanent business arrangement that would last as long as the recruit stayed in Nutrilite. Ordinary direct sellers now had the ability, for the first time, to build a sales organization that could generate residual income. Like bestselling authors, oil tycoons, or Wall Street investors, Nutrilite distributors could now gain leverage from the efforts of other people. Many achieved stunning success under the new system.

MULTIPLY YOUR EFFORTS

Rehnborg's key breakthrough was to allow Nutrilite representatives to draw compensation not only from the sales of their recruits, but also from the recruits of their recruits, and so on. This multilevel arrangement offered staggering potential for growth. You could now recruit others to do your *recruiting* for you, not just your selling. Each new salesman (or "distributor") that you brought on board now doubled your ability to recruit others. Simple arithmetic demonstrates how this doubling power works to the network marketer's advantage. Any time you multiply a number by the same quantity over and over again—whether you are doubling, tripling, quadrupling, or whatever—you are said to be increasing that number *geometrically*. The strange magic of geometric progression offers multilevel sales leaders the chance to grow their businesses at breathtaking speed.

GEOMETRIC GROWTH

Consider how you would respond if someone offered you the choice between $100,000 in cash or a penny that was guaranteed to double each day for a month. Those who understood the arithmetic would have no trouble deciding. They would ask for the penny, because they would understand that, after thirty-one days of doubling (assuming that the first doubling began on day one) the penny would have multiplied to over $21 million. That's geometric growth. Multilevel marketing puts the same mathematical force to work in building your business.

Let's take a hypothetical case. Suppose you recruited five people in your first month. Then, in your second month, each of your recruits brought in five more people. If the process continued, without interruption, for six months, you would end up with 19,530 distributors in your *downline* (the MLM term for the total number of people generated by your recruiting efforts). Now suppose each person in your downline purchased $100 worth of inventory each month. If you drew a 10 percent commission from each sale, your total commissions, in your sixth month, would be $195,300. And those commissions would keep on growing, month after month.

UNLIMITED POTENTIAL

Of course, this is a highly simplified and idealized example. No business proceeds like clockwork. The dropout rate is high among MLM recruits. Most people would have to go through a lot of trial and error before they could find five good people capable of going out and recruiting five more. For that reason, most network marketers earn only modest incomes. But for those special few with the energy, vision, and tireless persistence to break through every obstacle, multilevel commission structures offer a unique opportunity to build a sales organization that grows in geometric progression, year after year. Many succeed in doing just that.

> But for those special few with the energy, vision, and tireless persistence to break through every obstacle, multilevel commission structures offer a unique opportunity to build a sales organization that grows in geometric progression, year after year.

We've come a long way since the days when Indian trappers would pay one beaver skin per canoe for the privilege of joining a trading party. Multilevel marketing has raised the Leverage Principle almost to a science. Companies that employ MLM today routinely achieve growth rates unheard-of in conventional business.

"Most business editors get excited when they find a company whose sales or profits have 'soared' 20 percent in the last year," writes Duncan Anderson, editorial director of *Network Marketing Lifestyles* magazine. "But in network marketing, growth rates of 100 percent annually are not unusual, in the early, expansive phase of a successful firm."

THE COMING WAVE

In short, the opportunity has never been greater. Those who choose network marketing today gain a special advantage.

They enter the industry at the precise moment that it is embarking on a powerful new phase of evolution. For reasons that will be made clear in succeeding chapters, I have named that phase Wave 4. It marks the end of network marketing's infancy. No longer is MLM perceived as an immature business, rife with scam artists hawking get-rich-quick schemes. Today, blue-chip corporations such as Citigroup, MCI, and IBM confidently sell their services through multilevel sales forces. This powerful business strategy has become a linchpin of the twenty-first-century economy.

In the pages ahead, we will learn why corporate America has embraced this new strategy so enthusiastically. We will see how network marketing fits hand in glove with the needs of our burgeoning Information Society. Most important of all, we will find out how you and your family fit into the Wave 4 Revolution; how this radical new method of work may someday provide the key to your financial freedom; and what specific steps you will need to take in order to walk the path of Wave 4 success.

PART TWO WAVE 4

The Wave 4 Revolution

CHAPTER 4

Acres of Diamonds

Many centuries ago in Persia, a farmer listened enthralled while a storyteller wove him a yarn. The tale concerned something called a "diamond." According to the storyteller, a diamond was a "congealed drop of sunlight," a gem so precious that any man who discovered a mine of them would be richer than any king. The farmer had never heard of diamonds before. But now that he had, he burned with desire to lay his hands on such a treasure.

It happened that this farmer owned many fields and orchards. He was a wealthy man. Yet from the moment he heard about diamonds, he felt like a pauper. The one thing in life that he coveted, he could not have. The thought of all those diamonds lying undiscovered, somewhere in the world, tortured him in his sleep. So one day he sold his lands and set out on a quest. The farmer wandered through Africa, Palestine, and Europe in search of diamonds. At last he arrived in Spain, a bitter old man, dressed in rags. Overwhelmed with despair, he threw himself into the sea and drowned. Never once, in all his travels, had he so much as glimpsed a single diamond.

Meanwhile, back in Persia, the man who had bought his fields made a startling discovery. He found a diamond embedded in a black stone. Further investigation revealed that there were literally acres and acres of diamonds concealed beneath his property. In time, that humble farm came to be known as the diamond mine of Golconda, the richest ever found. If only the greedy farmer had been content to stay at home! The wealth he craved would have been his for the taking.

HIDDEN TREASURE

This story was first popularized by Dr. Russell Herman Conwell, a minister, educator, Civil War hero, and one of America's greatest inspirational speakers. Until his death in 1925, Conwell toured the country, exhorting audiences to open their eyes and to see the opportunities right in front of them. Rather than run off to the big city, Conwell preached, people should stay put and make the best of what they found, right in their own home-towns. Conwell's "Acres of Diamonds" lecture, delivered some six thousand times, made him the most beloved and sought-after speaker of his day.

"I say to you that you have acres of diamonds in Philadelphia, right where you now live. . . ." Conwell once told an audience in that city. "Out of the 107 millionaires worth $10 million [in 1889], 67 of them made their money in towns of less than 3,500 inhabitants. . . . It makes not so much difference where you are as who you are. . . . If you cannot get rich in Philadelphia, you certainly cannot do it in New York."

> ". . . It makes not so much difference where you are as who you are . . . If you cannot get rich in Philadelphia, you certainly cannot do it in New York."

Conwell believed that the capacity for success lay within each of us and did not depend on our surroundings or circumstances. Seventy-five years after his death, Conwell's message has acquired a special relevance for our burgeoning Information Society. More than ever, the best opportunities can be found right in our own backyards, in our own home offices, on our own personal computers. But you would hardly know it from the attitudes of most people. All too many of us contemplate the Death of Jobs with an ever-deepening dread. We see the future as a high-tech wasteland, where only the highly trained elite will find work. Yet precisely the opposite is true. For those who understand Conwell's lesson, the Wave 4 Revolution offers acres of proverbial diamonds, concealed under our very noses.

THINKING POOR

Lisa Wilber learned Conwell's lesson the hard way. When we last met her, Lisa was weeping in her trailer, having just paid her last $46 to the electric man. Self-pity was her ever-present companion. Like the farmer in Conwell's story, Lisa envisioned herself as poor and had done so for most of her life. Her father was a janitor and her mother a secretary. They were hard-working folk, who had always managed to put food on the table and a roof over their children's heads. But the glamour and excitement that Lisa craved could not be found in her parents' house.

Magazines and television only whetted Lisa's appetite. She would glue herself to the TV, gazing spellbound at the intrigues and power plays unfolding each week on *Dallas* and *Dynasty*. Lisa spent hours studying her parents' coffee-table picture books about the Kennedy family: the fine houses, the cars and boats, the sunny faces, the happy children, the languid afternoons in Hyannisport. How different it all seemed from her drab existence in rural Massachusetts!

Somewhere out there was a wider world, Lisa told herself, a world of money and opportunity. She vowed that she would partake of that excitement, someday. But for now, life was just a blur of chores and schoolwork. The only break seemed to come on those rare and special occasions when the doorbell rang for Lisa's mother, and a familiar voice announced from the porch that the Avon lady was here.

A DREAM OF WEALTH

"Ever since I was a little girl," Lisa recalls, "I always wanted to be the Avon lady."

Like the characters Lisa admired in *Dallas* and *Dynasty,* the Avon lady seemed at home in the world of money and commerce. Sharply turned out in a business suit, she would open her sample case and get right to the point. "She didn't come for chit-chat," Lisa recalls. "She came to do her job. She was a businesswoman. Very professional. I looked up to her for that."

Lisa longed to navigate the business world with that same ease and confidence. To her, Avon Products represented a corporate fairy godmother, a mysterious force capable of transporting her to a better world. Lisa loved the products. Her very first lipstick came from an Avon catalog. She also knew that Avon was a multibillion-dollar company, with a history going back to 1886. Its blue-chip reputation spoke of money, power, and status—the three things Lisa coveted most. If only she could become an Avon lady, Lisa thought, then perhaps she too might acquire some of those attributes for herself.

MENTAL HURDLE

Lisa's business instincts were not off the mark. Avon Products did indeed represent the future, notwithstanding the fact that it was one of America's oldest corporations. The direct-selling movement Avon had helped pioneer back in 1886 was only now beginning to fulfill its potential. Economic revolution was in the air. And Lisa was destined to play an important role in that coming upheaval.

But first, she had a mental hurdle to overcome. Lisa had to learn the lesson of Acres of Diamonds. Like the greedy farmer in Conwell's story, Lisa was never satisfied with the opportunities at hand. Her restless spirit kept her always on the prowl for something easier, better, and quicker. Consequently, she was ill-prepared to make a success of her Avon business.

Lisa joined Avon when she was only eighteen years old. Yet as with most things she tried, the novelty wore off quickly. Selling Avon products just didn't seem to bring in the kind of money Lisa wanted. She worked the business, year after year, on a part-time basis. But Lisa never gave it her full attention and, consequently, never earned more than a few hundred dollars per month. Most of her time and energy went into finding other ways to survive.

WELL-WORN PATHS

Lisa's quest for the proverbial pot of gold took her down many well-worn but empty paths. Convinced that she needed technical knowledge to succeed, Lisa put herself through school, completing two associate's degrees in management and data processing. Convinced that hourly pay was the most reliable form of income, Lisa earned her keep by working every sort of odd job, from cleaning houses to waiting on tables. When things got tough, Lisa sought escape through travel. She drifted far and wide across the world, from Mississippi and South Carolina to the island of Guam.

Through all these changes, Lisa's Avon business atrophied. Her punishing schedule left little time for selling. And her constant travel made it hard to keep customers. Ambition was never lacking in Lisa. She did not shrink from challenges. But her energy was scattered in a dozen different directions. Like the foolish old farmer in the story, Lisa encountered only struggle and hardship wherever she went.

ROCK BOTTOM

When she was growing up in Massachusetts, Lisa often felt poor. Yet her notion of poverty amounted to little more than having cheaper clothes than the other kids at summer camp. Only when she left home did Lisa finally learn what it meant to be broke. In Charleston, South Carolina, she went for three months without lights or hot water after failing to pay her electric bill. Lisa was exhausted all the time. Her job, classes, and Avon business kept her going around the clock. One night, while working late in a minimart, Lisa fell asleep at her cash register. The neighborhood was so bad that police surrounded the store, with guns drawn, thinking that Lisa had been shot.

"Hardly a day went by that I didn't tell myself, I can't take this anymore," Lisa remembers. "I was lucky I didn't have to compromise my principles. I had to work some icky jobs, but at least I never had to do anything illegal."

The Treadmill

Lisa was *underemployed*. No matter how hard she worked, she could not earn enough money. As the Death of Jobs gains momentum, underemployment is spreading with epidemic speed through our society. More and more people try to make up for the jobs they've lost by working several part-time gigs at once. But they soon find themselves on a treadmill. Their round-the-clock work schedules consume their time and energy, but give nothing back. Because they work for linear wages, their efforts offer no chance for growth. Most underemployed people dream only of landing a steady job again, with normal hours, decent pay, and good benefits.

Unfortunately, steady jobs will only grow harder to find as the twenty-first century progresses. The quest for regular employment will seem as quixotic in the years ahead as the search for gold mines did to Russell Conwell's generation. Conwell urged his contemporaries to forget about striking the Mother Lode and to busy themselves, instead, with more practical occupations. Someday soon, a new generation of Conwells will arise to offer that same advice to job seekers of the Information Age. These forward-looking people will advise us to put aside romantic and foolhardy notions about landing a good job, to stop wasting precious time on resumes and interviews, and to get busy with the more realistic task of building a self-sustaining, residual income.

DEAD END

Like most underemployed people, Lisa dreamt only of finding a good job. And in time, she did. After returning to New England, Lisa found work as a secretary in a New Hampshire computer firm, located only a couple of hours' drive from where she had grown up. Lisa's new job paid what, to her, was the incredible salary of $20,000. Two years later, she married. Lisa's luck seemed to be changing at last.

But her newfound happiness was based on a shaky foundation. Unknown to Lisa, the Death of Jobs was already stalking the land. It struck without warning, two weeks after her wedding. Lisa went to work that day only to learn that she and her entire department had been laid off.

"I cried all the way home," Lisa recalls. "Everyone in my department was crying. I was in love with that job. It paid full dental, full medical. I had no idea what I was going to do now."

Lisa's husband cut firewood for a living, earning barely enough to survive. Jobs were scarce in New England in the late 1980s. Talk of hard times and recession filled the papers and TV. After all the years of scraping and starving, Lisa could not believe that she was penniless once more. She broke down completely when she got home, wailing and rolling on the floor of her trailer before her befuddled bridegroom. "I pretty much pitched a fit," Lisa admits. "I'm not proud of it, but that's what happened."

A BLESSING IN DISGUISE

As usual, Lisa saw only the hole and not the donut. What she saw was poverty, recession, unpaid bills, a dingy trailer park, and an underemployed husband. Lisa looked back upon her travels, like the greedy farmer in the story, and concluded that all had been in vain. She had wandered to the ends of the earth and back. She had explored every path that was open to her. But God Himself seemed to block her every move. No wonder Lisa rolled and rolled on the floor that day, clenching her fists and kicking her feet. No wonder she wept as if life itself were coming to an end. But in fact, life was only just beginning for Lisa. She did not realize it yet, but "acres of diamonds" lay very close at hand. All she needed was to open her eyes to see them.

CHAPTER 5

The Four Waves

The Old West offered fabulous opportunity for pioneers, in the form of huge tracts of land that could be obtained for little or no money. A different, but no less precious, resource is available on the cyber-frontier—unlimited access to residual income. This was the resource that lay waiting for Lisa Wilber in such untold abundance.

Lisa had been fortunate on two counts. First, she had enrolled in a turnkey opportunity—Avon Products—that was destined to take a commanding lead in the Wave 4 Revolution. Second, she had lost her job at the precise moment that this revolution was getting underway. Fate had been kind to Lisa. Network marketing had been building momentum for more than fifty years by the time Lisa discovered it. But only now was the industry reaching its climax. The four waves of MLM's evolution can be broken down as follows:

WAVE 1 (1945–1979)—The Underground Phase
WAVE 2 (1980–1989)—The Proliferation Phase
WAVE 3 (1990–1999)—The Mass Market Phase
WAVE 4 (2000 and beyond)—The Universal Phase

CON MEN AND VISIONARIES

Wave 1 began in 1945, when Nutrilite introduced its first network marketing plan. This was the industry's Wild West phase, when neither law nor order prevailed. Con men thrived alongside genuine visionaries. Companies grew with reckless abandon, some honestly, others not. At the same time, government regulators targeted MLM companies with equal recklessness, often making up the rules as they went along. The chaos of Wave 1 came to an end in 1979. After a long and acrimonious investigation, the Federal Trade Commission ruled that Amway Corporation—and, by implication, network marketing in general—was a legitimate business, not a pyramid scheme.

Encouraged by the friendlier legal climate, the industry entered what I have called Wave 2. Breakthroughs in computer technology allowed entrepreneurs to start and run network marketing companies from their desktops. The 1980s saw unprecedented growth in the sheer number of start-ups.

GROWING PAINS

But even as network marketing proliferated in the 1980s, it still suffered from growing pains. MLM recruiters lured new prospects with the promise of unlimited opportunity. But few people could afford the time, money, or effort to make the business work. The average Joe, working the business part-time, often dropped out in frustration, after spending his money buying inventory that he didn't know how to sell. Those who made fortunes in MLM tended to be the super-salesmen, the gifted entrepreneurs, and the highly motivated, driven personalities.

Former IBM salesman Don Held experienced firsthand the rigors of networking during the Wave 1 and Wave 2 eras. Starting his Amway business in 1969, Don built his downline the hard way. Not only did he have to recruit and train new distributors, but he had to hand-write their commission checks each month. The 900-square-foot house he shared with his wife and six children was transformed into a warehouse. Every bulk order from his downline had to be processed, packaged, and shipped by hand. During the summers, when Don's children were out of school, the whole family would pile into a 32-foot motor home and travel the country like gypsies, building the business as they went. "Network marketing, in those days, was as primitive as a Model-T," Don recalls. "Most people today would not do what we did back then."

For Don, it worked. He was blessed with the inner drive and persistence it took to succeed despite every obstacle. After two years of working the business part-time, Don was earning $60,000 per year from Amway—double his old IBM paycheck. He was free to quit his job. Don became a millionaire within five years.

Nowadays, Don takes life at a slower pace. He spends a lot less time working, and a lot more playing. When he's not catching marlin and sailfish from his 32-foot sportfishing boat down in Florida, Don is hunting moose in the Canadian woods, or visiting with his children and grandchildren. He divides his time equally between four different houses— soon to be five, when his log cabin in the Smoky Mountains is finished. Don paid his dues for thirty years. Now he reaps the rewards. Every year, his Amway downline yields hundreds of thousands of dollars in residual income. But Don often wonders how much more quickly he might have achieved his dreams had he started out today. "It's a whole lot easier for those fellows now," Don muses.

THE AUTOMATED DOWNLINE

Like other multilevel companies, Amway revolutionized its methods in the 1990s. Customers now order products from an 800 number and receive shipments directly from the company. All a distributor has to do is collect his commission check, issued each month from a company computer. Prospecting videos, audiotapes, teleconferences, and satellite TV broadcasts have largely automated the recruiting process. Dedicated voice mail systems have streamlined communications within downlines. Fax-on-demand services have freed upline leaders from having to answer repetitive questions. Three-way phone calls let raw recruits listen in, while their more experienced sponsors close new prospects. Compensation plans, too, have been made easier, with larger commissions flowing to distributors for less work.

"The same amount of work is worth more money today, because of the bonuses they have," says Don. He points to a couple in his downline, Joe and Doris Shaw, who became Diamonds—one of the highest achievement levels in Amway—after only twelve months in the business. "I've got people in my organization who are making, in their second year, what I made in my tenth year," Held says.

The Wave 3 era had begun.

MASS-MARKET MLM

Wave 3 innovations made MLM fully accessible to the masses for the first time. They lowered the cost of working a multi-level business, both in time and money. As a result, millions of people flocked to the industry—people who would never have considered it before. Of course, the Wave 3 Revolution did not guarantee millions in residual income to every distributor. No business can do that. But for that vast majority of MLMers who worked the business part-time, these innovations made it easier to earn the few hundred extra dollars of spending money that they needed each month. For most people, that is enough to make the business worth doing.

A DECADE OF GROWTH

In future years, the '90s will be remembered as the decade when network marketing became a serious industry. According to a June 23, 1995, article in *The Wall Street Journal*, the total number of network marketers in the United States increased 34 percent between 1990 and 1994. The same article states that the number of full-time distributors doubled between 1993 and 1994 alone.

It was during the 1990s that network marketing spilled over the U.S. borders for the first time, spreading, en masse, into foreign countries. Many large MLM firms grew more quickly in China, Korea, and Japan than they did in the United States. Overseas growth reached such feverish proportions by mid-decade that the MLM sector temporarily outpaced all the rest of the U.S. economy put together. A weighted measure of publicly traded MLM stocks called the *Upline* Index actually outperformed the Dow Jones Industrial Average and the S&P 500 by nearly 80 percent in 1995.

THE NEXT WAVE

These developments did not go unnoticed by the Fortune 500. All through the 1990s, corporate America kept a watchful eye on the revolution taking shape in its midst. But with the caution endemic to large bureaucracies, most blue-chip corporations hesitated to involve themselves directly. Network marketing, for all its tens of billions of dollars in sales, remained a pariah in the corporate world.

> In future years, the '90s will be remembered as the decade when network marketing became a serious industry.

All of that changed, however, as the year 2000 approached. The closing years of the 1990s saw a quantum shift in the perception of network marketing. Suddenly, major corporations were jostling one another for access to MLM networks. Wall Street analysts praised multilevel marketing in their reports. Blue-chip companies rolled out MLM subsidiaries and formed strategic alliances with existing MLM firms. The race was on to cash in on the network marketing phenomenon.

What brought about this sudden change? As with all profound innovations, corporate America did not embrace network marketing voluntarily. In fact, Fortune 500 CEOs resisted as long as they could. But time was working against them. Conventional advertising and marketing strategies no longer worked. Market share was evaporating before an onslaught of interactive media, proactive customers, and global competition. Like so many millions of MLM distributors, corporate CEOs experimented with network marketing out of desperation, not choice. But once they had tasted of its fruits, they found they could not resist coming back for more. Thus began the fourth and most powerful phase of network marketing's evolution—the conquest of corporate America.

CHAPTER 6

The End
of Shopping

In the spring of 1999, a company called AllAdvantage.com emerged on the Internet. It is an MLM opportunity like no other. You don't sell a product. Instead, you just agree to install a so-called "Viewbar" in your Web browser. Whenever you access the Web, the Viewbar will display advertising messages from various client companies across the bottom of your screen. AllAdvantage.com will pay you 50 cents for every hour that you surf the Web with the Viewbar installed, and lesser amounts per hour for each person you recruit into the company, down to five levels.

"Get paid to surf the Web," says the company's home page. But, of course, you are not really being paid to surf the Web. You are being paid to grant AllAdvantage.com the right to sell advertising space on your computer screen. It is as if the Fox Network suddenly offered to pay you fifty cents for every hour you spent watching *Ally McBeal* or *The X-Files,* as compensation for allowing the network to interrupt your program every few minutes, with a string of commercials.

How far we have come from the golden age of Madison Avenue! A generation ago, advertisers ruled the roost. Captive audiences sat helpless before a barrage of televised images. Ad agencies funneled their messages, at will, straight into the consumer's mind. But now the roles have reversed. It is the consumer who controls the information flow, while the advertiser resorts to ever more desperate means to seize his attention. The average person today is exposed to 145 commercial messages daily—a 36 percent increase since 1960. But the chances of any one advertiser making an impact have plummeted. Armed with remote controls, today's consumers now flit from one cable station to the next, bypassing all the commercials. As the number of media outlets proliferates—from cable TV to the Internet—advertising messages are lost in the ever-widening datastream.

A FORTRESS MENTALITY

Channel-surfing is only one of many ways that people today protect themselves from commercials. To the alarm of advertisers, more and more people are adopting a fortress mentality toward psychological intrusions of any kind. They pay premium subscription fees for noncommercial cable stations. They withhold warranty applications, lest they wind up on mailing lists. They fast-forward through the promotions and trailers on rented videos. They delete commercial e-mail messages without reading them. They screen out unwanted calls from their answering machines. Nearly one in seven American households today has an unlisted phone number.

It's all part of the cocooning trend, foretold by marketing consultant Faith Popcorn more than a decade ago. Americans are retreating into cocoons, says Popcorn, because they are overwhelmed by the frenetic pace and social chaos of the Information Age. They seek a quiet, private retreat where they do not have to see, hear, feel, or do anything except by their own choice. "Cocooning is about insulation and avoidance," she writes in *The Popcorn Report,* "peace and protection, coziness, and control—a sort of hyper-nesting."

GUNS AND ROSES

Fearful of burglary, terrorism, serial rapists, killer viruses, pollution, traffic, and media overload, Cocooners seek tranquillity in a number of ways. Some emphasize physical protection of hearth and home. "Look for major growth in 'paranoia' industries," says Popcorn, "home security systems, anti-snooping devices, computer watchdog systems linked to private guards and emergency help." Popcorn notes the sharp rise in gun sales to women as a quintessential cocooning trend. In her latest bestselling book, *Clicking,* co-written with Lys Marigold, Popcorn observes: "Nearly 4 million Americans now live in gated communities—with ever taller, thicker, higher walls being built each week."

Cocooners also use more subtle methods for controlling and ameliorating their environment. Some equip their homes with "smart" technology, allowing them to open doors, adjust thermostats, or activate lights and appliances by preset program or remote control. Others outfit their bathrooms as "virtual mini-spas," complete with saunas, whirlpools, and heated towel racks. Still others pour their energy into sewing, gardening, and other traditional methods of feathering the hyper-nest. "Antique fabrics—which remind us of a cozier past—have soared in value . . ." write Popcorn and Marigold in *Clicking.* "We're spending small fortunes (more than $25 billion annually) on gingerbread gazebos, wisteria arbors . . . underground sprinkler systems for ever greener grass, and other gardening paraphernalia."

SHOPPING-PHOBIA

With all the effort Cocooners pour into building safe, secure, and comfortable hyper-nests, they are understandably reluctant to venture outside of them. "When Cocooners do leave their homes, they take the Cocoon with them," write Popcorn and Marigold. Cars are thus equipped with coffee-cup holders, faxes, phones, shiatsu cushions, and six-disc players. Corporate offices are furnished with dining rooms, couches, and piped-in Gregorian chants. Barnes and Noble superstores allow customers to sip cappuccino in lounge chairs, while browsing books at their leisure.

Despite all these inducements, the true Cocooner still knows there is no place like home. And that is bad news for retailers. "It's the end of shopping," Popcorn observes. "It's tough to go to stores with kids. It's a very cold environment." Depending on where you live, it can even be dangerous. Popcorn and Marigold note: "A recent survey showed that 33 percent of consumers have changed their shopping habits because of fear of crime. Of these, 43 percent no longer shop after dark."

"THE STORE WILL COME TO US"

The twenty-first century will see profound changes in shopping habits, Popcorn predicts. "Instead of going to the store," she says, "the store will come to us." Consumers have already taken drastic strides in that direction. Billions of dollars have been diverted from conventional retailers into catalog sales, televised home shopping, and virtual stores on the Internet. Network marketers play an ever-increasing role in that shopping revolution.

"In the future, we'll be looking at network marketing the way we look at regular marketing today," says Popcorn. "There's going to be a lot of respectability for this thing." Popcorn has observed this trend in her New York–based Brain-Reserve consulting practice, which serves top-drawer clients such as IBM, Campbell Soup, American Express, and Eastman Kodak. A few years ago, Popcorn notes, BrainReserve clients routinely dismissed her urgent warnings to prepare for the Information Age—two key facets

> Network marketers play an ever-increasing role in that shopping revolution.

of which, she told them, would be competition from the Internet and MLM. "They would say, 'Oh, we're not worried about the Internet. We're not worried about network marketing," Popcorn recalls.

Then consumer sales conducted over the Internet more than doubled in two years, leaping from $3 to $7 billion. Popcorn's clients sobered up quickly. "Now when we do our futurescapes, showing clients who their most worrisome competitors are likely to be ten years out, we often point to network marketers," she says. Popcorn's clients are far more inclined to heed her warnings now. She sees a growing awareness, among corporations in general, of the power of MLM. "They're saying, well, I'd better take a look at this huge, emerging marketplace."

THE MAGIC BULLET

AT&T was one of the first corporate giants to get its nose bloodied by network marketers. In the five-year period beginning in 1987, AT&T lost 15 percent of its long-distance market share to MCI and Sprint (then called US Sprint). You would never know it from reading the mainstream business press, but both of these upstarts had a secret advantage, a veritable magic bullet that enabled them to grow faster and penetrate markets more forcefully than their lumbering competitor. That magic bullet was network marketing.

MCI sold its long-distance service through Amway Corporation. "We became 25 percent of MCI's business the first year we joined them," recalls Amway distributor Don Held. Sprint enjoyed similar success, marketing its service through an MLM company called Network 2000. "In the three and a half years beginning in March 1988," says Jim Adams, former executive vice president of sales and marketing for Network 2000, "we acquired more than 4 million customers for Sprint—a $500 million a year revenue stream. The Network 2000 independent marketing representatives were ten times more effective in acquiring customers than Sprint's telemarketing groups."

To this day, MCI continues selling through Amway. As for Sprint, disputes over billing and commissions ultimately resulted in a fallout with their MLM vendor (which finally ended in a $91 million settlement in Network 2000's favor). There is no doubt, however, that the alliance, while it lasted, was critical to Sprint's success. I interviewed Sprint executive William Plikaitis, for *Success* magazine in 1990. As group manager for US Sprint's Consumer Services Group, Plikaitis supervised the MLM program. He was effusive in his praise both for Network 2000 and for multilevel marketing in general. "There's no better way today to get your product right in the consumer's face," Plikaitis told me.

WORD-OF-MOUTH

AT&T learned the hard way that network marketing is a fearsome competitor. But for innovative executives, it offers opportunity as well. MLM presents a solution to one of the most critical problems facing corporate America. "If there's one urgent business lesson marketers will have to learn . . ." warns Faith Popcorn, "it will be finding new ways to reach the hyper-cocooned consumer. . . . Don't expect consumers to come to you anymore. You'll have to reach them in the cocoon itself."

No marketing method does this better than MLM. Even the most elusive Cocooner will still lend an ear to the occasional friend, relative, associate, or co-worker who recommends a particular diet supplement, investment plan, or Internet service provider. If handled properly, the sales pitch raises no eyebrows and provokes no backlash. Word-of-mouth marketing penetrates the thickest psychological defenses, with the efficiency of a uranium-sheathed armor-piercing shell.

"Nobody wants to go to stores anymore, and network marketing has the solution," Popcorn concludes. "Network marketers are going right into the cocoon. They know how to invade the home, without being thought of as invaders."

CHAPTER 7

The Word-of-Mouth Factor

For Paul Zane Pilzer, cocooning is far more than a concept in a book. It is a destructive force of nature that nearly ran his company into the ground. Like so many entrepreneurs and corporate executives today, Paul saved his business only by turning to network marketing. In so doing, he set his company on the road not only to recovery, but to unparalleled growth.

Paul is no ordinary businessman. He is a respected and brilliant economist. At age twenty-three, he became the youngest vice president at Citibank. Paul served as an economic adviser to Presidents Reagan and Bush. He warned Congress of the impending $200-billion savings and loan crisis, years before official Washington was willing to listen. Although a professor of economics, Paul disdained academia and set out to test his theories in the marketplace. He amassed a personal fortune of tens of millions of dollars through real estate development and wrote smash bestsellers on economics, such as *Unlimited Wealth, Other People's Money,* and *God Wants You to Be Rich.*

THE NEW BREED

On the surface, at least, Paul seemed a most unlikely convert to MLM. The industry had long been associated, in the popular mind, with blue-collar dreamers, infomercial junkies, and hucksters in leisure suits, out for the quick buck. But such stereotypes were already out of date by the time Paul entered the industry. The new breed of networker was a sophisticated, highly educated professional, searching for a profitable niche on the cyber-frontier. And Paul fit that profile with admirable precision.

Paul's long and winding road to MLM success began in 1989, when he produced his first CD-ROM—an inspirational program based on a videotape in which Paul traded economic ideas with popular motivational speaker Anthony Robbins. The success of his *PowerTalk* CD gave Paul an idea. Why not use this new medium for educating children? Paul felt that the undivided attention children normally reserved for video games could be channeled into their algebra lessons, if only those lessons could be enlivened with exciting, interactive graphics. Paul's vision was well ahead of its time. The potential market was enormous. But Paul's game plan lacked a crucial component that nearly cost him everything.

> The new breed of networker was a sophisticated, highly educated professional, searching for a profitable niche on the cyber-frontier.

THE PROBLEM

Paul had not figured out how to penetrate the cocoon. And without such a strategy, his business was doomed. Paul would spend years attempting to sell his educational CD-ROMs through conventional channels, such as direct mail, retail stores, and schools. His Dallas-based firm, Zane Publishing, poured $25 million into marketing. But every distribution channel lost money. In order to make a sale, Paul had to penetrate not one, but three mental barriers. First of all, most parents did not see the need to get personally involved in their children's schoolwork. That was the schools' job, they thought. Secondly, parents did not understand why they should waste their money experimenting with this newfangled medium. And, finally, customers had no way of discerning, in the few seconds it takes to make a retail buying decision, how Paul's CDs were better than competing brands. Deeply cocooned in their established routines, they ignored Paul's flyers and in-store displays. Cocooners viewed such come-ons as nothing more than psychological intrusions, in a world already oversaturated with advertising media.

PERSON-TO-PERSON

A solution to this problem was already available, but Paul knew nothing about it. He did not realize that what he needed was a personal sales approach. Paul needed salesmen who could get right in the customers' faces, hold their attention, gain their trust, and explain, in great detail, the benefits of this technology. In short, he needed word-of-mouth marketing.

> Network marketers, on the other hand, looked upon word-of-mouth marketing as a science.

The mainstream business world offered no strategy for delivering personal testimonials, face-to-face. Conventional marketers looked upon word-of-mouth promotion as a *result* of good advertising, not a strategy for conveying it. They assumed that a good ad campaign would generate a buzz. But a buzz, by its nature, was thought to be as unpredictable and uncontrollable as the weather.

Network marketers, on the other hand, looked upon word-of-mouth marketing as a science. They knew that, through hard work and the application of certain well-known principles, a word-of-mouth buzz could be generated, time and again, with reliable and often lucrative results. This was, in fact, precisely what network marketers did for a living. It would be some years before Paul even realized that multilevel marketing existed. But once he did, he would quickly become one of the industry's most fervent advocates.

THE DISTRIBUTION FRONTIER

Paul was introduced to the industry by a happy accident. One day in 1991, an Amway distributor named Don Held sat down and listened to an audiotape version of Paul's *PowerTalk.* On the tape, Paul explained to Anthony Robbins that the big money in the 1990s was to be found not in building better mousetraps, but in finding better ways to distribute those mousetraps.

On the tape, Paul offered a memorable example to illustrate his point. He recalled a famous scene from the movie *The Graduate,* in which a well-meaning businessman offers career advice to Ben (the character played by Dustin Hoffman). The advice takes the form of a single word: "Plastics." Back in the 1960s, that was good advice. The best money, in those days, was to be made in figuring out ways to reduce the cost of manufacturing. One way of doing this would be to make objects from plastic rather than metal. By 1991, however, this opportunity had largely disappeared.

Advancing technology, Paul explained, had driven the production cost of an item down to where it typically represented less than 20 percent of the retail price. That left little room for reducing production costs further. Distribution costs, on the other hand, now accounted for a whopping 80 percent of an item's price. There was plenty of room left to push these costs down. For that reason, Paul explained, the big opportunity now lay in finding ways to *distribute* products more cheaply.

THE MLM CONNECTION

Paul did not know it at the time, but one of the best ways to reduce distribution costs is through network marketing. Unlike a conventional sales force, MLM distributors receive no compensation beyond their commission. Their word-of-mouth advertising can penetrate markets more effectively than conventional, multimillion-dollar ad campaigns, while costing the manufacturer next to nothing.

Despite all his credentials as an author, presidential adviser, economics professor, and entrepreneur, Paul did not know these basic facts. Indeed, he had never heard of network marketing. But listening to the *PowerTalk* tape, Don Held grasped the connection right away.

"He was saying that the big money now was in distribution," Don remembers. "When I heard that, I said, 'My God, that's what we're in!'" Don tracked down the famous economist and retained him to speak at an upcoming Amway rally.

THE AMERICAN WAY

Paul Zane Pilzer, of course, had never heard of Amway before. But behind the scenes, this company had been quietly revolutionizing American business since 1959. That year, two boyhood friends from Grand Rapids, Michigan—Rich DeVos and Jay Van Andel—broke away from Nutrilite Products, Inc. The pair had made a fortune distributing vitamin and mineral supplements for Carl Rehnborg's original MLM company. But DeVos and Van Andel thought they could do better on their own. Using an improved version of Rehnborg's MLM compensation plan, they formed a new entity that they called the Amway Corporation.

Having served in the Army Air Corps during World War II, DeVos and Van Andel were fiercely patriotic. They were also committed Christians, reared in the stern Protestantism, which their immigrant forefathers had carried over from Holland. From the beginning, the partners intended that Amway would epitomize America's old-fashioned virtues. Its very name was an abbreviation of the American Way. Amway's revival-style sales rallies, to this day, open and close with sing-alongs of *God Bless America* and *The Star Spangled Banner,* to the accompaniment of Old Glory waving on a giant video screen; its distributor force is composed, in large part, of devout churchgoers. God, country, and multilevel marketing find a happy synthesis in the Amway worldview.

INTO THE UNKNOWN

Amway's formula has proved remarkably successful. What began as a tiny enterprise, selling a biodegradable all-purpose cleaner called Frisk, has now grown to a $5.7-billion transnational corporation, with 3 million independent distributors worldwide, offering more than 6,500 different products and services, and managing one of the largest retail Web sites on the Internet. Amway's research and manufacturing facilities alone encompass eighty buildings, totaling 4.2 million square feet. DeVos and Van Andel appear routinely on the annual lists of America's wealthiest individuals, published in *Fortune* and *Forbes* magazines.

Paul knew nothing of these matters when he agreed to speak at his first Amway rally. To him, it was just another convention gig, but Paul had unknowingly taken the first step on a journey that would one day lead him to the cutting edge of twenty-first-century innovation. He was going where no mainstream economist had gone before. Had they known what he was up to, Paul's old professors at Wharton Business School would undoubtedly have frowned with disapproval. Yet they would also have marveled at the stunning opportunity Paul was about to uncover.

8

The Distribution Freeway

When Paul Zane Pilzer arrived at the St. Louis convention center to address his first Amway rally, he was immediately taken aback. The crowd of 3,500 was electric. Pep talks, testimonials, and a live performance by country and western star Crystal Gale whipped them into a frenzy. "I was a little intimidated," Paul admits. How would these people react, he wondered, to having their Saturday night festivities interrupted by a boring lecture from an economics professor? Would they pelt him with tomatoes and boo him from the stage, like irate patrons of an old vaudeville show?

Somehow, in the boisterous atmosphere of the rally, it did not seem out of the question. But shortly after he mounted the podium, Paul realized that his fears were groundless. The crowd proved surprisingly attentive. "When I got on stage, they turned the lights up a little, everybody took out a pad and paper and started taking notes," he recalls. "They got very serious. I felt I was with my students, prepping for a final."

BEYOND THE RAZZMATAZZ

Paul had received his first lesson in the culture of network marketing. Beneath all the razzmatazz, MLMers are a serious bunch, hungry for new ideas, and deadly earnest about making money. Paul hunkered down with a group of twenty top sales leaders after the lecture and talked economics until dawn. "I was overwhelmed by their dedication," Paul remembers, "by their desire to learn."

Paul was learning, too. He had spent weeks before the convention studying Amway and marveling at its diverse products, rapid global expansion, and word-of-mouth marketing strategy. Why had he never heard of this company before, Paul wondered? For that matter, how had this entire industry managed to escape his notice? "If I set out to design a new business, taking advantage of all the theories and emerging trends in my book *Unlimited Wealth*," says Paul, "that business would be network marketing." Paul resolved to make the study of MLM one of his top priorities in the years ahead.

> **B**eneath all the razzmatazz, MLMers are a serious bunch, hungry for new ideas, and deadly earnest about making money.

CUSTOMER RESISTANCE

For all his enthusiasm, it would be many years before Paul fully grasped the potential that MLM offered his own fledgling CD-ROM business. He would spend eight years on a wild goose chase, trying to market his discs through every conventional method available. "I wish I could tell you I saw Amway as the opportunity from the very beginning," says Paul. "But I didn't. I thought it was going to be retail—an error which ultimately cost us a fortune and almost the company itself."

Paul tried every trick he knew to sell CDs. He did mass mailings. He met with school officials, trying to arrange bulk orders. He talked Blockbuster Video into giving him free rein to hawk his CD-ROMs in fifty California stores, using any type of display or product mix that he liked. The experiment failed, three times in a row.

"It was so frustrating," Paul remembers. "We couldn't build customer loyalty." Without a salesman on the premises, Paul was at a keen disadvantage. It was hard enough getting people to buy educational CD-ROMs in the first place. But even those customers who did, often failed to distinguish one brand from another the next time they visited the store. "If they came back," Paul complains, "they were just as likely to buy a competitor's product, which was often inferior."

IN THE COCOON

What Paul needed was to get inside the cocoon. He needed to win people's trust and hold their attention long enough so he could tell his story. Only slowly did it dawn on Paul that network marketing might be the key. After his 1991 speech in St. Louis, Paul emerged as an MLM celebrity. He spoke at scores of Amway and other MLM conventions. Now and then, at speaking events, Paul would strike up conversations with top-level sales leaders and tell them about his CD-ROMs. Many asked for samples to try with their own children.

"I started giving away the products to the Diamonds, the top fifty leaders in Amway," Paul remembers. "It wasn't long before the children and grandchildren of all the Diamonds were using them. So they went to Amway Corporation and said, 'We should be distributing these.'"

THE INTELLIGENT DOWNLINE

In conventional marketing, decisions are made at the top and passed down to the sales force. But an MLM downline has a will of its own. Made up of independent business owners, acting in free and voluntary association, the downline often takes the initiative in identifying and exploiting opportunities well in advance of the corporate office. "It's a strength of network marketing," says Paul, "that if distributors believe in a product or service, they can pull it into the organization."

So it was with Paul's PowerCDs. He started distributing them through Amway in 1996. Sales took off immediately. With each passing year, Paul's other income streams dwindled away to nothing. But sales through Amway swelled until MLM distribution accounted for every penny of his $8 million revenues. Paul bowed to the inevitable in 1998, reorganizing his company to distribute exclusively through Amway. "We have failed at retail," he admits. "We have failed at direct mail. But we have succeeded beyond any of our expectations in selling directly, through Amway."

WAVE 4 DISTRIBUTION

Paul Zane Pilzer had gained a glimpse of the future. In a world without shopping, more and more corporations will contract with firms such as Amway to deliver their products straight into the consumer cocoon. Indeed, many brand-name companies have already taken this step. Products and services from a multitude of firms now reach the customer through network marketing sales forces, which may or may not be linked to the manufacturer in a subsidiary relationship.

IBM, for instance, is now selling Internet training programs through Big Planet, a division of NuSkin International. Dupont and Conagra teamed up in 1988 to form a bio-technology venture called DCV. After separating from its parent companies in 1997, DCV launched a network marketing subsidiary called Legacy USA to sell proprietary nutritional products. In May 1999, the $572-million nutritional giant NBTY (formerly Nature's Bounty, Inc.) acquired a Dallas-based MLM company called Dynamic Essentials Incorporated (DEI), to use as a marketing arm.

"We have observed the explosive potential of network marketing," says NBTY chairman, president and CEO Scott Rudolph, "and we believe we have a strong opportunity for growth with the DEI team." After years of watching competitors such as Rexall Sundown use MLM to achieve lightning-quick market penetration, NBTY decided it was time to join the Wave 4 Revolution.

MODEL FOR THE FUTURE

Perhaps no MLM firm better exemplifies the Wave 4 model of third party distribution than Amway. The company sells cars for GM, Chrysler, and Ford; appliances for Hotpoint and Whirlpool; and long-distance service for MCI. "Our catalog today looks like a small version of the Sears catalog," says Don Held.

> **W**ave 4 networkers will provide a Distribution Freeway through which thousands of client corporations will move their wares.

With its virtual mall on the Internet and its catalog of 6,500 products and services, Amway Corporation is showing the way to the future. Entrepreneurs, in the early days of MLM, would invent better mousetraps and use network marketing to carry those mousetraps to market. But MLM companies of the future will be more like Amway. Their main business will be selling everyone else's mousetraps. Wave 4 networkers will provide a Distribution Freeway through which thousands of client corporations will move their wares.

THE TROLL AT THE BRIDGE

In its forty-year evolution, Amway Corporation epitomizes the transition of network marketing from Wave 1 to Wave 4. Its founders, Jay Van Andel and Rich DeVos, began in classic entrepreneurial style, by introducing and selling a better mousetrap—a biodegradable cleaner called Frisk. But their company has evolved into a high-tech conduit for moving everything from Kellogg's cereals to Whirlpool dryers straight into the customer's home, bypassing the retail store entirely.

Just as Paul Zane Pilzer saved his business by making a strategic alliance with Amway, corporate America will ultimately be forced to bargain with network marketers for access to their Distribution Freeway. Like the troll at the bridge in the old Scandinavian folk tale, the MLM industry now guards one of the twenty-first century's most sought-after conduits for delivering goods and services. And, like the troll, it will demand its own price for access to that pipeline.

"I will argue, as an economist, that most of the products that worked in the past were discovered by blind luck," Paul concludes. "But the new network marketing does not depend on luck. It's about finding the best products and distributing them, regardless of who makes them. That's a system that will work consistently, in the future, on an ongoing basis."

The Growth Gap

"**I**'m not going to do it," said Lisa Wilber. "There's no way I'm going to work this program." Lisa was talking to her district manager at Avon. She had been called in, along with other sales leaders, for a special conference. There, the district manager explained that Avon was introducing a new compensation plan—an MLM plan, to be exact—and that she wanted Lisa and the others to try it. But Lisa dug in her heels.

The year was 1992. Four years had passed since Lisa had lost her job and had thrown a tantrum on the floor of her trailer. They had been hard years for Lisa, but good ones. With great effort, she had finally managed to get on her feet, with her Avon business. But Lisa was haunted each day by the fear that her gains might be taken from her. She had fought like a tigress for what she had. Lisa was determined to hold onto every scrap of it. And nothing that her district manager said would ever persuade Lisa to risk her business on some hare-brained MLM scheme.

TURNING POINT

Even now, Lisa can remember with painful clarity how she felt when she first got the news that she was laid off from her secretarial job. She remembers weeping all the way home and throwing herself on the floor in despair. "Honey, it's just a job," her husband Doug exclaimed. "Why are you carrying on like that?"

For Lisa, though, it was more than a job. All her hopes were pinned on that $20,000-a-year salary. She knew that Doug's meager earnings from wood cutting would never cover their mortgage and car payments. Until Doug found something better, they were in desperate straits. Lisa felt, at that moment, like one of the first homesteaders on the prairie. Before her lay a hostile wasteland, filled with perils. And it seemed to Lisa that the only helping hand she could rely on was her own.

"What about that Avon thing you've been doing?" Doug suggested. "Why don't you try building that up?" Awash in self-pity, Lisa did not at first see the wisdom in Doug's proposal. After all, she had been working with Avon for seven years, without success. Why should she expect anything different now? Yet something made Lisa pause that day. Desperation had opened her mind and stilled her usually ferocious pride. As Lisa dried her tears, it occurred to her that Doug just might be right. She had never really given Avon a fighting chance. She had never made up her mind to work the business, day in and day out, on a full-time basis, and to pour every ounce of her strength into it. What would happen if she did?

HIDDEN TREASURE

Lisa's mind wandered, at that moment, to one of her favorite motivational tapes, *Lead the Field* by Earl Nightingale. On the tape, Nightingale recounted Russell Conwell's famous story about the farmer who discovered diamonds beneath his fields. To illustrate the principle, Nightingale related a true tale about a gas station owner who once discovered acres of proverbial diamonds hidden in the most unlikely of places—his own filling station!

According to the story, the man looked out the window of his gas station one day and saw a customer waiting for his gas to be pumped. It was a familiar sight. But on that particular day, something clicked in the owner's mind. While the customer stood idly, with his hands in his pockets, it occurred to the proprietor that this gentleman had money to spend, and time to spend it, but nothing to spend it on. The owner subsequently stocked his gas station with snacks and sundries, thus inventing the first gas-stop convenience store.

Lisa realized that her position was not unlike that of the man in the story. She had been a part-time Avon lady since the age of eighteen, as familiar with her Avon business as that gas-station owner had been with pumping gas. Yet as with the man in the story, Lisa had failed to see the full scope of her opportunity. Until now, that is. The day she lost her secretarial job, something finally clicked for Lisa. She began to look at Avon with new eyes. "I started thinking that maybe my Acres of Diamonds are right here, in the job I already have," Lisa recalls. On the spot, she resolved to pour her full-time efforts into Avon.

TWO INCOME STREAMS

Avon Products, at that time, was a conventional direct-selling company. It did not use a multilevel marketing plan.

> Lisa formed a business plan that would allow her to exploit both income streams at once: linear income from direct sales and residual income from recruiting.

But the company was experimenting with a recruiting program that allowed sales reps to build an organization one level deep. Introduced in 1984, Avon's Sponsorship Earnings Program permitted representatives to recruit new sales reps and to draw a 5 percent commission from any inventory purchases made by their recruits. Lisa formed a business plan that would allow her to exploit both income streams at once: linear income from direct sales and residual income from recruiting.

To hone her recruiting skills, Lisa called her district manager and asked to accompany the woman on prospecting calls. Lisa also made sure that her advertisements offered both the products and the business opportunity, so prospects could take their pick. On the side of her broken-down Yugo, for instance, Lisa painted the slogan "To buy or sell Avon," along with an 800 number.

TOTAL MARKETING

Avon representatives did not usually promote their businesses with such gaudy displays. The Avon culture encouraged a more low-key approach. But Lisa saw no reason why she shouldn't avail herself of every conceivable marketing tactic. "I wanted to do all the things that a regular business does," Lisa recalls. "If you hired an electrician, wouldn't you expect him to drive up in a vehicle that was lettered?"

Lisa took out classified ads and went on the road, setting up booths at every flea market in her area. She printed business cards and stickers, setting a goal of hanging ten stickers each day, wherever her steps carried her. Some ended up on community bulletin boards and in public restrooms, others on restaurant tip trays. Lisa even transformed herself into a walking promotion. "I had the word *Avon* embroidered on all my shirts, and put the Avon name on my pocketbook," says Lisa. "Later, I put a light-up Avon sign on the roof of my car, and an Avon sign on my house. My mailbox is shaped like a lipstick."

Lisa's efforts paid off. Her income grew slowly, but steadily. Though years would pass before she succeeded in replacing her secretarial salary, Lisa quickly earned enough money to begin paying off bills and climbing out of debt. For her, it was a dream come true. Maybe Earl Nightingale had been right after all, Lisa thought. Maybe the acres of diamonds she sought were closer than she realized. But no sooner had Lisa begun to enjoy her new success than an unexpected threat materialized.

THE GEOMETRIC GROWTH GAP

Avon's Sponsorship program offered genuine residual income, but the program was hopelessly out of date. Unlike multilevel plans, it allowed sponsors to collect commissions only from their first generation of recruits. Avon sponsors were thus denied access to the geometric growth available from multilevel organizations.

A gap in earning potential consequently developed between Avon and its MLM competitors. This gap would grow increasingly worrisome to Avon executives as time went by. Sales leaders came to shun Avon as a second-rate opportunity. They preferred the rich payoffs of fast-growing MLM firms. Through its own choices, the grand old cosmetics company had effectively excluded itself from the network marketing gold rush of the 1980s. And with the best talent flocking to competing companies, the strain was beginning to show.

"IF YOU CAN'T BEAT 'EM, JOIN 'EM"

A revolution was underway in the direct selling industry. By the time Lisa was summoned to that 1992 sales conference, many older companies had already yielded to the pressure of MLM. Some went out of business. Others decided, "If you can't beat 'em, join 'em." The statistics tell the story. In 1990, fully 75 percent of the Direct Selling Association's member companies worked on straight commission. But by the end of that decade, the number of conventional firms had shrunk to less than 23 percent. MLM plans are now used by more than 77 percent of the DSA's member companies.

In the midst of this transformation, Lisa was called into that special sales meeting. "We have a new program called Leadership," the district manager announced. She explained that the program was similar to Sponsorship but better, because it allowed sponsors to get paid even for people recruited by their recruits. Lisa listened to the pitch in stony silence. Although the district manager never used the words "multilevel marketing," Lisa knew exactly what she was talking about. After 106 years of conventional direct selling, Avon Products was going MLM.

THE IMAGE PROBLEM

Lisa was frankly horrified. "I made a big point of letting them know that I wasn't going to do it," she recalls. Over the years, Lisa had been approached many times by MLM recruiters. She resented their hard-sell tactics and despised their fly-by-night, get-rich-quick programs. Time after time, Lisa had seen MLM firms lambasted in the media as pyramid schemes. She had always felt blessed to be associated with a high-gloss outfit like Avon, whose century-old reputation and conservative tactics protected it from negative press.

"What if Avon gets a bad name from this?" Lisa thought. What if 106 years of good will went spiraling down the drain, in a swirl of scandal? Clearly, Avon executives had not thought this through properly, Lisa concluded. "I thought they were just trying to keep up with the other companies," she says. "It seemed like a bad idea."

ACRES OF GRAVEL

Lisa left the sales meeting that day with a heavy heart. The acres of diamonds she had sought to discover in Avon were turning out to be acres of gravel. At least, that's how she saw it. But Lisa could not have been further from the truth. What she failed to realize was that network marketing was even then changing its image. Its perennial role as scapegoat for the business press was coming to an end. And the day of MLM's ultimate triumph was close at hand. Lisa was destined to play a very personal role in that triumph. Her impact on the Wave 4 Revolution would be considerable. Yet thanks to Lisa's relentless penchant for self-pity, it would be many years before she understood just how abundantly she had been blessed.

A Competitive Edge

T he first Avon lady in history was Mrs. P. F. E. Albee of Winchester, New Hampshire. She was hired in 1886 by a man named David H. McConnell, to sell a new line of scents and skin creams. As a door-to-door book salesman, McConnell had discovered that his female customers often appreciated the free bottles of perfume he gave them more than they did the books he peddled. So McConnell and his wife, Lucy, formed a new company to meet this demand. It was based in New York City, but they called it the California Perfume Company, to evoke the fragrant blossoms characteristic of that state.

McConnell's company owed much of its success to the efforts of Mrs. Albee. She ranged across a huge sales territory that encompassed much of the northeastern United States. Selling the product and recruiting women for the business, Mrs. Albee planted the seeds for what would become one of the largest direct-sales forces in the world. By the time McConnell's company changed its name to Avon Products in 1950, it was doing more than $25 million in sales. Today, more than 2.6 million independent representatives follow in Mrs. Albee's footsteps, selling Avon products in 135 countries and raking in some $5.1 billion in revenues.

MAKING A DIFFERENCE

Avon's early success illustrates one of the great strengths of a direct-selling force—the freedom it gives to rank-and-file members to make a difference. Independent sales reps have a far better chance of reaching their potential than salaried employees. They have the freedom and motivation to build their own businesses through innovative methods. In some cases, such as that of Mrs. Albee, a single go-getter can influence the destiny of a multibillion-dollar corporation.

Even greater leverage for individual innovators can be found in multilevel organizations—as Lisa Wilber would soon learn. Since childhood, Lisa had idolized Mrs. Albee. "I knew she was from Winchester, New Hampshire, which wasn't far from where I grew up," Lisa recalls. "I admired her for being a businesswoman. And I was drawn to Avon because it was a company of women, running businesses on their own." Lisa could hardly have suspected, though, that she would one day grow up to play a role in Avon's evolution not unlike that of the legendary Mrs. Albee.

> Avon's early success illustrates one of the great strengths of a direct-selling force—the freedom it gives to rank-and-file members to make a difference.

THE SELLING BARRIER

Stubbornness was one quality that Lisa had in abundance. Month after month, she slogged ahead on her sales rounds, refusing to have anything to do with Avon's new MLM program. But in time, her determination began to wither. It dawned on Lisa one day that she had spent a year and a half selling Avon full-time, but had never managed to earn more than $15,000 per year. For that, she toiled eighty hours each week, spending much of her life on the road.

Lisa finally had to face the fact that Avon's conventional sales program wasn't working for her. "Even at the top earning level of 50 percent," she says, "in order to earn $100,000, you had to sell $200,000 worth of product. That's one heck of a lot of lipstick." Ultimately, Lisa gave in. She signed up for Leadership in 1993.

THE SKUNKWORKS

Without realizing it, Lisa had joined a skunkworks. This is a group of mavericks who band together, within a corporation, to pursue some special project outside the mainstream. Groundbreaking achievements often arise from skunkworks. The Macintosh computer, for instance, was developed by a group of inspired innovators, working quietly among themselves within Apple. But the skunkworkers pay a price for such freedom. Often they are shunned by more buttoned-down colleagues and viewed as oddballs, weirdos, and rebels. The skunks are kept segregated, lest their noxious aroma contaminate the rest of the company.

A similar dynamic occurred at Avon. Soon after the Leadership program was installed, a new president who lacked enthusiasm for the experiment took charge. Leadership was allowed to continue, but only quietly and unobtrusively, as a skunkworks. "Multilevel marketing, back then, was viewed as a pyramid scheme," remembers Walter Bracero, head of Avon's network marketing program. Bracero admits that MLM's poor public image contributed to the company's lukewarm support. "We played it low key and didn't push it very hard."

BIRTH OF A LEADER

In the midst of a multibillion-dollar sales organization consisting of millions of people, Lisa found herself unexpectedly isolated and alone. "They weren't doing training," says Lisa. "They weren't coming out with any sales materials. They didn't offer any awards for people in Leadership. It was pretty much being ignored."

Lisa stood at a crossroads. If she wanted her MLM business to work, she would have to do it on her own. And that meant becoming a leader. In her old Avon business, Lisa had been responsible only for herself. But now she had to make sure that all her recruits did well, or her downline would not grow. Lisa's fate depended on her ability to train and motivate others. "In multilevel marketing, your own glory isn't important," says Lisa. "It's the glory you can get for your downline. If you make them successful, your own pay will take care of itself."

SUPPORT, SUPPORT, SUPPORT

Many Leadership representatives complained about Avon's neglect of the program. But Lisa had grown weary of complaining. Self-pity had gained her nothing but poverty in the past. She was determined to take control of her destiny. In fact, Lisa realized that Avon's apathy toward Leadership gave her an advantage. "I could blaze my own trail with Avon," she says, "I could work the business the way I wanted and see if it paid off or not. I didn't have somebody over me demanding that I follow the proven formula."

With no corporate infrastructure to rely on, Lisa decided she would just have to build her own. She started a newsletter for her downline, filled with tips and inspirational stories. She sent chocolates to her people on their birthdays and postcards to remind them of key events. She also started a "thousandaire" club for people selling more than $1,000 in a two-week period and awarded certificates to top achievers. Lisa made frequent visits to downline leaders in other states and offered training seminars. "I learned that the three most important things about Leadership are support, support, support," says Lisa. "This business is about supporting your downline."

THE POWER OF PERSISTENCE

Even with all this activity, success did not come right away. It took tireless persistence for Lisa to get through her first couple of years in MLM. She earned only $12,000 during her first year in Leadership and ended up reinvesting most of that back in the business. "I was afraid I was putting my money into a dead horse," Lisa recalls.

But the geometric growth started kicking in during the second year. Lisa's income more than doubled, to $32,000. It subsequently rose to $58,000, $89,000, $137,000, and $174,000 in successive years.

Today, Lisa's financial worries are long gone. Her husband built a successful construction business in the meantime, and the Wilbers' combined earnings have given them a freedom they could never have imagined before. "Six years ago, if someone said, 'Let's go out to lunch,' I had to worry whether I could pay for it or not," says Lisa. "Now, my husband can say, 'Let's go to Paris,' and we can do it, without thinking about the cost." At long last, Lisa has found her Acres of Diamonds.

GROWING LIKE A WEED

As she changed her own life, Lisa also helped transform Avon Products. Company executives took notice of Lisa's success by her fourth year in the Leadership program. "They started calling me and asking me to send them copies of my newsletter and other materials," she says. In fact, Avon was preparing for a major policy shift. For five years, it had allowed the Leadership program to grow like a weed. Now Avon began canvassing top leaders, like Lisa, to learn how corporate headquarters could adopt their successful strategies. The change came to a head in April 1998.

"We met with our Leadership representatives," says Bracero, "and announced that we were taking a more aggressive, motivational approach, really getting out there and supporting our representatives and promoting the opportunity to the public. Since then, we have doubled the number of Leadership representatives."

NO MORE SKUNKWORKS

Avon will not disclose how many on its sales force are MLM distributors today, but some estimate that 10 percent of the company's domestic direct selling force of 500,000 are enrolled in Leadership. And that percentage is likely to skyrocket in the years ahead. Bracero says that Avon is making its network marketing program "one of our key priorities for 1999." The skunkworks is no longer a skunkworks.

Just as the wild-eyed technicians behind the Macintosh remade Apple Computer in their own image, so Avon's MLM pioneers have transformed that company into a Wave 4 prototype. Avon's blue-chip trademark and global infrastructure ensure that it will be a powerhouse in twenty-first-century network marketing.

> Avon's blue-chip trademark and global infrastructure ensure that it will be a powerhouse in twenty-first-century network marketing.

A NEW CREDIBILITY

The conversion of Avon Products is but one example of the Wave 4 movement transforming corporate America. For years, Fortune 500 executives observed the MLM phenomenon from afar but dared not touch. Now, emboldened by network marketing's growing respectability, they are finally starting to cash in on it themselves.

"Multilevel marketing has become more credible today," says Bracero. "Entrepreneurs are seeing that they can make significant incomes by networking. There's really no limit to the earning potential. The Leadership program gives us a competitive advantage among our direct-selling competitors. It will put us on equal ground, for attracting entrepreneurs."

11

The Big Bang

I own a bookstore. But I never work there. I never run the cash register, sweep the floor, fret over inventory, or haggle with the landlord. In fact, the only thing I do is cash my check each quarter when it arrives in my mailbox. Like thousands of other people around the world, I'm an Amazon.com associate. To buy a book through my Web site at www.richardpoe.com, a customer simply hits a button. Amazon.com takes care of the rest. It takes the orders, processes the credit cards, and delivers the merchandise. The program costs nothing to join. At the end of each quarter, Amazon.com pays me a small commission on each purchase. I don't have to do a thing.

No, it's not a network marketing opportunity. But Amazon.com exemplifies the growing trend, among conventional corporations, to adopt more and more MLM-like strategies. As the Wave 4 Revolution transforms corporate America, the line between MLM and conventional business grows increasingly fuzzy. More and more companies are eliciting referrals from customers, recruiting customers as distributors, and treating employees like entrepreneurs.

If current trends continue, today's massive corporate bureaucracies will soon shatter into a galaxy of sole proprietorships, connected only by the Internet and fed through a network of invisible supplier relationships. Self-replicating businesses such as Amazon.com will abound. People will work from home, in the midst of their loved ones. And multilevel marketing will emerge as a dominant strategy for organizing those millions of newly independent business owners. Look for that explosion to come in the next few years. I call it the Big Bang.

UNBUNDLING CORPORATIONS

Of course, there's nothing new about the Big Bang theory. Futurists such as John Naisbitt and Alvin Toffler have been predicting a wholesale unbundling of large corporations for years. But only recently have experts begun to recognize that network marketing will play a role in that process. Barry Carter, the author of *Infinite Wealth,* was one of the first people to see the connection. Carter predicts what he calls a "mass privatization"—a wholesale transfer of assets from corporate and government bureaucracies into the hands of rank-and-file workers. Rather than slaving away for a salary, men and women of the twenty-first century will work for themselves, earning an income commensurate with their efforts.

"We already have our first mass privatization enterprises," says Carter. "Network marketers own their own businesses, receiving a percentage of whatever income each produces from sales. Network marketing has proved that it has staying power and has gained legitimacy. To date, only the network marketing industry has succeeded in offering a viable business opportunity, based on the mass privatization model."

MINDLESS ROBOTS

Carter is not involved in network marketing. Presently, he is a forty-two-year-old manager for a Fortune 100 company. As an executive, engineer, and management consultant for corporations ranging from IBM and Revlon to Hughes Aircraft, Carter has spent most of his life navigating the maze of corporate bureaucracy. And he was often appalled by what he found there. "I have worked in manufacturing environments where improper electrical assembly by a production worker could literally kill a customer," says Carter. "When I mentioned this fact to the production workers, they were shocked. They simply weren't aware of the gravity of their work."

People in corporations functioned like robots, Carter concluded, sleepwalking their way through prescribed routines without reflection, vision, or hope. What was missing from their lives was a sense of ownership. Workers and managers alike labored to benefit others, not themselves. Superior work rarely resulted in superior pay. Two hundred years after Adam Smith wrote *The Wealth of Nations,* it seemed that free enterprise had yet to touch most people's lives.

"There's not much difference between a corporate bureaucracy and a communist one," Carter observes. "Both are designed to squash initiative." Over the last two decades, legions of management gurus have sought to alleviate this problem. Yet their ministrations have had scarcely more effect than a witch doctor's rattle. "I have worked with virtually every fad management program of the past twenty years," says Carter. "I have done quality circles, management by objective, self-directed teams, horizontal organizations, worker empowerment, and all the rest. But none of them really worked. They were just Band-Aids on a gaping wound."

NATURAL EMPOWERMENT

The problem, Carter realized, was the corporation itself. As long as people served giant bureaucracies, they were no better than serfs. True freedom came only to those who owned and controlled their own businesses. But how could tens of millions of corporate employees suddenly become business owners? Where would they get the capital, the customers, the know-how? Was there enough demand in the economy to support that many businesses?

Conventional wisdom said no. It said that entrepreneurs working from home would be crushed by mega-corporations offering better service at lower prices. But Carter rejected conventional wisdom. He saw that fundamental forces in the economy were already eating away at the giant corporation, like termites. Carter believed that employees would soon gain their freedom, without the aid or intervention of a single management guru. The change would come naturally and spontaneously, from the collapse of Big Business. And it would arrive sooner than anyone expected.

IN SEARCH OF HORATIO ALGER

Back in 1931, a young British economics student named Ronald Coase traveled to the United States. He hoped to encounter the freewheeling spirit celebrated in Horatio Alger's classic rags-to-riches novels. But instead, Coase found Americans flocking to corporations like sheep, in search of steady jobs. What had happened to the fabled spirit of American entrepreneurship? "Why," Coase asked, "in a free-enterprise economy, would a worker voluntarily submit to direction by a corporation instead of selling his own output or service to customers in the market?"

In seeking an answer to that question, Coase wrote a paper called "The Nature of the Firm." It would one day earn him a Nobel Prize. In the paper, Coase concluded that corporations found it cheaper to hire full-time employees, because the transaction costs of doing business with outside suppliers were too high. In other words, it was cheaper to hire a secretary than to contract with an outside typist for each and every letter. Would-be Horatio Alger heroes therefore had no logical customers in the corporate world, because their services were overpriced. The cold logic of economics left them no choice but to submit, hat in hand, to the personnel department, in hope of a salaried position.

SMALLER IS BETTER

But today, the reverse is true. As Paul Zane Pilzer explains in *God Wants You to Be Rich,* "If Coase were to write this same paper today, he might come to exactly the opposite conclusion." Technology has reduced transaction costs so deeply that it is now cheaper and easier for corporations to farm out most work. Low phone rates, free e-mail, overnight delivery services, and instant computerized invoices facilitate collaboration, even between people thousands of miles apart. Today's economics dictate that "most large corporations should have far fewer employees, and many large corporations should not exist at all," according to Pilzer.

> Technology has reduced transaction costs so deeply that it is now cheaper and easier for corporations to farm out most work.

And, indeed, that is precisely what is happening. Major corporations are downsizing, and smaller companies are seizing more business. "Already 50 percent of U.S. exports are created by companies with 19 or fewer employees. . . ." writes John Naisbitt in *The Global Paradox*. "The Fortune 500 now account for only 10 percent of the American economy, down from 20 percent in 1970."

THE SWARM FACTOR

Scientists studying flocks of birds with high-speed film made a remarkable discovery. They found that birds react faster to subtle movements of the flock than they do to signals from their own brains. As the flock veers to avoid a predator, each bird takes about 1/70th of a second to mirror a neighboring bird's change of direction. That is less than the reaction time of an individual bird. The flock veers, swoops, and changes shape like a living thing, gracefully evading the predator. Yet no intelligence guides it. It is driven solely by the mindless reaction of each bird to the movements of its neighbor. "The flock is more than the sum of the birds," concludes *Wired* executive editor Kevin Kelly in his book *Out of Control.*

As the economy shatters into ever-smaller units, it, too, is beginning to exhibit what Kelly calls flocking or swarm behavior. A network of millions of small units can react faster and more decisively in the marketplace than a lumbering bureaucracy. "Mathematics says the sum value of a network increases as the square of the number of members . . ." writes Kelly, in *New Rules for the New Economy.* "Thus a thousand members can have a million friendships." Whether in man or beast, it is the sheer number of random relationships between individuals that gives the flock its fluidity. The more units you have in a network, the more relationships can form between them. And the more relationships you have, the faster and more effectively the whole network responds to the marketplace.

CENTRIFUGAL FORCE

Corporations today are spinning apart, as if by centrifugal force. A race is on to see which company can splinter into the smallest units, fastest, thus transforming itself from bureaucracy to swarm. At stake in this strange race for self-dismemberment is life itself. "Huge corporations like IBM, Philips, and GM must break up to become confederations of small, autonomous, entrepreneurial companies, if they are to survive," writes Naisbitt in *The Global Paradox.*

Thus, Asea Brown Boveri has split into twelve hundred different companies, employing about two hundred people each. AT&T has divided itself into twenty subdivisions, each responsible for its own profit and loss. But these are only half-measures, says Barry Carter. The advantage, in today's economy, belongs not to those companies that manage to split into scores or even hundreds of different parts, but to those that explode into millions. The Swarm Factor will achieve its full intensity only when each individual worker gains autonomy and can fly through the marketplace as freely as a bird in a flock. Therein lies the power of mass privatization.

"As one organization in one industry converts to mass privatization," says Carter, "the entire industry will fall like dominoes, one company at a time. Either they will be forced out of business, or forced to mass privatize."

THE NEXT FRONTIER

To illustrate, Carter points to the book industry. Amazon.com achieved lightning-quick market penetration by unleashing a swarm of independent associates, who spread the company logo to every corner of the Internet. Major book chains had no choice but to follow suit. Barnes and Noble, Borders, and other book chains not only created competing Web sites, but offered associate programs similar to that of Amazon.com.

> The advantage, in today's economy, belongs not to those companies that manage to split into scores or even hundreds of different parts, but to those that explode into millions.

Indeed, the last few months have seen an explosion of copycat programs on the Internet, going far beyond the book industry. At www.associate-it.com, would-be entrepreneurs can choose from more than a thousand different affiliate programs, in businesses ranging from real estate and flower deliveries to classified advertising. Some programs, such as buyMLMtools.com even offer multilevel compensation, allowing affiliates to recruit other affiliates and collect commissions on their sales. Jupiter Communications, Inc. predicts that affiliate programs will account for 24 percent of e-commerce sales by 2002.

Carter applauds the affiliate model as a prototype of mass privatization. Indeed, he himself is an Amazon.com associate. But Carter acknowledges that such online businesses do not yet provide sufficient income to replace a corporate salary. The Big Bang of mass privatization will occur only when strategies are developed for providing living income for thousands of people at a time. So far, says Carter, only MLM companies seem to have mastered this trick.

"Network marketing has its limitations," says Carter. "It provides private ownership only in sales and marketing, and most people are not sales people." Nevertheless, Carter believes that MLM has made an impressive start in pioneering mass privatization. "Network marketing is leading a revolution," says Carter. "It's a revolution that is destined to change not only the way we work, but how our children learn, how our families are structured, how we order society."

The Power of the Swarm

Delirium hit Wall Street on April 6, 1998. For the first time in history, the Dow Jones Industrial Average soared above 9,000 points. The financial press buzzed with excitement. Yet the most intriguing part of the story went untold. Pundits completely overlooked the small but critical role that network marketing had played in driving the Dow to new heights.

It all began with the largest corporate merger in history, announced earlier that day—an $85-billion deal between the world's second-largest bank, Citicorp, and the insurance giant Travelers Group. Together, they formed a new entity called Citigroup, which instantly took its place as the largest financial services company in the world. Citigroup boasted nearly $700 billion in assets and 100 million customers. Financial and brokerage stocks skyrocketed in response to the deal. Mutual funds with heavy stakes in the merger went through the roof.

THE SECRET CATALYST

So what did network marketing have to do with all this? In fact, it lay at the core of the Citigroup merger. One of the Travelers Group's most valued assets was an MLM subsidiary called Primerica. It acted as a distribution channel for a wide range of Travelers Group companies. Primerica sold everything from Smith Barney mutual funds to Commercial Credit loans and Travelers/Aetna property and casualty insurance. And it sold them with extraordinary vigor.

A January 1998 report from CIBC Oppenheimer called Primerica the "Travelers Group's primary vehicle for cross-selling." Donaldson, Lufkin & Jenrette Securities marveled, in a March 1998 report, that Primerica had managed to sell nearly 50 percent of all outstanding Commercial Credit loans. "In fact, Primerica sold more of a new series of Smith Barney Inc. funds in 1996 than Smith Barney," enthused the *Atlanta Business Chronicle* on February 14, 1997.

DOOR-TO-DOOR BANKERS

The Travelers Group, in short, had synergy. Its MLM sales force provided the perfect vehicle for moving financial services. And Travelers' numerous subsidiaries kept Primerica well supplied with offerings for its customers. "In fact, one of the things that drove the merger between Citicorp and Travelers Group," says Primerica CEO Joseph Plumeri in the April 1999 issue of *Network Marketing Lifestyles,* "was the chance to cross-sell financial products from all our potential sister companies."

Now that Primerica is in bed with the world's second-largest bank, Plumeri suggests that its agents may soon start hawking Citicorp checking accounts. "Your personal financial analyst can come to your house, deliver your checks, do a personal financial analysis, and help you plan your financial life, which now includes the banking aspect," he told *American Banker* in November 1998. "All of a sudden you've got bankers that are making house calls."

Just as she predicted the end of shopping in *The Popcorn Report,* Faith Popcorn predicts the end of banking, as we know it, in her new book *Clicking.* "Imagine . . . a bank where you always have an assigned individual who knows your name and your credit history . . . your 'private banker' . . ." she writes wistfully. Network marketing may soon fulfill that dream in an unexpected way—through Primerica.

"A MULTI-TIERED SYSTEM OF COMMISSIONS"

Long before the merger, Wall Street analysts had taken note of Primerica's innovative sales force. Yet many were so unfamiliar with network marketing, they did not know what to call it. They extolled Primerica's MLM pioneers in the clinical but wonderstruck terms of a lepidopterist encountering a new species of butterfly.

"Standard & Poor's views Primerica's agency force of over 110,000 . . . to be its primary competitive strength," said a typical 1997 S&P report. "The system is . . . very low-cost . . . yet the agents bear many attributes of a controlled system. Agent compensation is enhanced by a multi-tiered system of commissions that promotes new agent recruitment and allows each agent to build an organization for himself."

Many experts seemed unaware that MLM had been used for decades by a host of different companies. For example, when A. M. Best raised Primerica's rating from "A-" to "A" in December 1996, it explained, "This rating action reflects the progress the company has made in realizing the benefits of its unique distribution system. . . ." But, of course, Primerica's system was far from unique. It was only one of thousands of MLM networks criss-crossing the world at that point.

MASS PRIVATIZATION

With Primerica, the Wave 4 Revolution had come to Wall Street. On the surface, the mega-merger of Travelers and Citicorp looked like a consolidation of traditional corporate power—a move toward bigness rather than smallness. But, in fact, Citigroup was sliding inexorably toward mass privatization. It cut its workforce by 6 percent in 1998, laying off 10,400 people. And while Citigroup's conventional payroll dwindled, its MLM sales force grew, reaching 139,000 agents by 1999.

Like corporate America in general, Citigroup was cutting jobs but expanding entrepreneurial opportunities. It was availing itself of the power of the swarm. Primerica agents descended on the market like birds in a flock, targeting tiny or inaccessible niches that conventional marketers might have overlooked. Thousands of entrepreneurs acting in concert accomplished what the world's greatest financial giants could never achieve on their own.

> **P**rimerica agents descended on the market like birds in a flock, targeting tiny or inaccessible niches that conventional marketers might have overlooked.

MAN WITH A MISSION

Tyrone Taylor is part of the Primerica flock. For him, mass privatization is more than a concept. It has changed his life. Primerica helped Tyrone rise from a Xerox supervisor making $26,000 a year, to an entrepreneur with a six-figure income. Now he uses Primerica to fight a one-man crusade against poverty. Reared on the mean streets of Detroit, Tyrone's mission in life is to spread prosperity among his fellow black Americans.

"My downline is 98 percent African American," says Tyrone. "The only thing that separates a poor person from a rich person is knowledge. My passion is to produce financially independent people in my community." In the process, Tyrone has built a considerable degree of financial independence for himself. He earned more than $425,000 from his downline in 1998.

Things weren't always so cushy for Tyrone. He grew up on the east side of Detroit, the son of working-class parents.

"It was a tough environment," Tyrone remembers. His father was a janitor, and his mother a housewife. They struggled to make a decent home for their family. But they wanted their twelve children to have more. "They always told us to get a college education and a good job," says Tyrone.

CORPORATE DRONE

Unfortunately, the formula didn't work for Tyrone. By age twenty-seven, he had reached a dead end. As a production supervisor for Xerox Corporation, Tyrone worked six- and seven-day weeks. But the corporate hierarchy offered little room for growth. He began looking for part-time business opportunities.

An old college friend introduced Tyrone to a life insurance company called the A. L. Williams Corporation, founded in 1977 by ex-football coach Arthur L. Williams. It was a network marketing company. Excited by the chance to earn residual income, Tyrone went right to work building his downline. But his boss soon caught him handing out business cards on the job. "He told me that I either had to stop doing A. L. Williams, or leave," Tyrone recalls. "I was shocked. It made me feel like I was in prison, like some kind of slave to corporate America."

Tyrone promised to stop recruiting on company time, but he went right on building the business on the side. Six months later, Tyrone was making enough money to quit his job. It took him another two years to earn a six-figure income. "It was hard work," Tyrone recalls, "but I was passionate about what I was doing."

SQUEAKY CLEAN

Having joined the company in 1985, Tyrone watched it go through many changes. A. L. Williams was acquired by Primerica in 1988, which was subsequently swallowed up by Travelers Group Inc. in 1994, and finally by Citigroup in 1998. The company's culture changed along with its owners. "I think everything happens for a reason," Tyrone reflects.

"Art Williams was good for his time. He founded the company and got things going. But as we moved into the '90s, we needed a visionary who could professionalize us and give us a system for success."

That visionary turned out to be Joseph J. Plumeri, a Travelers executive who was appointed CEO of Primerica in 1994. One of Plumeri's first moves was to discipline the sales force, enforcing strict compliance with government regulations. Auditors scrutinized every agent. Those who wouldn't mend their ways were terminated. The result is a sales force more squeaky clean than its conventional competitors. At a time when the insurance industry is reeling from legal and regulatory actions, Primerica "stands above the fray," said the February 1997 issue of the insurance trade journal *Best's Review.* It touted Primerica as "a role model for its lawsuit-weary rivals."

Turnkey Systems

Plumeri next set up turnkey systems that would standardize and simplify the Primerica business. One of these was PFS University, a training program for new recruits. As many as 80 percent of Tyrone's recruits used to drop out after failing their insurance and securities licensing exams. Now that PFS University coaches Tyrone's recruits before the exam, their success rate has soared to about 45 percent.

Even more helpful has been a standardized selling tool called the Financial Needs Analysis (FNA). Primerica agents now have their prospects fill out an FNA questionnaire—a broad survey of the prospect's finances—as the first step in the sales process. The agents then take the figures home and run them through a computer program, which instantly reveals where the prospect's financial shortfalls lie.

A Cold Slap in the Face

"It's like a cold slap in the face," explains Primerica public relations senior vice president Mark Supic. The next time they meet with the prospect, the agents come armed with facts. They show the prospect the holes in his financial planning—the inadequacy of his present income to provide the dream house, the college education for his kids, or the comfortable retirement that he desires. "Once they see that shortfall," says Tyrone, "most people find themselves wanting to make some moves."

Those moves might take the form of buying insurance, investing in mutual funds, or taking out consumer loans—all available from Primerica. Or they might take the form of joining the salesman's own downline, as a Primerica agent. "If the person seems right for it," says Tyrone, "you suggest to him that one way to make up that income shortfall would be to come into the Primerica business."

ONE PERSON AT A TIME

As with all network marketing companies, Primerica's ability to turn customers into salesmen has enabled it to penetrate deeply into markets that would otherwise be closed. The Primerica program spreads through a community, one person at a time, by means of an endless chain of personal referrals, among friends, neighbors, relatives, and business associates. It brings the full battery of Citigroup services right into the cocoon—the cloistered sanctuary of people's homes, churches, and families.

Primerica has used its word-of-mouth strategy to reach the blue-collar and middle-income families disdained by most insurers. "Too many people in this business have told me, 'Oh, we can't afford to sell to anyone earning less than $100,000 a year,'" writes managing editor Edward Keenan, in the September 16, 1996 issue of the life insurance newsletter *Probe*. "Primerica . . . has made a bundle selling to the very people we've neglected."

BACK TO THE ROOTS

One of those neglected groups has been African Americans— who constitute some 20 percent of Primerica's top sales leaders.

"People in my market get really excited about Primerica," says Tyrone. "Most of them don't have a lot of money. They want to know how they can get out of economic bondage." Tyrone, his wife Carolyn, and their daughter Camille now live in a million-dollar home in the exclusive Detroit suburb of Franklin. But he hasn't forgotten his roots. Tyrone's business draws him back, again and again, to his old neighborhood in East Detroit.

"I speak at churches and a lot of different places where African Americans congregate," he says. "In my old neighborhood, you see a lot of banks and credit unions, but no brokerage firms. Children grow up seeing their parents work for thirty years and go to the bank and never accu-

> As with all network marketing companies, Primerica's ability to turn customers into salesmen has enabled it to penetrate deeply into markets that would otherwise be closed.

mulate anything, so they end up going the same route. No one is teaching them to invest. To be able to bring Smith Barney into my neighborhood is exciting to me."

NO MORE LAUGHTER

When Arthur L. Williams first brought out his MLM life insurance company in 1977, the industry laughed. An ex-football coach leading a part-time army of truck drivers, traffic cops, teachers, and factory workers hardly seemed much of a threat. But no one laughs anymore. The power of the swarm has stilled every jeer. A decade after his 1990 retirement, A. L. Williams's vision continues to rock the corporate world. Today, as we hover on the brink of the Big Bang—the explosion of corporate America into a million tiny entrepreneurships— Williams's prescience seems nothing short of inspired.

CHAPTER 13

The McDonald's Effect

Meg Kelly-Smith was living a nightmare. It had come upon her suddenly, without warning. Only a few months before, she had been on top of the world. As senior vice president of the nation's twelfth largest savings and loan, she managed a $12 billion real estate loan portfolio. Her husband, Jay Smith, was equally successful. For twenty years, he had run his own successful insurance services company in Marin County, California, just north of San Francisco. Both Meg and Jay were used to their five-figure monthly incomes. They assumed that the money would keep rolling in forever.

But it didn't. In the late 1980s, both Meg and Jay hit a bump in the road. The savings-and-loan industry bottomed out, along with the insurance business in California. "I saw my company in jeopardy," Meg recalls. Her husband was in even worse straits. The insurance providers and Wall Street firms for which he supplied processing services began delaying payments. Jay was stuck with over three hundred employees clamoring for paychecks and not enough income to cover them. He began selling off assets. "Instead of the employees working for him, he was working for them," Meg recalls. "He was liquidating his assets, but he couldn't keep any money for himself. After twenty years in business, Jay was afraid he would never be able to retire."

THE E-MYTH

Meg's husband had run smack into the E-Myth—the Entrepreneurial Myth. According to small-business consultant Michael E. Gerber, hundreds of thousands of people each year are bamboozled into thinking they can escape the corporate rat race simply by starting their own businesses. But for most, the dream of freedom proves as elusive as the Seven Cities of El Dorado.

The truth may take years to sink in. But when it does, it hits hard. "All of a sudden," writes Gerber in *The E-Myth*, "you are struck with the reality of your condition. . . . You don't own a *business,* you own a *job.* What's more, it's the worst job in the world." Unlike your corporate job, this one doesn't give you time off for vacations. It consumes you, seven days a week, twenty-four hours a day.

Hiring employees doesn't help. No manager ever seems good enough to take charge completely. You peer over everyone's shoulder as they work and step in to prevent disasters on a daily basis. In the end, you realize that you have sacrificed your life, your family, your peace of mind, and your health for the business. But what has it given you in return? More of your revenues seem to wind up in your employees' pockets than your own.

THE TURNKEY SOLUTION

Is there no escape, then, from the corporate rat race? There is, for those who know the secret, says Gerber. It lies in a new way of doing business, still poorly understood by most people. "There's a revolution going on today. . . ." Gerber claims. "The Turnkey Revolution. Not only is it changing the way we do business in this country, but it is changing who goes into business, how they do it, and the likelihood of success."

When you buy a new car, you shouldn't have to tinker under the hood. You should just turn your key and start driving. That's what the word *turnkey* means. In the business world, it refers to a system so perfectly crafted that it requires no tinkering, de-bugging, or trial and error. Just turn the key, and start making money. Gerber predicts that, in the years ahead, more and more people will attain entrepreneurial freedom through turnkey businesses. They will owe their success to a phenomenon that Gerber calls the McDonald's Effect.

ASSEMBLY-LINE BURGERS

The phenomenon takes its name from two brothers, Maurice and Richard McDonald. Back in 1948, they invented a new way of serving fast food. Their drive-in hamburger stand in San Bernardino, California, ran like a Detroit assembly line. It had a stripped-down menu, offering only burgers, shakes, and fries. Using simple, standardized procedures, they filled orders in record time. Customers flocked to the restaurant, which the brothers had named after themselves: McDonald's.

> That's what the word *turnkey* means. In the business world, it refers to a system so perfectly crafted that it requires no tinkering, de-bugging, or trial and error.

In 1954, a milkshake machine salesman named Ray Kroc visited the restaurant. He was so impressed that he made a deal with the brothers to franchise their concept. Kroc agreed to sell McDonald's franchises for a $950 fee. Once an outlet was up and running, the franchisee would pay Kroc 1.9 percent of his gross sales, of which about a quarter would go to the McDonald brothers.

Kroc's deal made history. More than 24,500 McDonald's stores span the world today, with systemwide sales of $36 billion.

IDIOT-PROOF

Some might assume that it was the genius of the McDonald brothers that lay behind the restaurant chain's extraordinary success. But they would be wrong. The original McDonald's in San Bernardino was a successful business, but not a turnkey one. Only a turnkey business could have worked consistently, time and again, under the management of more than 24,000 different owners. Ray Kroc made that possible. It was he who packaged the McDonald's concept into a viable franchise, unleashing, in the process, the unstoppable force that Gerber has named the McDonald's Effect.

After signing his deal with the McDonald brothers, Kroc memorized, step-by-step, every procedure they used in preparing and serving their food. He then set up a prototype store in Chicago to see if he could replicate their success. But it proved a daunting task. Rote imitation was insufficient to duplicate the McDonald's magic. Before his franchise was ready for market, Kroc had to make it idiot-proof. He had to de-bug every conceivable problem and provide back-up systems to circumvent them. By the time he was done, Kroc had rethought the concept from the ground up. It was a thankless task. But only because Kroc did all that thinking beforehand were his franchisees freed from having to reinvent the business, on their own. By the time they paid Kroc his $950 fee, the only thing left for them to do was to slip into the driver's seat and turn the key.

MAGNIFICENT OBSESSION

Kroc was obsessed. He demanded perfection in every detail. When his first batch of McDonald's French fries came out soggy and bland, he launched a full-scale investigation. Eventually, he figured out that the desert wind was drying out the McDonald brothers' potatoes, which were stored outside in open chicken-wire bins. That accounted for their unique crispy flavor. So Kroc set up an indoor curing system in the basement of his restaurant, where the potatoes were blasted by an electric fan.

Kroc perfected every detail of the McDonald's procedure in that first prototype store. In the process, he drove his manager, Ed MacLuckie, like a Parris Island drill sergeant. "Sometimes Ed MacLuckie would have forgotten to turn the sign on at dusk, and that made me furious," Kroc recalls in his autobiography, *Grinding It Out*. "Or maybe the lot would have some litter on it that Ed said he hadn't had time to pick up. Those little things didn't seem to bother some people, but they were gross affronts to me. I'd get screaming mad and really let Ed have it. . . . Perfection is very difficult to achieve, and perfection is what I wanted in McDonald's. Everything else was secondary for me."

BEYOND FRANCHISING

Ray Kroc's magnificent obsession irritated employees, who had to feel the lash of his tongue. But it blessed thousands of franchisees with the gift of a successful business. In exchange for a one-time fee and a small percentage of sales, McDonald's owners today gain a proven system, a valued trademark, and the massive advertising clout of a multibillion-dollar corporation. Kroc did not invent the full-format franchise, but he raised the technique to a science. Following in his footsteps, franchised businesses now account for an estimated 50 percent of all U.S. retail sales, according to the International Franchise Association.

> Turnkey systems have shown the same McDonald's-like ability to replicate themselves thousands of times over, even in non-franchised businesses.

As the twenty-first century dawns, the McDonald's Effect reverberates far beyond the boundaries of traditional franchising. Turnkey systems have shown the same McDonald's-like ability to replicate themselves thousands of times over, even in non-franchised businesses. Network marketers, for instance, gain the benefit of proven systems and trademarks, just like franchisees. But they replicate even faster. Swifter still is the spread of e-commerce Web sites, cobbled together with links to preexisting affiliate programs. Already, the Turnkey Revolution is upon us. And it has arrived just in time. As traditional jobs vanish and would-be entrepreneurs run afoul of the E-Myth, turnkey systems may well provide the most realistic alternative.

A WAY OUT

"With the downsizing of big companies, the whole economic structure of work is becoming different from anything it's ever been before," says Michael Gerber. "But it's not going to be six billion people out on the streets selling pencils. People are going to have to have a system, a framework, a context." Gerber predicts that turnkey businesses such as franchising, multilevel marketing, and Internet affiliate programs will provide much of the support structure necessary for easing the transition from a job-based economy to one built on mass privatization and self-employment.

Gerber's consultancy, the E-Myth Academy, based in Santa Rosa, California, teaches small business owners to become more like Ray Kroc, streamlining and standardizing their procedures into turnkey systems that can then be sold, franchised, or handed over to managers. But the fact is that most people would rather be a franchisee than a Ray Kroc. They would rather buy into a turnkey system than invent one from scratch.

This is the choice that Meg and Jay faced when their own careers hit a road block. Both were experienced and highly trained managers. Both could have built a company from the ground floor and run it in their sleep. Both were potential Ray Krocs. But Meg and Jay were tired of the rat race. They wanted no more worlds to conquer. All they desired was a way out. The Turnkey Revolution would provide that escape route, in a way that would astonish both of them.

CHAPTER 14

The Virtual Business

"For seven years, Jay and I hardly ever saw each together," Meg recalls. Not only were they both working high-powered jobs, but Meg commuted six hundred miles to work in San Diego. She came home only on weekends. When trouble hit their businesses, it came almost as a relief. Now they had the perfect excuse to break their routine and to seek a less punishing way of life.

By 1989, both Meg and Jay had taken the plunge. Jay had sold his business, and Meg had quit her job. Neither had a clear idea of what to do next. On five things only were they firmly agreed: first, they wanted to find a business that they could build together as partners; second, they wanted to be part of a growing industry, with a lot of upside potential; third, they did not want to deal with a single employee, ever again; fourth, they did not want to invest a lot of money; and fifth, they wanted to make residual income. "We didn't want to risk the money we had left," says Meg. "We were willing to work hard for five or six years, to build up the business with sweat equity. But after that, we wanted it to produce residual income." In short, they had set themselves a nearly impossible set of goals.

DUE DILIGENCE

It did not take long for Meg and Jay to discover that conventional business methods offered little hope of fulfilling their plan. To earn residual income, they would have to get paid for other people's efforts. And that meant either hiring a lot of people—which they had promised themselves not to do—or buying pieces of existing businesses, which meant risking a lot of money. "The last vehicle left was network marketing," says Meg. "We weren't exactly thrilled when we came to that conclusion. We didn't know much about network marketing, but the one thing we thought we knew was that it was bad."

Like many conventional businesspeople, Meg and Jay had formed their opinions about MLM mainly from lurid exposés in the media. Yet now they felt obliged to research the industry objectively. They combed the law library for everything they could find on MLM. They solicited from the attorney general a list of companies that had been shut down, and analyzed them to find out exactly where they had gone wrong. "By the time we were through doing our research, we understood the concept was viable and that the math worked," says Meg. "If you could get involved with a company that met the legal guidelines, and that offered a product or service you felt comfortable with, it gave the potential of getting paid for a lot of other people's efforts."

MLM ODYSSEY

Meg and Jay spent the next six months investigating more than seventy different MLM companies. They combed the ads in trade publications, such as *Moneymaker's Monthly.* They flew around the country, visiting various companies' headquarters. "Jay used to joke that we met a lot of nice people but, unfortunately, most of them did not have a clue how to run a business," says Meg. Again and again, they found companies that were successful at selling products but utterly inept at handling their own growth. "Their own success would kill them," says Meg, "because they didn't do the back office work. They didn't have the capital to build inventory or deliver. They couldn't track the sales. By the time commissions came due, they were long gone."

Meg and Jay were also put off by the products. Most companies seemed to offer consumables, from skin cream and herbal supplements to dog food. Meg disliked the idea of asking people to change their buying habits, especially in favor of products that were often more expensive than their store-bought counterparts. In some cases, the companies used pre–Wave 3 methods—they still required distributors to stockpile and deliver their own inventory. Meg and Jay could not imagine trying to talk their well-heeled, executive friends into filling up their garages with cartons of moisturizer. "After one trip where we looked at five different companies," Meg recalls, "I told Jay that I had decided that if you had to rub it on your skin or swallow it, I just wasn't going to do it."

THE NEW FRONTIER

Unknown to Meg and Jay, the object of their quest was even then unfolding right before their eyes. The hottest business headlines of the day were about telecommunications. Ever since 1934, the American Telephone and Telegraph Company—AT&T—had enjoyed a government-enforced monopoly over the phone industry. Then, in 1974, a company called Microwave Communications Inc. (MCI) brought suit against AT&T, challenging its monopoly. The U.S. Justice Department followed up with its own antitrust action. AT&T finally agreed, in 1982, to shed its local phone business and to compete on the open market for long-distance customers. The plan went into effect in 1984.

Two companies, MCI and Sprint, quickly became AT&T's biggest rivals, largely through the use of MLM sales methods. The success of network marketing companies, such as Amway and Network 2000, in selling their long-distance service went largely unnoticed in corporate America. But astute entrepreneurs saw a new frontier in the making. One of these was Texas oilman Kenny A. Troutt.

AN INNOVATIVE STRATEGY

An all-around entrepreneur, Troutt had tried his hand at the insurance, construction, and horse-breeding businesses before getting into oil. He took a beating in the 1980s when oil prices tumbled from $50 to $15 per barrel. Casting about for a new idea, Troutt focused on the feeding frenzy for long-distance phone service. A network marketer named Steve Smith convinced him that MLM was the key to cracking that market. The two men became partners in 1989.

Troutt had founded Excel Communications, Inc. the year before. Based in Dallas, the company operated on a simple concept. Unlike Amway and Network 2000, which acquired customers for MCI and Sprint, Excel would get customers for itself. It would shop constantly for the best prices and service, switching customers from one carrier to another at will, wherever the best deals turned up.

A TWENTY-FIRST-CENTURY BUSINESS

In his research, Jay Smith had already identified telecommunications as a growth business. At $52 billion in sales (in 1989), the industry was projected to hit $1 trillion by 2005. "Jay realized that it was going to be the industry of the millennium," says Meg. "Also, telecommunications had never had a down quarter in 150 years." An Atlanta company was reselling commercial long-distance service for AT&T. Meg and Jay decided to team up with it, to sell AT&T service through an MLM downline, much as Network 2000 had done for Sprint.

But the business proved daunting. Meg and Jay targeted big companies, with phone bills between $1,000 and $10,000 a month. That meant long sales pitches to corporate executives, involving complicated breakdowns of calling patterns and rate structures. "It was a very complicated business," Meg recalls. "Highly technical."

DUPLICATABILITY

Meg and Jay landed corporate customers with ease, but recruiting people for their downline was another matter. "There weren't many people who could do what we did," Meg admits. "So we couldn't build a large sales force." The business offered no turnkey system. It depended entirely on Meg's and Jay's unique skills. Though it turned out to be a great sales job for Meg and Jay, it offered little hope of leveraging other people's efforts—the key to massive residual income.

What they needed was a *duplicatable* business—one that could be replicated time and again, by people at different skill levels. And that meant it had to be simple. In the long-distance business, the simplest sell was the residential customer. You just signed him up, and never thought about it again. For that reason, Meg and Jay took note when a friend told them about a little Texas company called Excel Communications that was selling residential long-distance service through MLM.

SOUL-SEARCHING

"It was rather amusing," Meg remembers. After flying down to Dallas in 1990, they found that Excel Communications consisted of five employees and a few desks crammed into an office. The sales materials used by its representatives were photocopies of photocopies. Yet, Meg and Jay were intrigued. Crude though it was, the business seemed duplicatable. Anyone could do it.

Meg and Jay found they had some soul-searching to do. Every corporate instinct in their bodies told them to steal Excel's concept and do it themselves. Both had extensive experience doing back-office work for banks, insurance companies, and Wall Street brokerages. "We were probably better equipped to do the back office than Kenny was," says

Meg. "We could easily have replicated what he had done." But did they really want to? For the first time, Meg and Jay forced themselves to stop thinking like corporate executives. They reminded themselves of their goals: no employees; no financial risk; residual income. And it slowly dawned on them that, in the strange new world of the Turnkey Revolution, this tiny company with its Lilliputian office might be just the thing they were looking for.

KEEP IT SIMPLE

"We started reviewing all the reasons we got involved in network marketing," Meg recalls, "and the biggest advantage was the lack of employees." Why not let Excel have all the headaches of running an office? Why not let them negotiate rates with carriers and fight over billing? By leaving these responsibilities to Excel, Meg and Jay would be free to turn all their attention to building a downline. They could build their Excel business as large as they wanted, without having to rent a single office suite or hire a single employee. In effect, they would create a virtual corporation—a multimillion-dollar enterprise that existed nowhere except in the intricate chain of commission relationships stored in Excel's computer. That was exactly what they had dreamed about. Meg and Jay went to work on it in the summer of 1990.

"We made lists of people we knew and started recruiting," says Meg. "It was different from before. Now we didn't need people who were highly technical or had special sales skills. We took anyone who wanted to make extra income. And we looked for people who knew a lot of other people, so we could get their referrals." Their downline grew rapidly. By the end of the year, Meg and Jay had shut down their commercial long-distance business and gone full-time with Excel.

A BITTERSWEET VICTORY

Nobody knows what tomorrow may bring. The stunning success that Meg and Jay experienced with Excel took a bittersweet turn in 1995. Suffering from a heart condition, Jay passed out in an airport and died of head injuries from the fall. Meg was devastated but nonetheless grateful for the five good years they had enjoyed together, as partners in Excel. "We started this business so we could have more time together,"

> She and Jay matched their previous five-figure monthly incomes after only four years in Excel. But this time, the income was residual. It kept coming in, whether or not they chose to work.

says Meg. "We just had no clue that the time would be so short. When Jay passed away, it showed how important it was for us to do this."

Those five years with Excel had also ensured that Meg would have no financial worries in her widowhood. At age fifty, she still builds her Excel business but no longer needs to. She and Jay matched their previous five-figure monthly incomes after only four years in Excel. But this time, the income was residual. It kept coming in, whether or not they chose to work. "This business left me financially secure for the rest of my life," says Meg, "and probably for generations to come."

THE TURNKEY LIFESTYLE

As for Excel, it went on to become the fastest-growing telecommunications firm in history. By 1996, when it was listed on the New York Stock Exchange, Excel's annual sales had grown to $1.4 billion—a 200 percent increase from the previous year. Excel is moving constantly to expand its product lines, in keeping with Wave 4 trends. Already, it offers paging service, calling cards, and Internet access, in addition to residential and commercial long-distance service. Electrical service will not be far behind, Troutt predicts. Having merged with the Canadian firm Teleglobe Inc., in 1998, Excel now belongs to a conglomerate with combined annual sales of about $3.5 billion—the fourth-largest long-distance phone company in North America.

Meg Kelly-Smith is very glad today that she chose to work her business the turnkey way. Her virtual corporation of tens of thousands of Excel distributors works night and day with little supervision, enriching Meg even as the distributors build their own businesses. Meg enjoys reading about Excel's mergers and acquisitions in the *Wall Street Journal.* But she enjoys even more being able to fold up the paper and sit back in her Sausalito home, taking in a panoramic view of the Golden Gate Bridge. As she contemplates Excel's adventures in the global marketplace, she revels in the fact that people other than she must shoulder the burden of running that multibillion-dollar giant. Deep in her heart, Meg has embraced the Turnkey Revolution.

CHAPTER 15

The Techno-Edge

Technology is where the rubber meets the road, in the Wave 4 Revolution. As the twenty-first century dawns, network marketing is driven increasingly by advances in telecommunications. Rank-and-file networkers display an intimacy with cutting-edge technology that puts most corporate executives to shame. They work each day in the decentralized, virtual workplace that most managers and organizational scientists only read about in books.

The typical network marketer interacts with hundreds—even thousands—of people all over the world in the course of his normal business. Customers, prospects, and associates are just as likely to live in Malaysia as in the next town. And networkers use much the same methodology to recruit their Malaysian prospects as their neighbors down the street. Prospects are notified of the opportunity through mailings, ads, Web sites, or e-mail. If they want further information, they can get it automatically via fax-on-demand or e-mail auto-responder. After making personal contact, by phone or e-mail, the network marketer may direct his recruits to a teleconference or satellite TV conference, where thousands of prospects at a time may participate in a recruiting rally, led by the company president. Within downlines, network marketers coordinate their efforts constantly, using pagers, cell phones, Web site announcements, fax, e-mail, and voice broadcasts.

INTERNETWORKING

Shrewd observers noticed years ago that network marketers were leading the way in commercial applications of the Internet. At a time when corporate America dismissed the Net as all hype and no substance, MLM distributors were building downlines through Web site promotion and e-mail blasting. "Network marketers are one of the few groups actually doing successful commercial business on the Internet," observed John Fogg back in 1996. Fogg is the founding editor of MLM trade publications *Upline* and *Network Marketing Lifestyles.* "You've got people out there with downlines of 1,500 to 2,000 people built solely online," he pointed out.

What was true in 1996 has become even truer today—by several orders of magnitude. "Network marketers look at every edgy opportunity," says Faith Popcorn. "In the future, network marketing will have more and more of a web angle to it. Network marketers are best at reaching people in the cocoon. But a lot of cocooners are on the Web nowadays, and network marketers are responding to that challenge."

> Within downlines, network marketers coordinate their efforts constantly, using pagers, cell phones, Web site announcements, fax, e-mail, and voice broadcasts.

According to Walter Bracero, head of Avon's network marketing program, "MLM is about networking, and there's probably no quicker way to establish a network than through the Internet today. We are looking at leveraging the Internet very heavily." Avon has already made a good start in that direction, with Avon.com named the top retail Web site of 1998 by *Computer World.* Even America Online has become a hotbed of recruiting activity, through its MLM message boards.

MLM ONLINE

Many network marketing firms have launched retail stores on the Internet. Amway, for instance, has rolled out Quixtar.com, a virtual mall selling thousands of goods and services from different companies. To order from Quixtar, customers enter the PIN numbers of the Amway distributors who referred them. Those distributors automatically receive a commission from the customers' purchases. Companies such as Worldwide Internet Marketing (www.futurenet-online.com) not only sell products through their Web sites, but also the Web-TV devices customers use to access those sites. Big Planet offers a soup-to-nuts package that includes Internet access, training for Web site construction, and Web hosting.

One fast-growing site is MLM.com, launched in 1997 by Craig Wennerholm and his partners. Its Discussion Forum provides a popular meeting place for people with ideas, opinions, and observations to share about network marketing. Visitors can get updates on MLM company stock prices, corporate anouncements, and other news. By the end of its first year, MLM.com had already broken even on its operating costs, through ad sales, and was well on its way to turning a profit, with 100,000 hits per month.

Wennerholm observes that network marketers continue to lead the field in Internet commerce. "Back in 1996," he says, "MLM'ers were using Web pages mainly as electronic brochures. Now we're seeing more and more companies using e-commerce capabilities. It has become an interactive tool to process orders and new applications, to query databases for customer information, or even to notify people of upcoming events. I really think that's where the industry is going." Many companies already allow distributors to get updates on their sales and downline genealogies, via Web site.

TECHNO-RELIEF

All these high-tech advances have made a dramatic impact on network marketers' day-to-day lives. MLM veteran Michael S. Clouse, for example, remembers the bad old days, when he used to spend half his life on the telephone, acting as a human relay system for new product announcements and other company bulletins. Each time an announcement came down from headquarters, Michael remembers, "my wife and I would spend twenty minutes on the phone with each person in our downline."

Then Michael joined a company called The Peoples Network (TPN), a Dallas-based firm that sold subscriptions to the Success Channel, a proprietary satellite TV network. Nearly every distributor in the company owned a satellite dish. On most days, the Success Channel ran motivational programming by self-help gurus, such as Brian Tracy, Jim Rohn, and Og Mandino. But the real attraction came on Monday nights, when distributors would tune in to hear TPN president Jeff Olson address the sales force. These broadcasts covered everything from new products and special promotions to training events, conventions, and changes in the compensation plan. They largely relieved upline leaders, such as Michael, from the need to convey routine information to their downlines.

THE ULTIMATE TEST

For Michael and other TPN leaders, the satellite broadcasts vastly improved their quality of life. They were able to digest their dinners in peace, instead of rushing to the phone to start their nightly call marathons. They could leave town for a few days, without returning to find a voice mailbox stuffed with plaintive queries from their downlines. Even prospecting became easier. Instead of dragging potential recruits to hotel meetings, they could invite them over on Monday night to sit back and watch a TPN sales event right in the Clouses' own living room.

In the old days, Michael had felt like a robot much of the time, repeating the same tired old sales mantras and company bulletins until his voice went hoarse. Now he had become a human being. He was free to turn his attention to a network marketer's real job—building a network, one relationship at a time, and helping his downline improve sales.

It was all very encouraging. But the real test of TPN's innovative approach still lay ahead. In September 1998, the company entered a crisis serious enough to have brought many MLM firms to the brink of destruction. Its state-of-the-art telecommunications, however, enabled The Peoples Network not only to weather the crisis, but to thrive on it.

CHAPTER 16

The Wired Downline

The meeting opened on a somber note. An attorney reminded everyone that they had signed nondisclosure agreements. Should anyone leak what was about to be discussed, he warned, federal securities law provided that that person could be prosecuted and jailed. "After we heard that, we knew that these guys were serious," says Michael S. Clouse, one of the TPN distributors in attendance.

It was September 1998, three days before The Peoples Network opened its annual convention in Dallas. Michael was one of two hundred leaders who had been summoned for a special advance briefing. Everyone knew that TPN president Jeff Olson was preparing a major announcement, but most believed it amounted to little more than a new product roll-out. No one suspected what was really afoot. The company that they had labored for more than three years to build was about to pass from existence.

A TOUCHY SUBJECT

TPN was being merged with another company, Jeff Olson announced. It would no longer exist as TPN. In effect, The Peoples Network would be absorbed by Pre-Paid Legal Services, Inc., a network marketing firm in Ada, Oklahoma, that sold a kind of HMO policy for legal clients. TPN's products would be discontinued. Its distributors would become Pre-Paid Legal representatives. Its Success Channel would be taken over by Pre-Paid. "I was stunned," Michael remembers. "I'd invested my blood, sweat, and toil in TPN for almost four years. I had an organization of 5,000 people. What if they all quit when they heard about this? How would I tell my wife, my kids? How would I pay my bills?"

Michael was not alone. Anger and confusion swept the room. Among network marketers, mergers are a touchy subject. Entire downlines have been known to vanish overnight when rank-and-file distributors fail to support a merger. Michael's recruits had joined TPN to sell subscriptions to a motivational television network. Why should they suddenly switch to selling legal defense plans, just because Michael asked them to? At the very least, an appalling attrition rate seemed likely. One way or the other, Michael and the other leaders knew that the fate of their downlines would be settled in seventy-two hours. That's when the merger would be publicly announced at the convention. Like condemned prisoners on death row, Michael and the others counted off the remaining days.

PERCEPTION VERSUS REALITY

Ironically, the merger was a godsend for TPN. Had the company not concluded a deal with Pre-Paid Legal, it would have been forced to find another merger partner with similar qualifications. Cold, hard business calculus demanded it. Commissions from subscription sales to the Success Channel had never sufficed to feed TPN's large and growing downline. Olson had added an extensive catalog of "lotions and potions"—vitamins, weight-loss products, and skin creams. But even these had failed to provide the magic bullet that TPN representatives craved—an easy-to-sell product that guaranteed consistent commissions.

Michael and the other leaders realized that Pre-Paid Legal had the potential to fill this gap. But would their people accept the decision? No matter what the numbers showed, the distributors would flee the company en masse if they got any whiff of something amiss. In the battle for the hearts and minds of the TPN downline, perception would prove more critical than reality. "We had instilled in our distributors the utmost faith that TPN was the answer," says upline leader Art Jonak. "They thought the company was going to be around forever." When they found out differently, their sense of shock and betrayal might easily descend into hysteria.

THE PRESENTATION

Olson stage-managed the announcement with an impresario's skill. Every detail was weighed for psychological effect. Before the convention, Olson had insisted that every leader get on the phone and press his distributors to attend. He wanted as many people as possible to hear the presentation live. Two hundred top leaders were briefed, in advance, and given three days to digest the news before the convention. Following the general announcement on the event's opening day, rank-and-file distributors would then have another four days left to discuss and debate the news among themselves before the convention ended.

The announcement itself was handled with kid gloves. First, Olson himself would break the news, cashing in on all the trust he had built through four long years of leading the company through thick and thin. In the process, Olson would bear the brunt of the crowd's anger and dismay. Only when the initial shock had passed would the presentation begin in earnest. Olson had pulled out all stops for this part of the show. A parade of Pre-Paid Legal bigwigs would take the stage to explain the tremendous marketing and financial clout of the merger partner. Founder and chairman Harland C. Stonecipher was the chief attraction, followed by the president, Wilburn Smith, and the chief financial officer, Randy Harp. TPN distributors would be treated to a full-blown corporate briefing from Pre-Paid's top movers and shakers.

THE MOMENT OF TRUTH

Reaction to the announcement was predictably volatile. When Jeff Olson revealed the merger, indignation swept the hall. "There was every range of emotion you could imagine," says Michael, " from tears to anger to people literally walking out. It came as a complete shock." But then Harland Stonecipher took the stage, and the crowd fell silent. Video cameras rolled for the Success Channel, as Stonecipher cleared his throat and began telling his story.

It all began, Stonecipher explained, back in 1969 when he got into a head-on traffic accident. Stonecipher's insurance covered the car and hospital bills. But when the lawyer's fees came due, he was on his own. "That gave me the idea," he later recalled, in the July/August 1997 issue of *Success.* An insurance salesman by trade, Stonecipher realized that middle-income people needed coverage for unexpected legal expenses, just as they needed health coverage. He started a new company to provide that service in 1972.

The company took its time getting off the ground. After introducing an MLM compensation plan in 1982, sales doubled from $4 to $8 million in a single year. But Pre-Paid Legal still suffered from a chronic cash shortage. Only in 1992 did Stonecipher finally resolve that problem, by offering Pre-Paid shares on the American Stock Exchange. Success followed quickly.

> For the five-year period beginning in 1993, Pre-Paid Legal was the number one offering on the American Stock Exchange, in terms of profit growth.

For the five-year period beginning in 1993, Pre-Paid Legal was the number one offering on the American Stock Exchange, in terms of profit growth. *Fortune* magazine, in its 1997 ranking, listed Pre-Paid Legal as the twenty-ninth fastest-growing company in America, with revenues of about $100 million, while *Forbes* rated the company number five in its November 1998 ranking of the 200 Best Small Companies in America. Pre-Paid Legal has been listed on the New York Stock Exchange since May 1999.

An Easy Sell

What drove Pre-Paid Legal's growth was a highly sellable product. In a society where more than 100 million lawsuits are filed each year, where people are three times more likely to be sued than to be hospitalized, and where two-thirds of the adult population have yet to write a will, the need for legal advice speaks for itself. But few middle-income people can afford it. Much like an HMO, Pre-Paid Legal brings lawyers' services within the reach of ordinary folk. For a modest fee, it offers full legal coverage, through a network of pre-approved law firms.

Michael S. Clouse saw the potential immediately. After four years of selling The Peoples Network, he was tired of swimming upstream. The Success Channel was exciting and sexy, with its cast of motivational superstars. But only hardcore personal development junkies seemed willing to invest in it. The lotions and potions sold, but they were up against fierce competition. More than 90 percent of existing MLM firms sold similar products. In Pre-Paid Legal, Michael saw a product that made hard business sense. "This is a product that you could sell to your mother," Michael says. "And whether she was seventy years old or fifty, she would see the value in it."

The Rumor Mill

Emotions ran high through the convention's first day. But by evening, it seemed clear that many distributors would accept the new product. Now the real challenge lay before TPN. How to reach the vast majority of distributors, who had stayed home? Within hours of the merger announcement, press releases would be on their way to the financial media. News stories would spark the rumor mill, and the phones would start buzzing.

Years before, such an information gap might have sufficed to destroy an MLM company. Dependent on telephone chains and printed newsletters for their information, network marketers often learned of corporate decisions only through the grapevine. They acted on rumor rather than fact. Decisions about staying with a company or leaving it would be made days or even weeks before reliable information had filtered down from headquarters. The Peoples Network, however, had the advantage of a twenty-first-century telecommunications infrastructure. Its state-of-the-art interconnectivity may well have saved it from disaster.

AUTOMATED SPIN CONTROL

Michael S. Clouse returned home from the convention, preparing himself mentally for a monumental job of spin control. His voice mailbox would likely be jammed with panicky messages, demanding to know what was going on. There would be wheedling, arguing, and hand-holding till well into the night.

But when he walked into his Seattle home, Michael met with a surprise. The messages on his voice mail were overwhelmingly positive. "People were saying, 'Wow, this looks like a fabulous product,'" he recalls. "They already knew the whole story." The presentation, in fact, had been broadcast on the Success Channel, twenty-four hours after it was made at the convention. Michael's downline knew exactly who Pre-Paid Legal was and how the merger would benefit them. Many had already registered as Pre-Paid Legal distributors, having pulled the applications from a fax-on-demand number.

Of course, other distributors were less complacent. They tended to be those who lacked satellite dishes. "It would take up to an hour, on the telephone, to explain the situation to each one," says Michael. "They would go through every range of emotion. I would have given anything if those people had had access to a satellite. It would have made my job so much easier."

THE VIRTUAL FAMILY

What followed was a two-week blitz of electronic hand-holding. TPN broadcast updates on the merger every night. All over North America, at 8 P.M. Eastern Time, tens of thousands of TPN distributors gathered around their televisions to learn what was happening to their company. "On average, it seemed to take about five days for each person to go through the emotions and come out positive," Michael remembers. "Those of us at the convention spent those five days surrounded by our friends. The people back home were surrounded by the TPN family, too, but on television. Jeff Olson was on every night, looking right into the camera, right into their eyes, and walking them through it."

Michael likens the experience to the day that Princess Diana died, and billions were united in grief by her televised funeral. But the broadcasts offered more than just emotional support. They also gave practical guidance for dealing with the business and bureaucratic snafus of the merger. "Every glitch in the process was explained, and solutions offered," says Michael. The broadcasts coached TPN distributors through the complex transition from selling satellite TV to selling legal services. They also served as a selling tool, in themselves. Distributors invited prospects to their homes to watch the broadcast and learn about the Pre-Paid Legal opportunity, even as the distributors themselves were learning about it. "The network taught us how to do it," Michael concludes.

NARROWCASTING

While the company was broadcasting via satellite, individual TPN distributors were narrowcasting to their own down-lines, via e-mail. Long before the merger, Art Jonak had set up a system of E-mail Alerts for getting news and information quickly to his people. Everything from updates on company events to training tips and sample prospecting letters was blasted to Art's downline—about two thousand people in thirty-five states.

Within two hours of the merger announcement, Art released an e-mail broadcast, informing his downline that he backed the merger 100 percent. "In a situation like this, if a leader doesn't make a decision within forty-eight hours, then he starts losing more and more people every day," Art observes. "Indecision can kill a distributor force." Interactivity was crucial to Art's strategy. The distributors must have a chance to express their doubts and ask questions, he realized. More than a hundred e-mails poured in, responding to Art's first alert. He responded personally to each message, asking respondents to plug into a special conference call the following night, during which Art would answer all questions. "The e-mails gave me a good guideline of what to cover on the conference calls," Art observes. "I saw which questions were coming up for most people. It helped me to make the conference a lot more powerful and effective."

As it turned out, Art's E-mail Alert had gone out just in time. Responses poured in, many from people who had already seen rumors about the merger popping up on the America Online network marketing message boards. The instantaneous connection Art had established with his downline enabled him to short-circuit these rumors and put out the worst fires, even before TPN got around to broadcasting its satellite program.

INTERCONNECTIVITY

Interconnectivity helped keep the TPN downline intact. Art lost about 50 percent of his rank-and-file distributors. On the surface, it seems like a hefty number. But many rank-and-filers tend to be inactive in the business anyway, even during the best of times. "Distributors come and go," Art observes, "but the core of your business is the leadership." Art retained a stunning 85 percent of his top sellers, recruiters, and business builders.

As many distributors struggled to make the transition to Pre-Paid Legal, the Success Channel shored up morale with a stream of ongoing success stories. "On the Monday night communications show," Michael recalls, "they would bring out people whose first Pre-Paid Legal checks ranged from $15,000 to $40,000 for the month. My own first check was double what my last TPN check had been." Many distributors did not enjoy such instant success with the new product. But the satellite broadcasts kept their eyes on the prize, and their minds off their sorrows.

A DARING MOVE

TPN's success in controlling its downline reinforced Harland Stonecipher's original instincts. For years, he had admired the way MLM companies such as Primerica and TPN used their satellite networks to train and coordinate their downlines. With nearly its entire sales force equipped with Primestar satellite service, TPN was the jewel in the crown of the interconnectivity revolution. "No other direct sales company has a satellite link between its president and every single distributor in the field," Jeff Olson had boasted in 1996. "That has never happened before. We have our own production facilities, our own uplink, and our own transponder. We have a private studio right next to my office so that twenty-four hours a day, seven days a week, I can walk right in there, turn on the camera, and talk to the field."

Stonecipher coveted that kind of personal contact with his sales force. In fact, he was so taken by Olson's system that he made a bold and risky decision to pay one million shares of Pre-Paid Legal stock to acquire it—even though the risk was high that the entire TPN distributor force might evaporate in the deal, leaving Pre-Paid Legal with nothing but the Success Channel. That channel alone, Stonecipher understood, would equip his giant company of 140,000 distributors with the interconnectivity he needed to thrive in the twenty-first-century marketplace.

STAYING THE COURSE

Always a visionary, Stonecipher did not flinch when Pre-Paid Legal stock tumbled at the news of his acquisition. "Pre-Paid Legal's acquisition of The Peoples Network and its Success Channel on Primestar earlier this month sent stock values roller-coastering to a year low of 14 . . ." reported *The Journal Record* on Monday, October 19, 1998. "The deal had some questioning the direction of the company."

> He understood, even if Wall Street analysts did not, that electronic connectivity was the bloodstream of a network marketing community.

Some people might have doubted, but Stonecipher held the course with icy determination. He understood, even if Wall Street analysts did not, that electronic connectivity was the bloodstream of a network marketing community. "We've just got to do what we've been doing," said Stonecipher in the face of the stock slide. "We're going to grow very rapidly, and people will understand why I bought the channel. This gives us the ability to communicate directly with our sales force and do it daily."

THE INTERACTIVE FUTURE

Within weeks of the merger, the dire predictions of Wall Street pundits faded as Pre-Paid Legal's sales skyrocketed, and its stock rebounded to $30 per share. The infusion of TPN distributors has brought a new energy to the sales force. "On the last day of October 1998," Michael recalls, "we brought in more business than Pre-Paid Legal had ever done on a single day, in their twenty-five-year history. It was like this great tsunami wave. These brand new distributors from TPN watched the channel, understood the product, got the paperwork, and just went to work. And they have been signing people up left and right. This is the easiest product sale I have ever experienced." As Pre-Paid Legal moves forward with its plan to saturate its own downline with satellite dishes from Primestar by Direct TV, the old Pre-Paid distributors are speeding to catch up with the TPN newcomers.

Satellite programs, such as TPN's, are only the beginning. As the Wave 4 Revolution proceeds, new technology promises inexpensive video conferencing for every downline. Stuart Johnson, whose Lake Dallas, Texas, company Video-Plus sells communications products and services to MLM companies, believes that network marketers of the future will receive real-time corporate videos of training sessions, company announcements, and opportunity meetings via the Internet—much as they now obtain these programs through expensive satellite broadcasts.

"All that's needed is more bandwidth," he says, "which is going to come from cable modems and higher-speed DSL telephone connections. Right now, there's only a million or two million homes, out of 100 million, that have that technology. But that's going to grow substantially over the next two years." When it does, you can be sure that network marketers will be at the forefront of this video revolution, hot-wiring their downlines for maximum interconnectivity and explosive sales.

17

What Is Wave 4?

We have spoken a great deal about the Wave 4 Revolution and its impact on corporate America. But what is Wave 4, exactly? In chapter 5, we defined the four waves of network marketing's evolution as follows:

WAVE 1 (1945–1979)—The Underground Phase
WAVE 2 (1980–1989)—The Proliferation Phase
WAVE 3 (1990–1999)—The Mass Market Phase
WAVE 4 (2000 and beyond)—The Universal Phase

During the first three waves, network marketing grew and thrived. Yet it always remained a kind of counterculture. Network marketers had no place in the corporate mainstream. They did not appear in financial journals or Wall Street analysts' reports. They were not mentioned in corporate boardrooms or business school symposia. Theirs was a world apart.

But as the Wave 4 era dawns, MLM has emerged from isolation. It is widely acknowledged today as a legitimate marketing tool. Its successes are noted in the business press. To an ever-greater extent, the general public views MLM as a realistic alternative to nine-to-five corporate employment. In short, network marketing has joined the mainstream. As more and more companies yield to the centrifugal pressure of mass privatization, MLM's influence is being felt universally through the business world, from Wall Street to Main Street.

THE WAVE 4 WAY

Unlike MLM firms in the past, Wave 4 companies are fully integrated into the corporate economy. They provide vital services to the Fortune 500, who move goods and services through MLM's Distribution Freeway. Wave 4 companies also provide real employment to an increasingly jittery workforce, worried about downsizing. They offer a living wage for full-time effort, a reasonable income for part-time effort, and virtually unlimited earning power for the ambitious and the driven.

> ... MLM's influence is being felt universally through the business world, from Wall Street to Main Street.

The simple-minded MLM concepts of the past promised these things but too often failed to deliver on them. Wave 4 companies have turned the dream into a reality. To accomplish this, they have had to evolve, over the years, in five critical ways. We can summarize the five hallmarks of a Wave 4 business strategy as follows:

1. **Interconnectivity**
2. **Infinite Momentum**
3. **Turnkey Systems**
4. **Sustainable Commissions**
5. **The Touch Factor**

Interconnectivity

The Wave 4 company provides state-of-the-art telecommunications for its distributors. Rank-and-file representatives use voice mail and e-mail broadcasts to coordinate their activities. Video and satellite TV conferences bring corporate messages into the home. Distributors access vital data at will, by means of fax-on-demand services and Web-based information retrieval.

Infinite Momentum

The old-fashioned "MLM junky" used to jump from one company to the next, trying to "catch the wave" or "get in on the ground floor" of a new start-up, just before it went into "momentum"—a sustained cycle of exponential growth. Of course, most companies never made it to the momentum phase. And those that did often died shortly after, once the momentum was spent. MLM junkies lived like gamblers, ever in search of the next big windfall. It was a poor formula for growing a business.

The Wave 4 company, on the other hand, provides opportunities for sustained growth throughout the entire life of the corporation. It does this, first of all, by opening foreign markets to the average distributor, so that rank-and-file business builders can draw from the unlimited pool of global customers. Systems are installed that make it just as easy to build and sustain a downline in Hong Kong as in the next state. Growth is also sustained through the constant introduction of new product lines and the launching of new subsidiaries and trademarks, so that distributors always have fresh markets to conquer.

Turnkey Systems

A turnkey system is any method or procedure that simplifies or automates part of the business, making it easier for ordinary people to operate. Such systems form the heart and soul of a Wave 4 company. Drop-shipping programs, for instance, automate the retailing process. Instead of stockpiling inventory, taking orders, and shipping products to customers, the Wave 4 networker just gives his PIN number to a customer, who then uses that number to order what he wants through a Web site or an 800 number, directly from the company. Prospecting for new recruits can also be automated, through recruiting videos, satellite broadcasts, and Web sites equipped with auto-responders. Many companies automate the training of new distributors by providing standardized, company-run programs such as PFS University.

Sustainable Commissions

Old-fashioned MLM companies tended to pay their top-level leaders high commissions and their low-level distributors very little. Wave 4 companies, on the other hand, balance their compensation plans so that part-timers and high-rollers alike can prosper. Those who work hard and rise high in the sales ranks still receive higher commissions. But Wave 4 companies also allow a hefty share of the profits to circulate among the lower ranks.

The Touch Factor

Have you ever called a computer company, seeking technical support, and found yourself listening to a recorded voice instructing you to go to such-and-such Web site, where you will supposedly find answers to all your questions? Then, when you got to the Web site, you couldn't find any reference to your particular question? The moral of the story is that automation has built-in limitations. As more and more people transact their daily business through interactive media, such as Web sites, the need for living, breathing human beings to guide them through the process and help them with problems only increases.

Futurist John Naisbitt called this paradox "High Tech, High Touch." As technology accelerates, he predicted, so will our craving for the friendly attention of human beings. Network marketing is uniquely equipped to meet that need, since it moves products via

> On the contrary, Wave 4 companies continually invent new ways to complement their high-tech advances with high-touch service, provided by flesh-and-blood distributors.

human relationships. Wave 4 distributors will never have to worry about being replaced by advancing technology. On the contrary, Wave 4 companies continually invent new ways to complement their high-tech advances with high-touch service, provided by flesh-and-blood distributors.

THE CONNECTIVITY STATE

In previous chapters, we have referred to Wave 4 networkers as "cyber-pioneers" and the freewheeling marketplace of the twenty-first century as a "cyber-frontier." The new economy will indeed be defined by a high degree of electronic connectivity. But do not assume that people need to become expert hackers to partake of the Wave 4 Revolution. Quite the contrary is true.

"Computing, in short, was never about data crunching," write Watts Wacker, Jim Taylor, and Howard Means in *The 500 Year Delta*. "Data crunching was the means; connectivity was the end. . . . Fax machines, modems, interactive TV, and Internet providers were all the means; connectivity was the end. . . . Connectivity is a state of existence, nothing more. The true end is what happens when things are in connection, what happens when connectivity itself fuses with information."

THE BLACK BOX

Digital connectivity, then, is the state of existence from which the Wave 4 Revolution springs. But we need not be technicians to interconnect. Consider the Apple iMac, the hottest-selling personal computer on the market today. All the software you need comes pre-loaded in the machine. All the hardware comes encased in a single unit. The customer just pulls it out of the box, boots it up, and starts computing.

The iMac is a black box—a device that is complex on the inside, but simple on the outside. So is the Wave 4 Revolution. Network marketers in the twenty-first century don't need to understand the complexities of product fulfillment, Web-hosting, commission-crunching, foreign currency exchange, and the like. The company takes care of all that. Like an Imac user, the Wave 4 networker has only to hit the "on" switch and start working. The skills he needs are not High Tech, but High Touch. They include the ability to form and manage relationships, to evaluate opportunities, and to exploit advantages in the marketplace. It is to the cultivation of these subtle crafts that the remainder of this book is dedicated.

Getting Started

18

Choosing a Company

The first step in your personal Wave 4 odyssey will be to find and join a network marketing company. But which one? A tough choice lies before you. Hundreds of companies vie for your attention, most of them start-ups. Among those start-ups, the failure rate is high—over 96 percent within the first year, according to an estimate by *Inside Network Marketing* author Leonard Clements, based on his analysis of company listings and surveys in trade publications. There is no way to remove risk from the entrepreneurial process, whether in network marketing or in any other business. But if you follow the procedure for evaluating MLM opportunities outlined in this chapter, you will be well equipped to make an informed decision.

STEP #1—EVALUATE THE PRODUCT OR SERVICE

To succeed, an MLM company must have a salable product or service. It must be competitively priced and, ideally, it should be hard to obtain from non-MLM sources. Ask yourself, "Would I buy this product, at this price, if someone offered it to me?" Consumable items, such as herbal supplements, are preferable to one-shots, such as burglar alarms and water filters. Once your customer consumes the first bottle of supplements, he has to come back for more. Services that involve

ongoing fees, such as insurance, also ensure a continuing
stream of commissions. Look for "transfer buying" opportunities. It is easier to persuade
people to transfer from one
brand to another of a product or
service they already use—say
from AT&T long-distance service
to your company's service—than
to convince them to buy some exotic new lotion or potion for
which they perceive no obvious
need.

To succeed, an
MLM company must
have a salable product
or service.

STEP #2—CHECK THE INDUSTRY GRAPEVINE

Online message boards are a rich source of industry gossip.
To find out what people are saying about a particular company, you can visit America Online. Type in keywords
"MLM" or "multilevel marketing," and you will find yourself in the Network Marketing and Direct Sales Forum. Select "Message Boards," then "Network Marketing Message
Boards." Now you can browse through boards on over two
hundred MLM opportunities, listed alphabetically by company name. You can also post your own messages, request-
ing information on particular opportunities.

To find other MLM postings on the Internet, go to
www.deja.com and type in the name of the company you are
investigating. You will get a wide selection of messages
posted on all kinds of different newsgroups. MLM.com also
offers a discussion forum. In evaluating industry gossip, beware of disinformation. Some people run down competing
companies, as a strategy for recruiting you into their own opportunities. Always consider the source.

STEP #3—CONSULT INDUSTRY WATCHDOGS

Three publications specialize in doing objective, professional
evaluations of MLM opportunities. My favorite is *The*

MLM Watchdog, published by Rod Cook, president of America's MLM Consultants (www.mlmconsultant.com and www.mlmwatchdog.com). He can be reached at: (800) 532-9810, P.O. Box 701125, San Antonio, TX 78270. *Market Wave Alert Letter* is published by Leonard W. Clements, author of *Inside Network Marketing* (Prima Publishing, 1997), tel: (800) 688-4766; e-mail: mwave@aol.com; street address: 7342 North Ivanhoe Avenue, Fresno, CA 93722.

Also reliable is *Network Marketing Today,* published by Corey Augenstein. Every year, Corey publishes a ranking of the top ten MLM companies. Tel: (305) 947-5600; fax: (305) 947-8655; e-mail: coreya@mlminsider.com; Web site: www.mlminsider.com; street address: Network Resources Enterprises, Inc., 3741 NE 163rd Street, Suite 123, North Miami Beach, FL 33160.

STEP #4—DO A MEDIA SEARCH

Find out what the news media say about your target company. You can do this, free of charge, at the library by searching the Lexis-Nexis database. You can also search Lexis-Nexis on the Internet for $24 per day. To register, go to www.nexis.com and select "LN reQUESTer" from the pull-down menu. Finally, you can search by phone, using Lexis-Nexis Express, which charges by the hour and by the amount of text printed out. Any articles found will be sent to you by mail, fax, or e-mail, as you request. Tel: (800) 843-6476; fax: (937) 865-7418; e-mail: lexis-nexis.express@lexis-nexis.com. Mailing address: P.O. Box 933, Dayton, Ohio 45401-0933.

STEP #5—CHECK FOR COMPLAINTS

Several government and private organizations keep records of complaints made against MLM companies. These include the state attorney general's office, the state Department of Consumer Affairs, the Better Business Bureau, the Federal Trade Commission, the Securities and Exchange Commission, and the Direct Selling Association in Washington, D.C.

Be cautious in evaluating complaints. Many companies generate complaints due to temporary problems that are later resolved. Whether or not the complaints were resolved is a far better indicator of a company's ethics than the sheer number of complaints. Also, some agencies fail to distinguish between complaints and inquiries. Every call is registered as a complaint, even if it is really just a request for information. Be sure to ask whether the agency distinguishes between actual complaints and other types of calls.

STEP #6—CHECK THE FINANCIALS

If your target company is listed on a stock exchange, you're in luck. Public companies are required by law to publish detailed reports on their finances. You can request an annual report directly from the company. Or you can obtain the company's financial filings from the Securities and Exchange Commission (SEC) or from Dun & Bradstreet at (800) 234-3867. SEC filings can be retrieved from the Internet, at www.sec.gov.

Most network marketing firms are private, however, which means that they are not required to divulge financial information. You will have to do some detective work. Dun & Bradstreet supplies data on some private companies, but not all. Try asking the target company directly for a P&L statement. Most will refuse. Call up the company's banker and ask whether the company is a borrowing customer, and whether it is timely in its payments. Also ask whether it has applied for credit, and whether or not the credit was granted. You can run a credit check on the company through credit reporting agencies, such as Trans Union, Experian (formerly TRW), or Equifax. Reports can be retrieved through the Internet. If you are not online, ask your banker for assistance.

STEP #7—CHECK THE LITIGATION HISTORY

Find out what legal actions your company and its principal officers have been involved in. What were the amounts of the judgments, if any? Have there been state or federal tax liens? Credit reports will list past judgments and lawsuits. Legal information can also be retrieved through Lexis-Nexis or from CSC Networks/Prentice Hall Legal and Finance Services at (800) 221-0770.

Step #8—Consider the Company's Growth Phase

How old is the company? Some networkers prefer to join start-up companies, because you can make big money fast by getting in on the ground floor of the next Amway or Excel—theoretically, at least. But how do you know the company you're joining will succeed? You don't. Only a small fraction survive the first two years. Those that do may or may not hit it big.

Even if you are lucky enough to choose a start-up that achieves "momentum"—the spurt of exponential growth that catapults it into the big time—your troubles are not yet over. Fast-growing companies inevitably attract the scrutiny of government regulators. At one time or another, virtually every large MLM firm has passed through what *Inside Network Marketing* author Leonard Clements calls the "scrutiny phase"—a period of intense investigation by government and media. The lucky ones escape with some bad press and a few hefty cash settlements. Most go belly-up.

In short, joining start-ups is a bit of a crapshoot. There is slower but safer money to be made with the industry giants. Like blue-chip firms in any industry, these tend to grow more slowly than start-ups. But they also tend to be safer investments, because they have already passed through the scrutiny phase and survived it.

Step #9—Look for Legal Red Flags

Before joining any company, you should assess the risk of government intervention. Some companies are more vulnerable than others. Beware, for instance, of companies that claim outlandish miracle cures for their products. They risk unwelcome scrutiny from the Food and Drug Administration. Also problematic are companies that promise a quick and easy path to riches, or that engage in "frontloading"— pressuring distributors to purchase large quantities of inventory. They risk being investigated as pyramid schemes.

Legitimate MLM companies will not place onerous purchasing requirements on new recruits. At most, they will ask recruits to buy a starter kit, at cost (usually between $10 to $50). These kits may contain videos, audiotapes, printed sales aids, distributor applications, product samples, and the like. Legitimate companies will also guarantee a 90 percent refund on all products that you wish to return. They will refrain from guaranteeing high levels of income and will make clear to new recruits that success comes only to those who work hard and sell lots of product.

Beware also of companies whose distributors boast too much about their earnings. Regulators will sometimes interpret such statements as an attempt to mislead prospects into thinking that everyone who joins the opportunity will make an equally large income. Wise companies play it safe by discouraging distributors from flashing their paychecks.

STEP #10—DO A WAVE 4 CHECKLIST

The first nine steps are designed to help you evaluate whether your target company is legal, ethical, and financially sound. But is it a Wave 4 company? Is it well positioned to thrive in the twenty-first-century economy? The following checklist will help you separate the innovative companies from the dinosaurs.

1. **Is the company "wired"?**

   Wave 4 companies offer discounted telecommunications services to their distributors, such as voice mail and voice broadcast service; Web hosting and Internet access; and newsletters available through fax, voice mail, or e-mail. Some companies even offer satellite television broadcasts and video conferencing.

2. What turnkey systems does it offer?

The Wave 4 distributor should have access to a wide range of labor-saving systems, including: high-quality printed sales materials; high-quality prospecting videos (available for $7 tops) and audiocassettes (for no more than $2); standardized training programs: teleconferences and satellite broadcasts, for prospecting and training; access to updated genealogies, group sales volume, instant order confirmation, and company announcements through fax, voice mail, e-mail, or Web site; tracking reports of customers' buying habits; direct fulfillment of customer orders through an 800 number or e-commerce Web site (drop-shipping); twenty-four-hour ordering, by credit card, with no minimum on the number of units ordered, and guaranteed shipment from the warehouse within forty-eight hours (with overnight delivery options available for an extra charge); a phone hotline to take distributor questions, so you don't have to handle all your downline's queries personally.

3. Is there a High Touch component to the opportunity?

The product or service should be one that lends itself to person-to-person selling. Those that require a good deal of lengthy explanation or personal testimonial, for instance, are well suited to Wave 4 distribution methods.

4. Does the company have a long-term growth strategy?

A single product or service, no matter how successful, will not sustain a Wave 4 company indefinitely. At the very least, your company should have plans drawn up for inducing infinite momentum through product diversification and international expansion. The Wave 4 company positions itself as a global Distribution Freeway, moving goods and services for a large number of third-party clients, on every continent.

5. Does it have a Wave 4 compensation plan?

The compensation plan is the commission structure of the company, through which your income is calcu-lated. Wave 4 companies offer a balanced plan that provides opportunity both for the little guy who works his MLM business on the side and the full-time business builder who aspires to achieve a signif-icant income. A full dis-cussion of comp plans can be found in the next chapter.

> A single product or service, no matter how successful, will not sustain a Wave 4 company indefinitely.

QUEST FOR PERFECTION

The Wave 4 company, as outlined previously, is an ideal. Few, if any, network marketing firms offer all these benefits simultaneously. If you demand perfection on every point, you will probably be disappointed. But your target company should, at least, have a Wave 4 vision and show evidence of moving in a Wave 4 direction. It should have a realistic timetable in place for modernizing telecommunications, ex-panding markets and product lines, improving turnkey sys-tems, and balancing compensation plans. Hold your target company to a Wave 4 standard, and you will find yourself well positioned for growth in the twenty-first century.

CHAPTER 19

Understanding
Your Comp Plan

How important is it to understand comp plans? Not at all, some will argue. Many successful MLM veterans boast that they have never given a thought to how their commissions were calculated. They leave such matters to the company computer. Instead of agonizing over bonuses and overrides, they invest their time and energy in building and training their downlines.

This approach has its merits. Compulsive brooding over pay plans can indeed distract you from your goal. The plans themselves tend to be complex and hard to decipher. You'll spend a lot of time unraveling them. And once you've succeeded, you'll discover that, most of the time, one plan turns out to be as good as another. "Comp plan design is without a doubt the most perception-oriented aspect of the business," says Leonard Clements, publisher of *MarketWave* and author of *Inside Network Marketing*. "There are tons of ways to make a plan appear more lucrative on paper but in reality have it pay no more than any other plan."

In short, the differences between comp plans have been greatly exaggerated. Some are more generous than others, to be sure. But it's a safe bet that any legitimate, growing company with a successful track record has a plan in place that is perfectly adequate to ensure your success—provided you put in the work. So the question arises, why bother analyzing comp plans at all?

HYPE REPELLENT

One reason is self-defense. Every network marketer today is bombarded with hype from rival companies—much of it centered around the issue of comp plans. The Internet abounds with MLM prospecting pitches promising easier, more generous pay plans. Many can seem quite alluring. If you are a beginner shopping for your first opportunity, you could easily be enticed into joining a company with poor products, slipshod management, flat sales, and an empty bank account simply because it promised a better "payout."

Even experienced networkers are at risk. Suppose you have a long, stable relationship with a particular company. You might feel that you're immune from comp-plan hype. And maybe you are. But what about your downline? What do you tell your prospects when they seek your advice about some rival company that claims to have an "easier" plan than yours? Many leaders are caught off guard by such questions. They have no idea how to respond.

"I'm pitched every single day of my life by other companies," says Kalyn Gibbens of Neways (whose story can be found in chapters 28–29). "And the people in my downline are pitched too. I make sure to teach my people about pay plans, so they know how to respond when someone tries to sell them on another plan."

SIX CRITERIA FOR CHOOSING A COMP PLAN

You don't need a Ph.D. in compensation plans in order to see through the hype. A few simple principles will suffice. Measure any plan against the six criteria listed below, and you'll get a pretty good idea of its pros and cons.

1. Potential Size of Organization

Your MLM organization grows in two directions—horizontally and vertically—wide and deep. Find out exactly what limits your comp plan places on the width and depth of your downline. Depth is the number of levels from which you are allowed to draw commissions. Width is the number of people you are allowed to place on your frontline. Matrix and binary plans limit your width. All other plans allow infinite width, but strictly control your depth to a certain number of levels. Be careful when calculating depth. You might look at two plans that claim to allow six levels each. But look closer and you might discover that one is a unilevel, that stops your commissions cold after the sixth level, while the other might be a stairstep/breakaway, that lets you draw commissions from twice as many levels, under certain circumstances. See below for a detailed explanation.

2. Qualifications

In order to qualify for commissions and bonuses, you will have to buy a certain amount of product each month, at wholesale. This is your minimum personal volume requirement. Most plans also require you to order additional product, each month, to qualify for certain commission levels. Find out what these qualifying amounts are. If the quotas are too high, you will feel pressured to buy more product than you can sell. If they are too low, your downline may feel little incentive to sell anything, buying only enough product each month to meet their personal needs. Some plans also require you to recruit a certain number of distributors, at certain levels, who have achieved a certain designated achievement level themselves, before you are allowed to collect the higher levels of commission. Make sure that these recruitment goals are realistic, if you wish to avoid frustration.

3. Front end or back end?

Some plans weight their commissions on the back end, others at the front end. The front end refers to the higher levels or the earlier part of the plan. These are generally the first people you recruit. If you receive higher commissions on your first people, that means you get your money faster and easier. The back end refers to the lower levels. These are generally the last people to join your organization—the people recruited by your recruits, and so on. Traditional plans pay the highest commissions on the lowest levels. That means you will have to work longer and harder before you start getting the really big commissions.

But, in fact, higher back-end commissions offer a great advantage for those dedicated workers who build deep organizations.

At first glance, it would seem more logical to go for the faster, easier commissions. But, in fact, higher back-end commissions offer a great advantage for those dedicated workers who build deep organizations. That's because it is the lower levels—the recruits of the recruits of the recruits of the recruits of the recruits of your orginal recruits—who will tend to be the most numerous. It is on the bottom levels that the full force of geometric growth begins to kick in. For a fuller explanation, see below.

4. Payout

Every company claims a certain level of payout. This is the percentage of total sales that the company "pays out" in the form of commissions to its distributors. Conventional wisdom holds that the higher the payout, the better the company. However, it is important to keep in mind that the more money the company

pays out, the less it keeps for itself, in corporate profits. If a company pays out too generously, it could find
itself facing cash flow problems. Higher commissions
will not help you, if the company offering them is tee-
tering on the verge of bankruptcy. The sales volume
and overall financial health of the company are far
more important than the payout.

"Seventy-five percent of zero is still zero," explains
Inside Network Marketing author Leonard Clements.
"A company with a great payout but poor sales is not
as good an opportunity as a company with a low payout but doing a large volume of sales." Keep in mind
also that some companies succeed in offering higher
payouts only by raising their product prices through
the roof. A company selling $25 bottles of shampoo
will have a hard time finding customers, no matter
how many distributors it attracts with high front-end
commissions.

5. Breakage

According to Clements, no company can really afford
more than a 60 percent payout—that is, 60 cents in
commission on every wholesale dollar. If it paid more,
it would be in danger of going broke. So when you
hear companies offering payouts of 75 percent or
more, you can be pretty sure that they have built some
breakage into their plans.

Breakage is the difference between what your
company promises to pay and what it really pays. The
fine print of most compensation plans will contain a
host of subtle stipulations whose purpose is to lower
your commissions, raise your qualifications, or disqualify portions of your sales volume, in certain circumstances.

For instance, it is natural to assume that all the
sales volume of your organization counts toward your

monthly quota. But does it? Many companies only count what they call your "unencumbered" volume, which is defined as volume from your personal group, but not from any of your breakaway legs. Then there are companies that translate your actual sales volume into what they call "bonus volume"—an amount that is often less than the actual sales volume (say $700 in bonus volume, compared to $1,000 in wholesale sales volume). When it comes time to calculate your monthly quotas, the figure they use is the bonus volume, not the sales volume.

Even more breakage is created through penalties. Many companies impose stiff penalties for failing to meet your quota. In some, you could be demoted down to a lower commission level—even the very lowest level, in some cases—the first month that you fail to make quota. Kinder, gentler plans will offer a grace period of several months before lowering the boom, giving you a chance to get your volume back up. And some plans are so gentle, they never demote you at all.

It's important to remember that there's nothing innately wrong with breakage. It's just an advertising ploy to make comp plans look more attractive, much as retailers price their wares at $9.99 instead of $10.00 to make them seem cheaper. Keep a sober eye on the company's real payout (after breakage) and ignore its hyped payout (before breakage). That way, you'll be able to make a responsible decision.

6. Type of plan

There are four major types of compensation plan that you will encounter, again and again, in the network marketing business, each with its own strengths and weaknesses. They are the Stairstep/Breakaway, the Matrix, the Unilevel, and the Binary. We will explore and compare the various plans below.

THE WAVE 4 COMP PLAN

In May 1994, *Upline* magazine editor-in-chief John Milton Fogg interviewed me on the subject of my just-released book, *Wave 3*. In the course of that interview, he put the question to me: "Is there a Wave 4, Richard?" I responded: "I think the next frontier of network marketing involves the compensation plans, where everyone will realize that comp plans can evolve . . . that there can be more money available to rank-and-file distributors who are doing a moderate amount of work."

I was referring to the fact that more and more companies, at that time, were beginning to pay out higher commissions on the front ends of their plans—that is, on the higher levels. As explained previously, this arrangement makes it easier for larger numbers of people to earn money faster—especially the little guy, who may never succeed in recruiting more than a handful of people.

I am happy to report that my prediction of May 1994 has withstood the test of time. The clear trend among MLM companies is to offer more generous commissions in the upper levels. In fact, it is hard to find a network marketing company that has not lightened its plan, to some extent, within the last few years.

THE FIRST LAW OF COMP PLANS

Some companies have taken this principle to an extreme. Instead of just beefing up their higher levels by a few percentage points, they have moved almost all of their commissions into the top two levels, leaving little or nothing on the levels below. At first glance, it seems like a logical step. If "easier" plans are the wave of the future, why not go whole hog and make your plan as easy as it can possibly be?

I wish it were as simple as that! Unfortunately, as will become clear in the following pages, an inexorable law of the universe—let's call it the First Law of Compensation Plans— seems to hold that every advantage you build into a comp plan will give rise to an equal and opposite disadvantage.

COMPRESSED PLANS

In the case of the so-called "compressed plans"—those that compress the bulk of their commissions into the top levels— the advantage is obvious: you get more money for the first few people you recruit. But the disadvantage is equally obvious: you get less money for your later recruits.

Let's say you work very hard, for months or years, to build a downline that is many levels deep. Now suppose (in an idealized example) that you end up with 3 distributors on your first level, 9 on your second, 27 on your third, 81 on your fourth, 243 on your fifth, 729 on your sixth, and so on. In the more extreme types of compressed plans, you might get hefty commissions on those first 12 people, considerably less on the 27 people on your third level, and little or nothing on the remaining hundreds of people below that. In short, you fail to benefit from the geometric growth on your lower levels.

Some companies address this problem by offering bonuses on the deeper levels. This can help, but let's face it: In an organization this deep, your advantage clearly lies in drawing higher commissions from the lower levels. Some will argue that the vast majority of MLMers don't have to worry about the lower levels, since most will never succeed in building an organization deeper than two levels. That may be true. But network marketing companies thrive on leadership. And potential leaders, who aspire to build large organizations, should think very hard before giving up earning power on their lower levels.

THE WAVE 4 MYTH

Unfortunately, some networkers have recently begun claiming that the compressed plan is the only type of MLM program that this author—Richard Poe—classifies as a "Wave 4" comp plan. Let me set the record straight.

First of all, I never stated that a company's "Wave 4" status depended on its comp plan alone. My book *Wave 3*— published in 1994—contained a chapter called "Wave 4 and

Beyond," in which the Wave 4 Revolution was clearly defined as a quantum leap in marketing technology, associated with interactive media. The Wave 4 Revolution covers a wide range of developments, from Internet marketing to product diversification strategies. The lightening of comp plans is an important part of that revolution, but only a part.

More to the point, I have never once stipulated that any specific percentage of commissions should be offered at any particular level or levels of an MLM company. It would frankly be irresponsible of me to make such exact prescriptions, in a business where there is so much room for legitimate disagreement, and where the long-term results of comp-plan innovations are often impossible to know.

A Delicate Balance

What I can say—and what I have always said—is that the overall trend, for the twenty-first century, is in the direction of easier plans. But just how easy those plans should become is a tricky question. Most experts agree that the best plans steer a middle course between the heavy quotas and minuscule front-end commissions of yesterday's plans and the more top-heavy of today's compressed plans. "Eventually, I predict, we'll see an adjustment back towards the middle," writes Clements, in the 1998–1999 "Annual Best Companies" issue of *Network Marketing Today*. "Pay plan designers will start shifting a portion of that huge second level down to the third and fourth levels." In short, Clements calls for a "middle-weighted" plan.

I agree. I think that the Wave 4 comp plan must provide a delicate balance between front-end and back-end commissions—yielding profits for part-timers, while at the same time offering sufficient rewards to attract full-time business builders. No doubt, a wide range of different plans will arise to provide these benefits, not just one particular type. The Wave 4 comp plan is an ideal—not an exact formula. Readers must weigh the pros and cons of each plan for themselves, and decide which one best suits their needs. This chapter is designed to help you do that.

THE FOUR TYPES OF COMP PLANS

Now let's get down to business. As stated previously, there are four major categories of compensation plan. None is innately better than the other. All have their peculiar advantages and disadvantages. The main ones are outlined below.

THE STAIRSTEP/BREAKAWAY PLAN

Description

These plans are structured like staircases, with each step representing a higher achievement level. The more product you purchase each month, and/or the more distributors you recruit who attain a certain achievement level, the higher you ascend up the staircase. The higher you rise, the higher your rate of commission (or the greater the number of generations from which you are allowed to draw earnings).

People in your downline are also ascending the same staircase. When they reach a certain designated achievement level, they and their downlines "break away" from your group. At that point, the volume of the breakaway group no longer counts toward your monthly quota and, in most cases, you receive a lower percentage of commission from the breakaway distributor and his group. However, you have the potential to make more money from a breakaway leg, even at a lower rate of commission, because you are paid on the total group volume of that breakaway distributor, rather than just on those distributors in his group who happen to fall within your normal pay range (see the Glossary at the back of the book for an explanation of technical MLM terms).

Advantages of the Stairstep/Breakaway Plan

• Unlimited earning potential

No plan matches the stairstep/breakaway in sheer earning power. Through "breakaways," people can build larger organizations and earn commissions from deeper levels than would generally be possible in other plans.

• Deeper pay range

In a typical six-level unilevel plan, you draw commissions from six levels, and no more. But a six-generation stairstep/breakaway could theoretically pay down as many as twelve levels. Let's say that someone on your sixth level breaks away. You would then collect a monthly override on the volume of his entire group—which may be six levels deep. That's twelve levels total.

> Through "breakaways," people can build larger organizations and earn commissions from deeper levels than would generally be possible in other plans.

• Bigger downline

The depth of a stairstep/breakaway may be impressive, but its width is virtually unlimited. There is no limit to the number of people you can recruit onto your frontline, and likewise no limit to the number your recruits may recruit.

• Company stability

After more than 50 years of network marketing, only a handful of companies have managed to survive in the marketplace for seven years or longer. Of those survivors, 86 percent were found to have stairstep/breakaway plans, according to a *MarketWave* study conducted in 1996. Why do so many of the industry Methuselahs have stairstep plans? Part of the explanation may lie in the fact that the stairstep/breakaway has simply been around longer than other types of plans. Binary plans, for instance, didn't even exist until ten years ago. But some industry experts have also speculated that the high corporate profits generated by stairstep/breakaway plans afford a financial safety cushion that increases the long-term survival prospects of companies that use them.

Disadvantages of the Stairstep/Breakaway Plan

• Delayed gratification

In all MLM plans, the benefits of geometric growth kick in most strongly on the deeper levels or "back end" of the plan. But it takes long, hard work to reach the point where you even have a "back end" to draw from. Just as stairstep plans offer the richest back-end commissions, in the form of overrides from breakaway legs, they also demand the hardest work and the longest delay before you are finally able to draw those back-end commissions.

• High monthly quotas

In order to ascend from one step to the next, most stairstep plans require that you buy a certain amount of product each month (and/or recruit a certain number of distributors who have attained a certain achievement level). The quotas rise, the higher you ascend. Moreover, as you build up sales volume in a leg of your downline, that leg eventually breaks away, and its volume is no longer counted toward your monthly quota. To meet your requirements, you must start all over again, recruiting more people and building up sales volume, in your personal group.

• Complexity

Stairstep/breakaway plans tend to be quite complicated, and new recruits have trouble understanding them.

• Top-heavy Commissions

Because they are back-end weighted, stairstep plans tend to reward the heavy hitters disproportionately. Some networkers call the stairstep/breakaway the "Republican" plan, because it tends to divert more money to top achievers and less to the rank and file. Nowadays, however, many stairstep plans are easing their requirements and moving more commissions up front, giving rise to a new generation of "soft" or "Wave 4" stairstep/breakaways.

The Matrix Plan

- **Description**

The typical matrix plan sets strict limits on both width and depth. In a 2×12 plan, for instance, you are allowed a 12-level depth, but a frontline that is only two people wide. The first two people you recruit will fill up your frontline. The third person will "spill over" onto the next level down.

Advantages of the Matrix Plan:

- **Spillover:**

Because the number of people allowed on your frontline is so small, virtually any ambitious recruiter will generate lots of spillover. If you recruit six people, for instance, into a 2×12 plan, four of them will spill over into your second level. Just as your spillover fills up the downlines of people underneath you, so your downline is being filled by spillover from above.

- **Easy to manage**

You are responsible for training and supervising everyone in your frontline. In plans with unlimited width, such as the unilevel or stairstep/breakaway, you can end up with 100 or more people under your direct supervision. But, in a typical matrix, there are never more than two or three people in your frontline.

- **Simplicity**

Matrix plans have no breakaways, and usually have few other complexities. In most cases (though not all) they are easy to understand and explain.

Disadvantages of the Matrix Plan:

- **Lazy downlines**

People in matrix plans often lure prospects with the promise of spillover—of letting someone else build your downline for you. This draws in a lot of recruits, but it also tends to attract people who don't want or expect to work.

• The Socialist Effect

Like socialist states, matrix plans tend to take from the rich and give to the poor. High achievers work just as hard, in matrix plans, as in other plans, but more of their commissions end up in the pockets of their downline—and often in the pockets of people who are doing little more than sitting around waiting for spillover.

• Limits to Growth

Unlike other plans, the matrix puts a strict limit on the potential size of your organization. A 2 × 4 matrix, for instance, will not allow you to have more than 120 people in your downline. Some companies attempt to alleviate this problem by permitting distributors to acquire more than one "profit center"—in effect, signing up multiple times, as if they were more than one person.

The Unilevel Plan

• Description

The typical unilevel plan does not have breakaways but, in other respects, it resembles the stairstep/breakaway plan. Like the stairstep plan, it sets a limit on the number of levels from which you can draw commissions, but no limit on width. As in the stairstep, you advance to higher achievement levels, earning higher commissions, by meeting specified monthly quotas.

Advantages of the Unilevel Plan

• Simplicity

The unilevel tends to be easy to grasp and explain, because it generally does not have such complications as breakaways.

• Unlimited Width

Like the stairstep/breakaway plan, the unilevel allows you to recruit as many people as you like into your frontline.

• **Spillover**

Many unilevel plans put their highest commissions on the third level. This gives distributors a strong incentive to stack more recruits on level three. In doing so, distributors are actually helping other people build up their frontlines, because every distributor's third level corresponds to someone else's first level.

• **Easy qualifications**

In a unilevel, all your sales volume counts toward your monthly quota. You do not have to worry about any of your volume "breaking away" and being disqualified. This makes it much easier to ascend the stairs to higher commissions.

Disadvantages of the Unilevel Plan

• **Limits to growth**

Unilevel organizations tend to be smaller, both in size and commissions, than those built through stairstep/breakaway plans. There are two reasons for this. In a stairstep plan, a distributor can draw commissions from deeper levels, by means of breakaways. But the typical unilevel pays only on a set number of levels. Stairstep plans enable you to grow your organization wider, by dividing up the burden of training and supervising your downline between you and your breakaway leaders. The typical unilevel, on the other hand, requires you to take direct responsibility for training and supervising everyone in your frontline. If you grow too wide, you can find yourself overwhelmed.

• **Laziness**

Many ambitious networkers tend to avoid unilevels, because of the limits they place on growth. These plans tend to attract a lot of people who join mainly so they can buy product at wholesale.

The Binary Plan

• **Description**

As in a "two-by" matrix plan, the typical binary plan allows you to have only two people on your frontline. You thus create an organization divided into two legs, generally referred to as a "right leg" and a "left leg." Commissions are typically paid only on the "weak leg"—whichever leg happens to have a lower sales volume, during the pay period in question. In most cases, no commissions are paid on the "strong" leg.

Advantages of the Binary Plan

• Fast money

Most plans pay commissions once a month. Binaries typically pay every week.

• Greater depth

Even though you only get paid on one leg, you receive commissions for the volume of the entire leg, not just for a few levels of it. This is a tremendous advantage. Suppose you are in a seven-level unilevel plan. If you happen to recruit a big fish on your eighth level, you're out of luck. He and his entire organization fall below your pay range. In a binary plan, however, you would make a commission from the sales volume of this big fish, whether he were on your twentieth level or your hundredth.

Disadvantages of the Binary Plan

• Runaway legs

Binary plans work best when both legs grow at about the same speed. But suppose one leg wildly outruns the other. Suppose, in an extreme case, that your strong leg did $50,000 one week, while your weak leg made nothing. You would receive no commission that week. And once a leg grows out of proportion, the disparity only tends to get worse, because the strong leg has more people and sales momentum than the weak one. Like a wild bronco, it runs away, out of control, generating oodles of cash for your company, but nothing for you. It should be noted that some binary plans alleviate the runaway leg problem by paying "matching bonuses" on the strong leg's volume.

• Incremental payouts

Some binaries (but not all) pay commissions according to predetermined levels or increments, rather than as a straight percentage of sales. Suppose, for example, that you made $1900 one week. You would expect your 20 percent commission to yield a $380 paycheck. But many binaries would calculate it differently. They would say that your $1900 falls somewhere between the two increments of $1000 and $2000, and then round off your sales volume to the lower of the two increments—$1000. Your 20 percent, for that week, would thus come to only $200. True, the remaining $900 of your sales volume would then be "carried over" into your volume for next week. But next week's volume would also be rounded off to the lowest increment, and more money withheld. So, in practice, the company always manages to keep a substantial portion of your commissions. Some binaries, it should be said, avoid this problem by paying a straight commission on the weak leg—one of the many ways in which binaries, like other types of plans, are beginning to reflect the Wave 4 Revolution.

No Easy Answers

If readers take away any lesson from this chapter, it should be that there are no black-and-white answers, when it comes to comp plans. Ten years of reporting and writing about network marketing have taught me a principle that we might call the Second Law of Compensation Plans—that for every expert on comp plans, there is an equal and opposite expert. My analyses, in this chapter, rely heavily on the advice I have received, over the years, from such experts as Leonard Clements, Rod Cook, Corey Augenstein, and Dr. Srikumar Rao. But none of these experts would agree on every point presented here, just as they do not always agree with each other.

What I offer is an amalgam of my teachers' wisdom, tempered by my own observation and judgment. You too must temper the advice in this chapter with your own common sense, weigh each plan individually, and choose the one that most closely meets your needs and goals.

CHAPTER 20

The Seven Pillars of Wave 4 Success

Turnkey systems are the engine of the Wave 4 Revolution. For that reason, twenty-first-century MLM firms do not demand heroic feats of entrepreneurial creativity from their distributors. They demand only that you work the system faithfully and tirelessly. This is accomplished by adhering to a few simple principles that I have named the Seven Pillars of Wave 4 Success.

PILLAR # 1—NEVER GIVE UP

Every success story in network marketing is a tale of endurance in the face of hardship and discouragement. The Wave 4 Revolution does not eliminate hard work. Turnkey systems are excellent tools, but they are only tools. A craftsman must still wield them energetically to get the job done. Do the work, and your business will grow. It may take years. There will be setbacks and disappointments along the way. But if you stay the course, you will reach your goal.

PILLAR #2—FIND A MENTOR

Network marketing is based on the sponsorship principle. The person who recruited you into the business—your sponsor—is in charge of training and managing you. But your sponsor may not always be qualified for the job. Sometimes you have to track up-line—go over your sponsor's head, to his sponsor, or his sponsor's sponsor—to find someone with the experience and skill to act as your mentor. Don't be shy. Keep searching until you've found the right person. Securing an able mentor should be your very first task in starting your Wave 4 business.

PILLAR #3—WORK THE SYSTEM

Your Wave 4 business is based on turnkey systems that were put in place long before you joined. The very fact that your company is successful means that its systems have proven themselves in the marketplace. Take advantage of this fact. Work the system, just as it is presented to you. Don't try to reinvent the wheel.

Of course, there might be several different upline leaders in your company, with different strategies for working the business. Follow the strategy taught by your particular mentor. If you want to get the most from the mentor relationship, don't fight with your teacher, and don't second-guess him. Be coachable.

> Securing an able mentor should be your very first task in starting your Wave 4 business.

Use his system, and become an expert at it. Someday, you may be successful and experienced enough to start developing your own unique approach. Then you will be an upline leader, too. But, as the old saying goes, you must learn to follow before you can lead.

PILLAR #4—TELL YOUR STORY

Every salesman is a storyteller. In most cases, salesmen tell nuts-and-bolts stories about the uses and benefits of the products or services they sell. Network marketers tell a different type of tale. They talk about themselves, their lives, and their goals, dreams, and aspirations. When you make your pitch to a prospect, you are trying to sell that person on the fact that he should follow in your footsteps. You are trying to persuade him to make the same career move that you did, by joining your company as a distributor. Your personal story is critical in inspiring him to follow you.

Your story doesn't have to be special. Just tell the truth, in your own words. Maybe your story is that you have just joined the company, that you're taking a big risk, that you don't know how it's going to turn out, but that you believe in it, and that Joe here (your sponsor) has been doing a great job teaching you the ropes. Then let Joe take over. Let him be the issue, rather than you. Your story will help Joe to make his pitch, because it shows the prospect that there are other people out there willing to accept Joe's guidance. As you become more successful, your story will improve.

PILLAR #5—KEEP IT SIMPLE

The key to network marketing is duplication. You persuade people to join your downline by convincing them that they can duplicate what you or your sponsor are doing. The more complex or difficult your business seems, the less duplicatable it will appear to your prospects, and the less likely they will be to try it.

If you go to a prospect's house, for instance, and spend two or three hours explaining the opportunity in detail, your prospect may shy away from the business simply because he does not want to have to do the same thing—spend two to three hours with each potential prospect. If, however, you simply hand your prospect a ten-minute recruiting video and say, "Call me in a couple of days with your decision," your prospect will conclude that this is a very simple business to work and will be more inclined to try it.

PILLAR #6—SIFT AND SORT

Don't waste time begging people to join your business. Reluctant prospects make poor distributors, even if you succeed in signing them up. The people you want are the eager beavers, those who are ready, willing, and able to start work now. A small but consistent percentage of your prospects will fit this category. Keep on looking until you find them. Sift out the chaff, as if shaking it through a filter. Then all you will have left are the strong, healthy kernels of grain.

PILLAR #7—SUPPORT YOUR DOWNLINE

Just as you relied on a mentor to get you started, your downline will rely on you. The more training and support you give to your recruits, the better they will perform for you. Leadership, in network marketing, is about making sure that the people you recruit have a good experience in your company and that they make money. You accomplish this by helping them sponsor other people and teaching them the same lessons your mentor taught you.

DECEPTIVELY SIMPLE

To the business-savvy, these seven principles may appear simple and naive. But the fact is, they work. As the remaining chapters of this book will illustrate, the Seven Pillars of Wave 4 Success are remarkably flexible and resilient. They apply to every business situation you will encounter in network marketing.

> The more training and support you give to your recruits, the better they will perform for you.

Men and women from all walks of life have succeeded in MLM. Some bring talent, education, and business experience to the job. Others bring nothing but their hunger for success. But all alike have the same chance of making it. In network marketing, the battle goes not to the gifted, the wealthy, or the highly trained. It goes to those who build their businesses upon the Seven Pillars of Wave 4 Success.

PART FOUR WAVE 4

Never Give Up

The Zone

Jeff Mack was through with MLM. As far as he was concerned, the whole industry was a scam. For fourteen months, he had poured his time, effort, and money into building a network marketing business. He had worked around the clock, harder than anyone else in his downline. Yet in the end, Jeff had nothing to show for it but $40,000 in credit card debt.

"I felt like a hamster on a treadmill," Jeff remembers. "I was always buying more product, to satisfy the demands of the compensation plan." In Jeff's company, you or your personal group had to order at least $3,000 in product from the company each month, in order to qualify as an "executive" or "director" earning top commissions. Generally, Jeff bought about $2,000 worth, while his personal group purchased the rest. But if Jeff's downline failed to meet its quota in any particular month, Jeff made up the difference out of his own pocket. In theory, most of this product was supposed to be sold to customers, at retail. But Jeff ended up buying far more than he could sell. His closet filled up with skin cream, while his bank account emptied, day by day.

THE REVOLVING DOOR

After fourteen months of this, Jeff was finished. His career as a would-be high-roller in network marketing had come to an end. "I put my tail between my legs and went back to the construction industry," says Jeff. His eight-to-five job as a civil engineer offered little hope of advancement, but at least Jeff was drawing a paycheck. As he confronted his credit card bills each month, Jeff vowed that he would never again be snookered into a network marketing deal.

Like hundreds of thousands of hapless souls each year, Jeff had passed through the revolving door of MLM. Rod Cook, the editor of *MLM Insider,* estimates that only about 25 percent of network marketing recruits stay in the industry past their first year. The rest, he says, "get burnt and go away with a bad taste in their mouths." Some experts set the failure rate much higher.

FIRE IN HIS BELLY

Had he been a different sort of man, Jeff might have resigned himself to life as another MLM statistic. He might have spent the rest of his days grumbling about the $40,000 he had lost. The dream of residual income that Jeff had harbored would have faded with each passing year, until at last it was gone.

But Jeff was not ready to give up. He had a fire in his belly, a burning desire to succeed. And Jeff's job as a civil engineer was never going to quench it. "I was twenty-seven years old," says Jeff. "I looked at guys in my industry who were thirty-five and forty, and I realized I was following in their path. And boy, I didn't like what I saw."

Jeff was determined not to enter middle age as so many of his colleagues had done, consumed by worries over money. But what were his alternatives? The more Jeff pondered this question, the more his thoughts turned back to network marketing. Had he really given it a chance? Had he lost that $40,000 because the industry was flawed—or because he himself had made poor choices? Jeff chewed at these questions like a pitbull at a rawhide bone. Painfully, almost grudgingly, he came around to the conclusion that MLM just might be worth a try, after all.

A SECOND CHANCE

An associate of Jeff's from his old MLM firm phoned him one day with some shocking news. Todd Smith, one of the top sales leaders in the old company, was jumping ship. He was joining a firm called Rexall Showcase. This was a new MLM division launched by a Boca Raton, Florida–based corporation, Rexall Sundown—a company born in a 1985 merger between Sundown Vitamins, Inc. and the venerable Rexall drugstore chain founded in 1903.

Rexall was one of America's leading brand names. It lent an unusual prestige to the line of vitamins and pharmaceuticals offered by Rexall Showcase—unusual, at least, by the standards of the MLM world in the early 1990s. Jeff wondered whether an opportunity with such a high-gloss trademark might be an easier sell than his last company. Even more intriguing was the chance to work with a heavy hitter like Todd Smith. If he was going to risk his time and money in yet another MLM venture, Jeff wanted a mentor of Todd's caliber to guide him past the shoals.

SOFT BREAKAWAY

Also alluring was the compensation plan. Rexall was pioneering a new type of "soft" stairstep/breakaway—one without the arduous monthly quotas and penalties that pressured so many networkers into stockpiling unneeded inventory. In Jeff's old company, you had to work your way up from a $2,000 to $3,000 monthly volume, over a five-month period, just to qualify for a 9 percent commission. If you missed your quota for two months, you lost your "executive" status and had to start all over again.

The Rexall plan, on the other hand, required only a $1,000 monthly volume to become a director. And there was no penalty for missing your quota. Once you attained a certain commission level, you kept it for life. Jeff realized that such a plan would be far less likely to sweep him into another whirlpool of credit card debt. It would also be easier for the people he recruited to work this plan, many of whom would be part-timers, without a lot of money or time to invest in the business.

A TOUGH DECISION

Despite these obvious advantages, Jeff faced a hard decision. His friends and family were painfully aware of his previous failure in MLM. If he went back to the business now, he would look like a fool in their eyes. All his life, Jeff had seen himself as the black sheep of his family. His grandparents had been hard-working immigrants from Lebanon, who had built a thriving apparel business by the sweat of their brows. Their stern work ethic had been passed on to Jeff's brothers and sisters, all of whom had excelled in school and gone on to become highly paid doctors, lawyers, and white-collar professionals.

> Virtually every great network marketing success story begins when a person decides that he no longer cares what other people think.

But Jeff was different. He had always been a dreamer. He never stuck with anything long enough to make it work. After flunking out of college, then later graduating with a bare 2.006 grade point average, Jeff had been forced to settle for a second-rate job. His ill-advised brush with MLM only deepened his father's conviction that Jeff was going nowhere fast. "I was a pretty big disappointment to him," Jeff admits.

THE DREAM STEALERS

Mark Yarnell, a top sales leader for Legacy USA, believes that one of the hardest tasks an MLM beginner faces is to maintain his commitment in the face of criticism by friends and family. Yarnell calls these well-intentioned naysayers the "dream stealers." Many an MLM neophyte has been driven to quit through pressure from those he loves and respects. "If you begin talking to your relatives and friends about this industry," write Mark and Rene Reid Yarnell in *Your First Year in Network Marketing,* "most of them are going to tell you that you've lost your mind."

For that reason, thick skin is a prerequisite for success in MLM. Virtually every great network marketing success story begins when a person decides that he no longer cares what other people think. Often, he reaches that point out of sheer exhaustion and desperation. This was clearly the case with Jeff Mack.

BEYOND SELF-CONSCIOUSNESS

With $40,000 in high-interest debt and not enough money to pay his rent, Jeff moved back in with his parents at the age of twenty-six. "At that age, after you've been out on your own, that's a pretty humbling experience," says Jeff. But it was precisely the stimulus he needed.

Stripped of his pride and backed against the wall financially, Jeff had transcended self-consciousness. He was in the Zone—that rarefied state when the only thing that matters is getting the job done. In Jeff's mind, nothing could supplant the raw urgency of survival, the need to win back his freedom and dignity. And, as it turned out, Jeff would win all these things and more through his Rexall business.

CHAPTER 22

Make It,
Don't Fake It

"Fake it till you make it," Jeff's upline advised him, in his old company. What this meant was that Jeff was supposed to invest in expensive clothing and other props to fool his prospects into thinking he was successful. By "faking it," the theory went, Jeff would attract so many prospects that his business would soon take off. Unfortunately for Jeff, he decided to follow this advice to the letter.

"I bought nice clothes and entertained prospects at fancy restaurants," Jeff recalls. "I got a cellular phone and was doing three-way calls and prospecting every chance I could get. My first cellular phone bill was $1,800. But my commission check that month was only $450." Jeff quit his engineering job prematurely, going full-time in MLM before he had a paycheck to justify it. It was only a matter of time before the whole house of cards came crashing down. Jeff's high-rolling lifestyle lasted only a few months. He learned the hard way that faking it and making it are two entirely different things.

LEAN AND MEAN

Things worked differently under Todd Smith's tutelage at Rexall. Jeff's new mentor taught a lean and mean approach to the business. "Todd taught me to be smart about what I spent," says Jeff, "and to make sure that I invested my time the same way I invested my money—in a way that would give me the biggest return."

Of course, Jeff's circumstances lent themselves to a Spartan approach, in any case. Deep in debt and living in his parents' house, he was forced to strip his business down to the bare bones. Jeff set up his office in the garage. He took a desk he had used in college and laid the headboard of his water bed across it. Then he strung a phone line through the ceiling from his bedroom. A single file cabinet held all his paperwork, such as commission statements and tracking information on prospects. "I shared my office with a rusty refrigerator and two cars," Jeff recalls. "It always smelled like antifreeze in there."

MASSIVE ACTION

Jeff then instituted what networkers call "massive action"—a sustained barrage of prospecting effort. The company Jeff worked for had gone out of business shortly after he joined Rexall. That left Jeff without a paycheck. But it also left him with a lot of time for prospecting. He was at his desk from 7:30 each morning till midnight, with only two short breaks during the day. "I grew up fast," says Jeff. "While my friends were going to concerts and playing basketball, I was making sacrifices. I was going to do whatever I had to do to make this business work. A lot of people thought I was crazy. I wanted to prove them wrong. That was the biggest motivator for me."

It was hard, lonely work making sales calls from his parents' garage. Discouragement dogged Jeff at every step. But he kept his spirits high by listening to motivational tapes. One tape set called *Take Charge of Your Life* by Jim Rohn taught him a lesson that would prove critical to his success. Rohn said that if you noticed another salesman closing a higher percentage of sales than you—say, 10 percent to your 1 percent—there was an easy way to close the gap. "Just talk to ten times more people," says Jeff. That principle became the cornerstone of his strategy.

WARM MARKET

Jeff drew up a list of friends, family, and associates. These constituted his "warm market"—the pool of potential prospects with whom he had a prior personal relationship. Conventional wisdom in network marketing holds that it is easier to recruit people from your warm market than from a pool of strangers.

But this is not always the case. Jeff's warm market proved peculiarly resistant. Those who knew Jeff had already seen him fail at one MLM opportunity and viewed him as something of a slacker. To make matters worse, many of Jeff's friends were poor prospects, because they were just as irresponsible as Jeff had once been. "These were guys who spent all their free time in the gym or socializing at night," says Jeff. "They didn't think about the future. For them, the future was Friday night."

COLD MARKET

Of the 160 people on Jeff's warm list, only five agreed to join Rexall. It was a discouraging result. But remembering Jim Rohn's advice, Jeff redoubled his efforts. He turned his eyes to the cold market—the pool of potential recruits outside his sphere of personal influence.

Many MLM trainers warn beginners to avoid the cold market. Strangers can be cruel in the face of unwanted sales pitches. "Making cold calls is one of the quickest ways to burn yourself out of sales," comments Hilton Johnson, president of MLM University, a network marketing consultancy based in Lauderdale-by-the-Sea, Florida. "In a cold call, you constantly face rejection and abuse. Making cold calls every day is like doing a stretch in prison." Johnson's advice holds true for most people. But Jeff was in the Zone. Rejection and abuse meant little to him now. Shame and

failure had incinerated every emotion, until all that remained was his burning desire to succeed.

COLD-CALLING

One of Jeff's tactics was to call people right out of the Yel-
low Pages. He targeted accounting firms, in particular, because their display ads often listed the individual CPAs in the
firm by name. "I would cold-call for six to eight hours a
day," Jeff recalls, "just trying to get people who would meet
with me for fifteen minutes or who would listen to an audiotape." Such calls bore a high risk of rejection, but the Rexall
name gave Jeff a psychological foot in the door.

"I am working with Rexall," Jeff would begin his pitch.
"We're expanding our operations here, in one of the new
preventive health divisions. Are you familiar with Rexall, the
pharmaceutical giant?" Most would say yes. Right off the
bat, Jeff gained a threefold advantage. First, he had gotten
an affirmative response from the prospect. Second, he had
linked himself with a respected brand-name. And third, he
had set the stage for his pitch by mentioning the pharmaceutical industry—a business widely perceived as prestigious
and lucrative. Even so, it was rough work. Jeff estimates that
he signed up one prospect for every 250 cold calls.

THE LUKEWARM MARKET

Not all of Jeff's calls were quite as ice-cold as that. Much of
his prospecting was done in what Hilton Johnson calls the
"lukewarm" market. This market includes people you've
spoken to once or twice, referrals from previous prospects,
or follow-up calls to people who have already reviewed your
promotional materials.

Jeff learned to use his cold calls to generate lukewarm
prospects. Even when a prospect turned him down flat, Jeff
would always seek a referral. "We're looking for professionals in this area who might be open to some new business
ideas," he would say. "Can you think of anybody you know

who might be interested in developing his own business?" Quite often, prospects would provide names and numbers. These became lukewarm prospects. When Jeff phoned them, he already had an edge, because he could honestly say that he had been referred by a friend or associate of the prospect.

CLASSIFIED ADS

Many networkers report a high success rate with classified ads. Such ads produce a multitude of lukewarm prospects, people who have already demonstrated an interest in your business by picking up the phone and calling you. Because Jeff was broke, he used classified ads sparingly but shrewdly. He kept word counts to a minimum to save money and paid close attention to the response rates from different types of ads.

> Many networkers report a high success rate with classified ads.

Jeff found from experience that the most effective ads were those placed in the employment section, rather than the business opportunity section, of the newspaper. A typical ad would read: "Manager with entrepreneurial spirit and corporate burnout needed immediately. We're a group of medical and business professionals, working on the expansion of a new division of a major health care company. Fax resume in confidence to . . ." When prospects called, Jeff would warn them that he was offering an entrepreneurial opportunity, not a salaried position. About 10 percent of his respondents would get angry when they learned it was MLM. But the majority were at least willing to listen. Jeff succeeded in recruiting about 1 to 5 percent of his ad respondents.

PERSONAL OBSERVATION PROSPECTING

Jeff also engaged in what he calls "personal observation prospecting." He would seek out environments where he was likely to meet business-oriented people, such as Office Depots and local Chamber of Commerce meetings. There, he would strike up conversations with likely-looking prospects. If they seemed promising, he would exchange business cards with them. But Jeff made a point of never trying to pitch anyone on the business at the first meeting.

"My goal was to build rapport," says Jeff. "I learned that rapport is the most important thing in the cold market. Ultimately, people will take time to listen if they like you." Personal observation prospecting proved to be one of Jeff's most successful strategies. He signed up about 10 percent of the people he prospected in this manner.

THE POWER OF PERSISTENCE

Jeff worked his business the hard way. Many networkers prefer the comfort of the warm market, or the anonymity of prospecting via Internet or direct mail. But desperation had infused Jeff with a boldness he never knew he possessed. For the first time in his life, he had confronted a great challenge and refused to back down. "People began to look at me differently," he recalls.

Jeff notes that when he travels the country now, giving training seminars and business briefings, he often asks the audience how many have been approached by network marketers who subsequently quit the business or switched companies within six months. Anywhere from 50 to 90 percent typically raise their hands. Their experience highlights the image MLM has acquired in many people's minds—that of an industry dominated by losers and quitters.

"When I first told people what I was doing, they expected me to be like every other network marketer they'd ever met," Jeff concludes. "They thought I was going to fail." But when these same people saw Jeff still in the game, a year or more later, many began to show a new respect. "I started to make money after the first year," says Jeff. "My self-confidence was high. I knew that I'd done something a lot of people would never do, and that was stick it out and not quit."

VINDICATION

Jeff's father was one of the first to notice his new attitude. "I don't understand what you're doing," his father told him, after watching Jeff sweat it out in his garage office, month after month. "But I can tell you're working extremely hard, and whatever it is, I know you'll be successful if you keep pursuing it this way."

His father was right. In his first year, Jeff earned $48,000—more than the $30,000 he had made at his last engineering job. Exponential growth kicked in the following year. "I started to see people in my business doing their own thing," Jeff recalls. "There were sharp, talented people in my downline now, people who were putting in time and had their own groups growing." Jeff's income rose accordingly, more than doubling in his second year to $100,000. By 1998, his seventh year in business, Jeff pulled $833,000 in commissions and overrides.

IT'S A WONDERFUL LIFE

Back when he was struggling in his father's garage, Jeff began dating a woman named Lisa. "Sometimes we'd go out and she'd have to pay," says Jeff. "If I took her to dinner, it meant going to Burger King." Working in a bank, Lisa held down-to-earth ideas about business. She viewed Jeff's MLM venture as a form of lunacy. "But she was supportive," says Jeff. "I sat her down one day and said, 'If you have faith in me, you'll hang in there, and you'll be glad you did.'"

Jeff and Lisa were married in his third year in Rexall. Today, they live in a 6,000-square-foot lakefront house with a private beach. His four-car garage houses a Cadillac, a Lexus, and a Harley-Davidson motorcycle. When Jeff started with Rexall, he had never traveled overseas. Now he frequents exotic cities like Hong Kong and Osaka for business and pleasure. His residual income has given Jeff a freedom he never could have imagined. Recently, after returning from a trip to Hawaii, Jeff took a few extra days off to drive his Harley up the California coast.

BEING THERE

For Jeff, the days of "fake it till you make it" are long gone. He has learned that dogged persistence is the only sure formula for success in network marketing. "I realized, at a certain point, that I wanted to have real success," says Jeff. "I didn't want to be one of these guys you always see in MLM who put on a front, dropping names and being in with the in crowd, while in reality they're leveraged up to the hilt. So I made a commitment that I was going to stick with it and make it work."

Jeff is thankful now that he didn't give up after his disaster with the first company. "The reason most people fail in this business," he concludes, "is that they get discouraged and quit. Being there when the dust settles is 90 percent of the game."

WAVE 4

Find a Mentor

CHAPTER 23

Role Models

Life has been good to Denson Taylor. Only three years after starting his Excel Communications business, Denson became a millionaire. His full-time chauffeur now drives him to and from the airport in a limousine, whenever his business calls him out of town. For more casual outings, Denson can choose from among his convertible Mercedes 500, his Lexus LS 400, or his Lincoln Navigator sports utility vehicle for rambling around with the kids. Most people would be satisfied with Denson's six-figure monthly income. But not only does Denson dream of increasing his cash flow to a million or more per month—he has a realistic plan for doing so.

How did he achieve so much in such a short time? Denson will be the first to admit that he is no business genius. Nor was he raised with any special advantages. A college drop-out, he was born to a working-class African American family in Memphis, Tennessee. His father drove a forklift in a warehouse. Denson's parents would have been satisfied to see him land a steady job with a good pension. But their son had loftier ambitions and the good sense to pursue them systematically. He attributes his success, more than anything else, to finding the right teachers and following their instructions to the letter.

THE DECISION

Denson's first role models, of course, were his parents. They were no-nonsense people who raised their three children with strong morals and a hard work ethic. "My parents were very high on discipline," recalls Denson. "They didn't tolerate for me to disrespect anybody, especially my elders. We went to church every Sunday. When we sat down to dinner, everybody was at the table, whether we were hungry or not. If I brought a C home from school, I was punished for six weeks."

Denson's parents provided a comfortable home for their children, but they paid a price for it. From an early age, Denson noticed the toll that his father's factory job took on him. "I saw him give his life to that company and never miss a day for twenty years," says Denson. "He'd be in a good mood on Friday, because he knew he had Saturday off. But by Sunday evening, his mood was worse. He was already thinking about work the next morning." One day, Denson's father called the family together and told them that his plant was closing down. He was out of work. The company later offered him a warehouse job, but for only half his previous pay. "He took it, because he felt he had no choice," Denson recalls. "I decided right then that I wanted to be an entrepreneur and be in business for myself. I did not want to be at a corporation's mercy."

MOVING ON

Denson had learned an important lesson about mentors. No matter how good your teacher or how vital the lessons he imparts, there comes a time when the student must outgrow the teacher. Take from each mentor what you can, but then move on. If you want to keep growing, you must find new mentors to guide you on each step of your journey. From his father, Denson had learned hard work, consistency, and self-respect. Yet his father could not teach him to be an entrepreneur, because he himself had never had that experience.

It did not take long for Denson to discover that his college instructors had limitations, too. A math whiz who studied calculus in high school, Denson opted for a business degree at Memphis State University. But his enthusiasm waned with each lecture. "I felt that I was wasting time," he recalls. "My goal was to be a millionaire, and I knew what college instructors made. It was hard for me to sit there and listen to them." To his parents' consternation, Denson announced that he was dropping out to become a real estate agent. "They warned me that I wouldn't have health benefits or a steady paycheck," says Denson. "But I didn't want any of that. I wanted to be rich."

MODELING SUCCESS

Wealth had fascinated Denson since boyhood. When he visited his well-to-do cousins, Denson took careful note of their fine house, their upscale neighborhood, and their gleaming new Cadillacs. "I was always a big dreamer," says Denson. "Being rich was always at the back of my mind." Denson knew instinctively that the way to achieve wealth was to surround yourself with people who were already achieving it. He planned his move into real estate shrewdly, joining a high-profile agency where he knew he would get training and support. Once there, Denson kept a sharp eye out for teachers and role models. "I surrounded myself with people who were already doing what I wanted to do," he says.

> If you want to keep growing, you must find new mentors to guide you on each step of your journey.

When the company offered a twelve-week training course, Denson threw himself into it wholeheartedly. "A lot of people in the class thought it was corny," he remembers. "They didn't pay attention and didn't do the assignments. But every week, I had my assignment done. Whatever they taught, I practiced it till I got it right." Denson memorized the sales scripts as if they were Holy Writ. He listened to the tapes over and over until he could mimic each inflection of the trainer's voice. "I started to sound like the guy on the tape," he says. Denson's efforts paid off. Within seven months, he was the number four agent in the office, earning six-figure annual commissions.

The Next Level

Yet Denson wanted more. When he showed clients through houses in ritzy neighborhoods, he would find himself coveting the very homes he was supposed to be selling. "I would walk through them and dream," he says. "I would say to myself, one day I'm going to have one of these." But that particular dream was still out of Denson's reach. He had a wife and children to support now. Bills were piling up. Denson's commissions were good but unreliable. One month he might make $50,000, the next only $12,000. "I used to tell my wife, we need to be making $50,000 every month to do what we really want to do," Denson recalls.

Then one day Denson got a call from a friend, a fellow realtor who made about $400,000 a year selling houses. The man invited him to a meeting, which turned out to be a business briefing for Excel Communications. Denson had had some brushes with MLM in the past. His mother had spent a couple of years selling part-time for an MLM perfume company, but had never made any serious money. Denson himself had dabbled for awhile in a company that sold skin cream, back when he was twenty-one. "But I never really understood the business and didn't get it off the ground," he admits.

A Leap of Faith

Others might have concluded from these experiences that MLM was not a viable business. But Denson looked upon his friend as a role model. Why would this man leave behind a $400,000 real estate business just to do Excel? Denson was intrigued. His whole strategy up till then had been to model successful people. This man was nearly four times as successful as Denson. If he was willing to try MLM, maybe his example was worth following. "It felt right," Denson concluded. "I didn't know a whole lot about the company or the industry or anything, but I dropped real estate right away and pursued it."

TRACKING UPLINE

Once again, Denson had found a role model and followed him on faith. But once more, he discovered that his new teacher had limitations. Denson's sponsor was almost as new to the business as he was. In order to excel, Denson knew he would have to find more experienced teachers. That meant tracking upline—going over his sponsor's head and working his way up the hierarchy until he found a leader willing to spend time with him.

Excel encouraged people to invite their prospects to business briefings—meetings that could be held in a hotel conference room, where you could give your pitch to many people at once. The company provided flip charts and scripted sales presentations for these meetings. All you had to do was follow the instructions and read the script, word for word. But Denson and his sponsor realized that if they wanted to give a really effective presentation, they needed help. So they tracked upline. They called around until they found a leader willing to speak at their meeting. Thirty people showed up for that first briefing, and several joined Excel on the spot. The results were so good that Denson persuaded the leader to come back and do a second meeting that same night.

A LITTLE HERE, A LITTLE THERE

Many people, when they think of the word *mentor,* imagine a close personal relationship spanning many years. But such relationships are rare in business. Most networkers have to take their mentoring on the fly, a little here, a little there, from a variety of different teachers.

Denson never found a single mentor who could take him in hand and offer him a soup-to-nuts success system. But he always kept attuned to the upper reaches of Excel's hierarchy. When the top leaders spoke, Denson heeded their words, whether they came through the medium of newsletters, tapes, or remarks at an Excel convention. Some of his most priceless lessons Denson gleaned from people who would never have recognized him in a crowd.

KEEP IT SIMPLE

One of Denson's long-distance teachers was Paul Orberson, the top sales leader in Excel. From his tapes and training, Denson learned the principle of Keep It Simple. Many new recruits in Excel are tempted to overwhelm their prospects with information. They lecture endlessly about the deregulation of the telecommunications industry and the tremendous potential for growth it offers in the twenty-first century. But Orberson taught that such monologues are a waste of time. People join MLM for one reason—to make money. What they need to know most is how to make it work.

> **M**ost networkers have to take their mentoring on the fly, a little here, a little there, from a variety of different teachers.

"You just focus on two things," says Denson, "financial independence and time freedom. They need to know how to operate the business, how to get paid, and then how to help other people get paid." The simpler your pitch, the more duplicatable it is—that is, the easier it will be for your recruits to emulate when talking to their prospects. Denson breaks down the business into simple modules for his newcomers. He keeps them focused on one easy step at a time. "I tell people we're going to help them make $1,200 in their first two weeks," says Denson. "All you have to do is sign up three reps, and help each of them get eight customers."

MEETING MANIA

Another way to keep it simple is to bring your prospects to business briefings. If you spend two hours at a prospect's house giving a personal presentation, you're sending the wrong message. Your prospect will get the impression that this is a door-to-door business that will require him to spend many hours making house calls. But if you invite your prospect to a forty-five-minute business briefing, sign him up, and then get him home within an hour and a half, he will have a completely different impression of your business. He will realize that he can build a downline simply by inviting people during the week to attend a single Monday-night meeting.

Enthused by the success of his first meetings, Denson began holding business briefings every night. Success was mixed. On some nights, he would get as many as 120 people. On other nights, he would be staring at an empty hall. Denson recalls one meeting at which only two people showed up—a member of Denson's downline and the single guest he had brought that night. Denson dutifully went through the whole presentation for the benefit of that single visitor.

THE TURNKEY BARRIER

Denson knew that the meetings worked. His business was growing steadily. But he could not shake the feeling that something was missing from the formula. Everything he had been taught suggested that the business ought to be simple to work. Yet keeping the meetings going every week was a punishing routine that left him spiritually, psychologically, and physically depleted. He was always rushing around, trying to find surprise guests from out-of-town, to keep the regulars from getting bored. And there was always the last-minute suspense of wondering how many people, if any, would actually show up. This emotional roller-coaster didn't seem to fit in with Excel's otherwise smooth-running turnkey culture. There had to be a better way, Denson told himself.

He was right. In the past, Denson had always managed to break through such impasses by finding new mentors. The same approach would work now. One of the top minds at Excel was already working on the problem. The solution he offered would turn out to be the key that would unlock Denson's boyhood dreams.

CHAPTER 24

The Turnkey Meeting

The vice president of marketing for Excel Communications was a man named Steve Smith. As described in chapter 14, Smith teamed up with Texas oilman Kenny Troutt in 1989 to launch Excel as an MLM opportunity. Unlike Troutt, Smith was an experienced network marketer. He knew the power of MLM and persuaded Troutt to use this innovative method to sell his long-distance service.

According to James W. Robinson in *The Excel Phenomenon,* Smith expected to receive a cushy corporate position once Troutt accepted his plan. Instead, Troutt threw him a curveball. "Steve," he said, "you've done such a great job convincing me that this plan can't fail—so that's how you're going to make *your* money!" Smith was flabbergasted. Troutt was telling him that he would have to live on nothing but his own commissions. He was flat broke and had a family to feed. But Smith took Troutt up on his challenge.

He traveled the country, holding business briefings and singlehandedly building the Excel downline from the ground up. Today, Smith is an extremely wealthy man. But he has never forgotten his roots as a rank-and-file networker. He knows what it means to build a business one prospect at a time. For that reason, when Smith came out with a new format for Excel business briefings in the spring of 1998, it had an unusual ring of authority.

THE SWAT TEAM

Smith had studied the most successful Excel sales leaders and culled the best of their strategies for conducting opportunity meetings. He combined these techniques into a turnkey system called SWAT, for Steve's Weekly Action Team. The 43-page SWAT manual laid out a procedure for growing one's Excel business through weekly business briefings. Every detail was carefully scripted. Nothing was left to chance.

When Denson Taylor first heard about the SWAT system in the spring of 1998, he was delighted. This was exactly the kind of hands-on guidance he craved. But many other Excel distributors took a more skeptical view. They picked through the manual, embracing those elements of the system they liked, but discarding those they didn't understand. For instance, Smith had spelled out exactly which songs to use as background music for different points in the meeting. But many representatives chose their own music. "A lot of the leaders decided, well, I'm going to do this part, but not that part," says Denson. "They didn't do the plan verbatim. Then, when they didn't see an immediate transformation in their businesses, they went back to doing things the way they had always done them."

THE GOOD STUDENT

For Denson, it was like the twelve-week training course he had taken in real estate all over again. By doing every assignment faithfully and working the program just as his trainers taught it, Denson had achieved success as a realtor. He now resolved to use the same approach in network marketing. "With someone as successful as Steve Smith putting this program together," says Denson, "I decided I was just going to be a good student and not question the technique."

In the weeks ahead, Denson restructured his business around the SWAT concept. He modeled Smith from afar. Denson's personal contact with the man was limited to a few minutes of conversation here and there at training conferences. But Denson wore his copy of the SWAT manual ragged by constant use. His meetings perfectly reflected Smith's method.

A CLEAR GOAL

At the core of Smith's concept was a subtle but crucial shift in perspective. Denson had previously looked upon his meetings as a kind of pep rally for his downline. It was just as important, in Denson's mind, to make the events attractive to his regulars as to the prospects they brought as guests. Consequently, Denson expended great energy bringing in outside speakers, in order to keep the presentation fresh and the troops enthused.

But Smith narrowed the goal. In his view, the meetings had but one purpose—to sign up new recruits. Everything else revolved around that objective. Because the regulars were already signed up, it was no longer necessary to keep them entertained. They were part of the team, not the audience. No longer did Denson have to knock himself out finding fresh speakers and devising new presentations. Denson himself could be the main speaker every week. The guests would never know the difference.

ENTHUSIASM

By redefining the regulars as part of the team, the meeting organizer gained leverage to enlist their active assistance. Every representative became an actor in an elaborate play, staged for the benefit of the prospects. Their job was to keep the enthusiasm level high. They were instructed to go out of their way to laugh at the jokes (even if they'd heard the same punchlines fifty times), to smile, nod, clap, and cheer at appropriate moments.

Smith told organizers to encourage an upbeat atmosphere, almost like that of a sports event or a revival meeting.

"Some people say it's not professional to clap and cheer during a business presentation," says Denson. "But this is not corporate America. Most people working jobs in America are broke, and that's the norm. We're trying to do something different from the norm. We teach people that it's okay to have fun, to be excited. You don't have to sit there being stiff and professional."

> "We teach people that it's okay to have fun, to be excited."

THE POWER OF MUSIC

Perhaps the most potent of Smith's innovations was the idea of using music at critical points in the meeting. Smith posted a list of specific songs on the Internet, along with instructions on how they should be used. Denson dutifully went out and bought every CD on the list. "The first day we inserted the music into the equation, we saw an immediate and dramatic result," Denson recalls. "There was more excitement in the room, more people getting involved."

Many of the songs Smith recommended were high-energy tunes with a heavy dance beat, like the music you might hear at an NBA basketball game. When speakers strode up to the podium, Denson would play pop hits like "YMCA" or "Pump Up the Jam" by Technotronic. He would open meetings with "Let's Get Ready to Rumble" by Michael Buffer and "Get Ready for This" by Unlimited. Then there were special songs for special purposes. "If a real conservative presenter is coming up," says Denson, "We'll put on 'Too Sexy' by Right Said Fred, and everybody just goes crazy. People just get a kick out of it. Nobody is ever bored."

IRON DISCIPLINE

Behind the fun and high spirits, however, is a strict format and an iron discipline. Meeting etiquette is rigorously enforced. That means designated SWAT team leaders are required to show up thirty minutes early for the meeting. Everyone must have a name badge, including guests. Meetings start exactly on time, at 7 P.M. Monday night, and must last no longer than forty-five minutes. Everyone is required to bring the necessary paperwork for enrolling new recruits. "You come with the assumption that you're going to sign people up right on the spot," says Denson.

Even the seating is regimented. The goal is to fill up the front rows first, so presenters aren't talking to large blocks of empty seats. Everyone must sit down during the meeting, and under no circumstances should anyone leave the room with a guest. Whatever conversation you wish to have with a guest, it will be more effective if it happens in the room, where the excitement level is high.

THE FORMAT

The format for the meetings is always the same. First, an announcer will start the meeting with a two to three minute introduction. Then the business presentation begins. It lasts twenty minutes and follows a prewritten script. To break the monotony, two different speakers give the presentation, each speaking for ten minutes. As they speak, a CD-ROM projector flashes graphics on a 12-foot screen—the same CD-ROM presentation that Excel representatives use on their laptops for one-on-one sales pitches.

After the presentation, the local leader hosting the meeting will take the stage for a few minutes to introduce Denson, who closes the meeting with his final remarks. At that point, leaders in the room arrange the chairs in circles, one circle for each leg of Denson's downline, and begin a Pow-Wow—an intense group discussion designed to answer the questions of prospects in the circle and get them signed up. While the Pow-Wows are going on, Denson circulates around the room, shaking hands and offering congratulations and encouragement to new recruits.

CREAM OF THE CROP

In one respect, Smith's SWAT approach breaks sharply with MLM tradition: there are no testimonials. Traditional opportunity meetings set aside time for ordinary distributors to take the podium and talk for a few minutes about their experiences in the business. Sometimes ten or more testimonials will be crammed into a single session. Smith eliminated this practice entirely. Not only does it take up too much time, but it degrades the quality of the overall presentation. Personal testimonials are often clumsy and emotional. The people giving them are a mixed bag, many of whom have enjoyed only mediocre success in the business.

"Steve says that we need to have the cream of the crop at the front of the room," says Denson. Between meetings, his group holds practice sessions, during which they take turns giving business presentations. Everyone votes on who presented most effectively. Only those of exceptional quality are allowed to take the podium during actual meetings.

CRACKING THE WHIP

Discipline does not maintain itself. It needs to be enforced. At one meeting, Denson noticed that only about two hundred people showed up—nearly 50 percent less than he expects on a good night. He immediately sent a voice mail broadcast to his group. "I thought I had a serious group of people here," Denson scolded them. "Maybe I don't. If you can't get excited about the possibility of being financially independent, maybe I need to start a new group."

The reaction was immediate. "They stepped up," says Denson. "The next meeting, they were there." You can't force people to show up, Denson cautions. But you can warn them that there will be financial consequences for their apathy. If they lose the support of their leader, Denson, they lose the chance to succeed in the business. That's a sufficient threat to keep most of them in line. The key to discipline, says Denson, is to impress on your group the need to work as a team. "I tell them, 'You can't create excitement by yourself. I can't create excitement by myself. The only way we can have an exciting meeting every week is for all of us to work together.'"

DUPLICATABILITY

When they come to a meeting, prospects receive a powerful message about the duplicatability of the Excel business. Each guest can see with his own eyes how effective the meeting is for recruiting. He can also see how easy it was for his sponsor to invite him and then to sit back, letting the meeting itself do the rest of the work.

As representatives gain experience and build their downlines, many will ultimately choose to take on the responsibility of hosting meetings themselves—but it is not obligatory. Most will remain part-timers. Their business will consist of recruiting people during the week and bringing them, each Monday night, to a single forty-five-minute event. For these people, the SWAT system offers a reliable infrastructure for building the business, with little time investment on their part.

> The key to discipline, says Denson, is to impress on your group the need to work as a team.

INSTANT RESULTS

When Denson switched to the SWAT format, the results were immediate. Attendance at Denson's old business briefings ranged from zero to 120. Under the SWAT format, total attendance jumped to the 300 to 400 range, with the number of guests varying from 70 to 200 on any given night.

Denson's commissions also skyrocketed. "I saw a pattern where my income started jumping $20,000 from one month to the next," Denson recalls. "It hit all of a sudden. Those numbers just came out of nowhere." Today, Denson's income fluctuates between $80,000 and $100,000 per month. "Steve Smith uses me now as a big example of what SWAT can do for your business," says Denson.

The Twenty-First-Century Meeting

Many networkers view the full-blown hotel meeting as a relic of MLM's past. New technology has made it easy for people to hold informal business briefings in their own living rooms with just a few guests. You can invite friends and acquaintances over to view a sales rally on satellite or Web TV, or listen to a company-sponsored teleconference via speakerphone. For many, this seems a far more attractive way to spend an evening than dragging yourself or your prospects out to the Ramada Inn on some dark, snowy night.

Denson believes, however, that there will always be a place for the live meeting in network marketing. "It keeps people plugged into the excitement," he says. "If I've got a brand new person who goes and makes $1,400 his first week in the business, I want everyone in my group to meet this person, face to face." Denson applauds Excel's plan to start using video broadcasts over the Internet, but he sees the new technology as an adjunct, not a replacement for the SWAT system. "I'll use the broadcasts to bring my Monday night meetings to my out-of-town groups," he says.

A Matter of Faith

What makes the live meeting work in the twenty-first century, says Denson, is the turnkey approach, exemplified by Steve Smith's SWAT system. The prepackaged format, the scripted speeches, the CD-ROM presentation, and the tightly enforced rules help standardize the process and eliminate bugs. As Denson's experience makes plain, the SWAT system works if you follow it faithfully, step by detailed step.

"It's just as if you're baking a cake, " Denson explains. "You may taste the flour before you mix it in and say, well, I don't like the taste of this, so I'm not going to use it. But flour is the main ingredient." Likewise, network marketers cannot judge, from the separate components of their mentors' success "recipe," which component will be most critical to the "cake" of success. A great deal of what it means to be a Wave 4 networker is to have the faith and courage to trust in your mentor, to believe in his system, and to give it a chance to work in the marketplace. Denson Taylor showed such faith. He has been reaping the rewards ever since.

PART SIX

WAVE 4

Work the System

Quest for a System

John Valenty was afraid. He had been brought up to believe that hard work guaranteed success, but now he wasn't so sure. John was working night and day, at the limits of his strength. Yet every month he seemed to slide deeper into debt. At the tender age of twenty-three, John had somehow managed to end up owing $100,000. "I was living beyond my means," he says. "And no matter how much I grew my business, my net income still was not sufficient."

Friends and lawyers urged John to declare bankruptcy. But this went against the grain of his upbringing. "I'm a responsible person," he says. "For me, debt was not a game. It wasn't something negotiable. I knew that if someone owed me $100,000 and reneged on the debt, it would end me. I couldn't do that to someone else, even if it was a big company."

John realized that he needed a system, a way of doing business that would multiply his personal efforts many times over. Only in that way could he build a residual income sufficient to turn his life around. "I knew there was something out there for me," says John. "I just had to find out what it was."

VICTIM OF THE E-MYTH

In chapter 13, we discussed Michael Gerber's concept of the E-Myth—the delusion that striking out on your own and starting a business will give you freedom. In fact, most owners of small businesses experience just the opposite. Their enterprises become taskmasters crueler and more demanding than any corporate boss. This was certainly the case with John Valenty.

He dropped out of high school in the eleventh grade to work his automotive repair business full time. Within a few years, John had a fleet of trucks cruising San Diego, doing on-the-spot repairs, and bringing in $30,000 in sales per month. But profits were thin, and John's high-rolling lifestyle expensive. By the age of twenty-one, he was deeply in debt and scrambling for a way out. He dabbled for awhile in a classified ad scheme he had seen advertised on an infomercial. But that, too, required a large investment of time and money. "The thing I didn't like about sales was that it all depended on your own effort," says John. "I knew that the answer for me lay in duplication of some kind, in utilizing other people's efforts."

WAVE 3

But how could he achieve such duplication? John knew about network marketing because his parents had worked a Shaklee business. Yet he had never paid much attention to it and knew little about MLM's inner workings. Now John began noticing that a large number of the classified ads in the newspaper were hawking MLM opportunities. Perhaps it was worth investigating, he thought. "Whenever I start something new, the first thing I do is go to the bookstore and get a book about it," says John. In this case, the book John found was *Wave 3: The New Era in Network Marketing* (by yours truly).

"I started reading *Wave 3*," John recalls, "and it hit me like a bolt of lightning. Network marketing was what I needed to do. This is what I'd been groomed for, all this time. The leadership, the duplication, the way it uses other people's efforts. I felt that it had just been put there for me."

A TURNKEY VISION

Especially intriguing to John was the description in *Wave 3* of a new type of MLM company, in which turnkey systems automated many aspects of the business. He dreamed of

He dreamed of running a downline on auto-pilot, a business so perfectly ordered that its high-tech systems and standardized procedures practically managed themselves.

running a downline on auto-pilot, a business so perfectly ordered that its high-tech systems and standardized procedures practically managed themselves. But did such a futuristic company even exist? John was determined to find out.

His first phone call was less than encouraging. John answered a classified ad for an MLM opportunity, but the woman who answered the phone seemed to know less about the business than he did. "She was like a deer in the headlights," John recalls. "She was very scared, very uncomfortable, and obviously didn't want to be talking to me." John only compounded the woman's insecurities by firing off a series of pointed questions about her business that she was unable to answer.

FOLLOW THE SYSTEM

It seemed to John that he had hit a dead end. How could this woman sponsor and train him, John asked himself, if she could not even answer basic questions about her own business? It was a disheartening introduction to network marketing. Yet John realized that a successful business system must allow for every contingency. If MLM really worked, in the real world, then it must come equipped with steps and procedures to follow in the event of mishaps or road-blocks. What procedure was appropriate to this situation?

John's mind wandered back to the only MLM system he knew—the one laid out in the book *Wave 3*. It occurred to him that the book had touched on exactly this sort of problem. But what had it said? "When you start out in network marketing, you're usually a poor advertisement for your company . . ." John remembered reading. "What can you do? *Track upline.* That means find a successful person in the levels above you who is willing to act as your mentor. Then use that person as the lure for new prospects."

DON'T MAKE YOURSELF THE ISSUE

That was the problem, John realized. No one had told this woman about tracking upline. Because she herself was inexperienced and therefore a poor advertisement for the business, her best move would have been to deflect John's attention away from her and toward her sponsor. "To tell the truth," she might have responded, "I just started out in this business. But I know someone who's been very successful in it, who can help you. Let me try to get him on the phone right now." If her sponsor had been available, she could have set up a three-way phone call right then and listened quietly while her sponsor gave the pitch. That was Wave 3 prospecting.

If John knew that, why didn't she? John was startled to realize that he had more insight into the business than she did, simply from reading a book. He decided to do his own tracking. "Do you have a sponsor?" John asked the woman. She did. "And what's his name?" John coaxed. It was Terry. With a little more wheedling, John got Terry's phone number. He had cleared his first big hurdle in MLM, simply by following the system.

GO TO THE SOURCE

"Terry was a dynamo," John remembers. "He was the kind of sponsor I had read about in *Wave 3,* a Mother Teresa type who doesn't get anything done for himself because he's always doing everything for everyone else." Terry was always available to John, coaching him, answering questions, or doing three-way calls with prospects. But John soon realized that

Terry, too, had his limitations. "He had a lot of hands-on experience and he could answer many of my questions," says John, "but, in some ways, I knew more about the business than he did, just from reading *Wave 3*."

John's previous business experience also helped. The prospecting system Terry taught was direct-mail lead generation. Instead of working the warm market or making cold calls like a conventional network marketer, Terry advised John to buy mailing lists from brokers and send out cassette tapes pitching the opportunity. This made sense to John. He had done a lot of direct-mail work in previous businesses. But he realized that Terry's knowledge of the subject was limited.

Three levels up from Terry, in the company's downline, was a well-known mail-order guru named Charles. It was Charles' system that Terry was teaching. "Terry thought it was so profound and original," says John. "But it was all the stuff that I had been doing at home in my other businesses, mailing out information packages and follow-up kits." It was time to track upline once more, John realized. Perhaps Charles had the turnkey system he was looking for. Perhaps direct-mail prospecting was the key to the automated downline.

The Right Platform

"Professional mailers spend thousands of dollars creating, testing, and producing high-class mailing packages. . . ." writes Tom "Big Al" Schreiter in *Turbo MLM*. "It takes money to play in the big leagues."

Schreiter's advice about network marketing through the mail is very simple: Don't do it! When you add up the cost of flyers, stamps, audiotapes, postage-paid return envelopes, and list brokers' fees, Schreiter warns, you can easily end up dropping $20,000 on a mere 50,000-name mailing. And although direct-mail professionals usually expect about a 2 percent return on their mailings, there is no guarantee you will get even that much. "There is no average return percentage in mail order," says Schreiter, "because there is no average mail order."

HIGH RISK, HIGH REWARD

For all the previous reasons, Schreiter advises that MLM recruiters—and especially beginners—stick with good, old-fashioned face-to-face prospecting. His advice is sound. No one should jump into mail-order without considering the risks. It costs money, and if your mailing doesn't work, you can lose your shirt.

But for those willing to incur the risk, the rewards can be great. An effective turnkey system for direct mail multiplies your duplication power many times over. It gives you access to huge numbers of people, over an unlimited geographical range. And it eliminates the psychological wear and tear of pitching people face-to-face or cold-calling on the phone. The trick is to reduce your risk by finding a system that yields a high return. That is what John Valenty set out to do.

AUTO-PROSPECT YOUR WARM LIST

Charles was a master of direct mail. His system worked. Under his tutelage, John quickly began building a downline through audiotape mailings alone. "A lot of people really mocked us about that," John remembers. "They said, 'Learn to work your warm market. Learn to sponsor. Learn to build in traditional ways.'"

But John realized that if you were successful in direct mail, your warm market would take care of itself. Friends and family would notice that your business was taking off. And the very fact that you had not pestered them about the opportunity would make it seem more attractive. "We would tell people, 'You don't have to talk to your friends and family,'" says John. "It's all done through direct mail lead generation." With that promise, John was able to re-cruit many people who would not have been interested in network marketing if they thought it required face-to-face prospecting.

FIND THE RIGHT MARKET

Yet John had problems with his company. It sold natural health products, such as algae capsules, to a highly special-ized niche of vegetarians, ex-hippies, and New Age health freaks. "It was a strange category of people," John recalls. "I didn't relate well. They weren't the kind of people that I wanted to eat dinner with or build my warm market out of." John found it hard to sell the opportunity outside of that narrow subculture. "It just wasn't as duplicatable as I wanted it to be," he says.

John also felt hampered by the anti-capitalist sentiments prevailing in the company. Many of John's fellow distributors professed to be more concerned about the environment than their income. Company etiquette discouraged speaking bluntly about one's financial goals. But John made no bones about his ambitions. He was in it for the cash, pure and simple. Night after night, he lay in bed, running projections with his pen, pad, and calculator, based on the exponential arithmetic he had seen in *Wave 3*. "My goal wasn't glamorous," he says. "I was attracted to the big numbers. I had to see if it was possible to make that much money. I would run the numbers literally every night. Every time I got frustrated, I would do it again. It gave me hope."

STEAK VERSUS SIZZLE

John knew that direct mail could work for him, but he needed the right platform. If only he could find a product that he believed in and a corporate culture that nurtured his ambitions, John told himself, his business would really take off. He began shopping for another company only three months after joining the first. It was a hard quest. John discovered that many companies promote the sizzle over the steak. At one meeting, he was bowled over by the professional speakers. "I'd never seen that before," he recalls. "I was captivated by the magic. I was under the ether."

John was cornered by a group of self-styled heavy hitters who tried to recruit him. But he soon realized they were "faking it" till they made it. "These guys were wearing $3,000 suits," says John, "but driving $1,200 Volvos or Toyotas. They weren't making money. It was so disheartening, because I wanted it to be real."

NO COMPROMISE

John was not shy about expressing his disappointment. "You guys are a big joke," he told the poseurs. "I'm outta here." John expected an angry response. But strangely, one of the men whom John had just insulted seemed to agree with him. Throwing up his hands, the man said, "That's it.

I'm out of here, too. I can't stand people walking out on me. This happens all the time." John and his new friend left the meeting together.

"What are you really looking for?" the man quizzed him outside. John thought for a moment. "I read this *Wave 3* book," he finally said. "I guess I'm looking for a company that's run the way Poe here says it should be." The man had never heard of *Wave 3*. But on John's recommendation, he went out and bought the book.

About three weeks later, he showed up on John's doorstep and offered him a curiously titled audiotape. It was called *I Hate Sales, Don't Like Recruiting, but I Love to Get Rich in Network Marketing.* The tape was produced by a representative for New Vision, a nutritional company based in Tempe, Arizona. John's friend assured him that this was the company he had been searching for, the platform on which John could build his automated downline. Turning the tape over in his hands, John wasn't so sure. But the title certainly caught his attention. Its promise of a turnkey, low-maintenance business seemed to fit his vision of a Wave 3 company. Maybe, John thought, just maybe, this was worth checking out.

CHAPTER 27

The Automated Downline

Since its founding in 1994, New Vision International, Inc. had had its growing pains. Its line of diet, skin care, and nutritional products sold faster than anyone had anticipated. When sales hit $500,000 per month, within the first six months, the company's computerized accounting system crashed. Rapid growth also taxed its phone system to the limits. Upgrade after upgrade failed to solve the problem. No sooner would New Vision change the phone system than call volume would jump again, making it obsolete. For a whole year, callers to corporate headquarters got mostly busy signals. Product orders were also delayed, because New Vision's suppliers could not meet the demand.

But Jason and B. K. Boreyko—the two brothers who founded the company—learned from their mistakes. They had been raised in the world of network marketing. Their parents had distributed for Matol and Amway. The Boreyko brothers knew that MLM success depended on giving support to the rank-and-file distributors. So they invested heavily in state-of-the-art technology, transforming New Vision into a model of twenty-first-century automation.

Distributors have twenty-four-hour access to the company's computer system via phone or interactive Web site. A

75,000-square-foot automated warehouse ensures rapid and reliable order fulfillment. Today the Tempe, Arizona–based company generates over $200 million in sales per year. Its lightning growth earned the Boreyko brothers the title of Emerging Entrepreneurs of the Year from Ernst & Young in 1998.

FILET MIGNON

When John Valenty joined the company in 1995, much of its twenty-first-century infrastructure was still being developed. But John saw a fast-growing company positioned for the future. "It felt like home to me," he recalls. "New Vision was very Wave 3. You didn't have to buy inventory. It was shipped direct from the company. They had a unilevel compensation plan that paid good commissions up front." John was somewhat less confident about his upline, however. The man who had produced the tape *I Hate Sales, Don't Like Recruiting, but I Love to Get Rich in Network Marketing* struck him as a little too glib, a little too pat, on their first meeting. His name was Bob.

"When I first saw him speak at a hotel meeting," John recalls, "I was turned off. He had a perfect, polished pitch, a perfect comeback for every objection." John had learned to distrust slickness. He wanted steak, not sizzle. "I put him on the spot and asked him how much money he was making," John says.

The man had only just started with New Vision. He had made only $3,500 that month, and $2,000 the month before. But then Bob pulled out his 1099 form from the previous year. It represented his earnings from a prior MLM company: $900,000. This was not sizzle, John realized, but filet mignon. He swallowed his pride on the spot. "I'd never known anyone who made that much money," he admits. "I said, 'Bob, tell me what to do. I'm desperate. I'll follow directions.'"

TWENTY TAPES, TWENTY PEOPLE

Bob's system was simple. "Take twenty of these audiotapes," said John's new upline, "and give them out to the next twenty people you come in contact with. If all of them don't get involved, maybe you shouldn't. Maybe it's not right for you."

The idea of getting twenty recruits from twenty tapes seemed preposterous to John. But he had resolved to follow the system. "I gave out all twenty tapes," says John, "and I followed up with the people and made sure they listened to the tapes." Only four signed up. "I felt like a miserable failure," says John. But to his surprise, Bob told him he had done well. His next assignment, Bob said, was to hand out twenty more tapes! At that rate, Bob told him, he was bound to build a sizable downline.

ONE STEP FORWARD, TWO STEPS BACK

The system was wondrously duplicatable, John realized. Instead of expending your time, energy, and self-confidence trying to talk people into joining your business, you simply handed them tapes. Those who were interested signed up. Then you sent out each of your recruits with twenty more tapes, to repeat the process. Product fulfillment was handled by the company. You never even knew how much product your customers were ordering until you received your monthly check.

It all seemed so easy, but there was a catch. John's commissions grew with excruciating slowness. "My first check was for $187," he says, "but my phone bill was $500." John tried to accelerate the pace by using direct mail. He sent out batches of one hundred tapes at a time, getting an average response rate of about 2 percent. "Of those, I would close about half," says John. That meant one recruit per hundred mailings, with an average initial product order of only $56.85 per recruit.

DEEPER LEVELS, HIGHER COMMISSIONS

It seemed hopeless. But one night, John sat down with his calculator. He knew, from reading *Wave 3,* that success in network marketing depended not so much on the number of people you recruited directly, as on how many people your recruits recruited, and their recruits in turn. The real money was generated on the lower levels of your organization, where the number of people was greater, the percentage of commissions larger, and the exponential growth more pronounced. "I started running the exponentials," says John, "and I saw that the trick was to get more people to send out more tapes."

> The real money was generated on the lower levels of your organization, where the number of people was greater, the percentage of commissions larger, and the exponential growth more pronounced.

All he needed, John realized, was to get a couple of people to commit to doing exactly what he was doing—recruiting ten to twenty people for every thousand mailings—and then get each of those two people to find another two people who would do likewise. If he could duplicate that kind of commitment down several levels in his organization, John saw that the exponential growth would make him rich.

THE WELCOME KIT

A small innovation proved crucial in turning John's business around. Drawing on his previous direct mail experience, John made up a welcome package to be sent to each person who responded to the mailings. Most respondents had little or no interest in building a business. They signed up as distributors solely in order to qualify for a wholesale discount, so they could buy the products. But John realized these wholesale buyers were a potential recruiting ground in their own right. He designed a welcome kit that would appeal specifically to their sluggish ambitions.

The kit contained a welcome letter, a business card from the recruiter, and some sales materials pitching the New

Vision opportunity. But most important, it contained four to six audiotapes, describing the health benefits of the products, and a written plea for prospects to hand out the tapes to people they cared about. "Maybe one in ten would do it," says John. "That was enough to get some duplication."

LOW-IMPACT PROSPECTING

The new system perfectly fitted the Wave 3 concept of "low-impact prospecting"—recruiting with a minimal amount of effort. When he first started using the welcome kit, John took the low-impact concept to an extreme. "We literally would not even talk to people about the distributor opportunity," he says. "We would just let the welcome kit do the talking."

Nowadays, John briefs his prospects on the business even before sending them a welcome kit. "I've found that it's better to ask right away," he says. At the end of the first conversation, John will ask, "Are you interested in earning a little extra money? Because I'm growing a business, and I could use some help." Even if they say no, they still get a welcome kit. But John has found that pitching the business beforehand increases the recruitment rate.

DISQUALIFYING PROSPECTS

Disqualification is a powerful prospecting strategy used by many networkers. It means not wasting your time begging people to join your downline. If you encounter any hint of resistance from the prospect, disqualify him immediately. Politely end the conversation and move on to the next prospect. Not only does this strategy save time and effort, but it prevents you from recruiting people who are going to be problems later on. People who have to be browbeaten to join your business will more than likely turn out to be complainers and quitters in the end.

John discovered the disqualification strategy by accident. Still in debt and struggling to keep his auto repair business going, John was overworked and underpaid. His desperation gave a peculiar intensity to his phone work. "Necessity is a radical thing," says John. "I was pushing very, very hard. I was hot. I didn't massage the prospect. It was either, 'You want to do this thing with me now or you don't.'" Nowadays, John has lost some of that edge, but he looks for it in his recruits. "I look for prospects who have so much need for this, they'll do anything to reach their goals," he says. "I'll put a motivated idiot up against a semi-motivated skilled person anytime."

GOING FULL TIME

The power of geometric growth started to kick in only two months after John began using the welcome kit. He had managed to persuade only eight people to follow his system, but that was enough. That month John made $2,087 in commissions, from a total sales volume of $25,000.

"That was like an Oreo to a T-Rex," he says. "But it was just enough to tell me that we're onto something." In his third month, sales volume quadrupled to $100,000, and John's paycheck reached $8,200. He made his decision then to shut down his auto repair business and go full time in MLM. "I gave away all my accounts and sold my trucks," John recalls. "That gave conviction to the people I was sponsoring, because they saw I was throwing away a business that was grossing up to $30,000 a month." Today, John is New Vision's top performer, making more than $1 million per year in net commissions.

WAVE 4 PIONEER

John's stunning success came from following the system. Once he found a methodology that made sense, he stuck with it doggedly until the numbers came in. John's commitment to the Wave 3 vision has made him a Wave 4 pioneer. After four years with New Vision, his quest for the perfect turnkey system has carried him far beyond audiotapes.

Nowadays John is assisted by such high-tech props as Earnware—an automated prospecting system that he developed. Equipped with Earnware, even John's greenest recruits can deliver consistent sales presentations, and track their results like pros.

John's distributors glean prospects using ordinary MLM methods ranging from word-of-mouth to business cards, brochures, postcards, flyers, Web sites, infomercials, or billboards on the freeway. But each member of John's organization also has a toll-free 800 or 888 phone number. When prospects call, in response to an ad, they are automatically linked to the computerized Earnware system.

A prerecorded message promotes the business opportunity or one of the New Vision products. At the end of the message, the caller can choose whether or not he wishes to place an order or receive a return call. In this respect, the Earnware system resembles conventional voice mail marketing. But the similarity ends there.

AUTO-TRACKING

With a normal voice mail system, most prospects hang up without leaving a message. You never even know that they called. But Earnware automatically captures every phone number. The information is then routed to an interactive Web site, where you can view a read-out, in real time, of who called and exactly how long each prospect listened to your recorded sales presentation. This critical information enables you to prioritize your callbacks scientifically. For instance, a caller who listens to 3 minutes of a 5-minute recording is probably a better prospect than one who hangs up after 30 seconds.

"With Earnware, the average network marketer can get above average results very quickly," says John. "Because the system is automated, it lets network marketers focus on relationships, building rapport, and training new representatives." John sells the system through his Carlsbad, California company, Earnware (www.earnware.com).

LIVING THE DREAM

Today John and his wife, Shelleen, live a dream life. But John will never forget how much struggle it took to attain it. "It was the loneliest time in my entire life," he says about his early days at New Vision. "Everyone to me was a prospect. I used everyone. I had no real friends. I borrowed money from my mom, my grandma, my best friend, just to squeak by and get marketing materials." But those days are over. "I've since made most of them millionaires," he says. "So I can sleep at night."

John hopes that others in his downline will not have to struggle as he did. He ruminates constantly on ways to improve and streamline his prospecting system. John's Earnware system has given flesh to his dream of an automated downline. But fancy software is no panacea. The lesson John learned, from his earliest days in network marketing, remains as true in the age of the Internet as it was when he was mailing out audiotapes, for a 1 to 2 percent response rate. The rule is: Find a system that works, and work it till you drop.

PART SEVEN

WAVE 4

Tell Your Story

CHAPTER 28

Story Power

Kalyn Gibbens of Eugene, Oregon was an MLM success. With 2,500 people in her downline and commissions between $2,500 and $3,000 per month, Kalyn knew she was doing better than most. So why did she feel like quitting? Kalyn wasn't sure. She only knew that a thick malaise seemed to have descended over her business in recent months. Her downline was torpid, apathetic. Month after month passed with little or no growth.

"My income had not gone up for about a year and a half," Kalyn remembers. "It was stagnating. It wasn't going forward. I really started thinking that maybe this wasn't the right company for me." Kalyn talked it over with her sponsor. After listening patiently, he said, "You can leave this company and go to another one where people are making money faster. But that doesn't mean you will make more money. Whatever company you're in, you take yourself with you."

SOUL SEARCHING

Kalyn was hit hard by her sponsor's words. She had always seen her MLM business as a test of character. Since the age of eighteen, Kalyn had gone from one network marketing firm to another in search of success. Some had turned out to be scams. Others had broken her with steep monthly quotas. But for twenty-four years, Kalyn had refused to give up. Was she now growing weak, Kalyn wondered? At the brink of success, was she beginning to lose heart?

"I began to wonder how much stamina I really had," says Kalyn, "how much I could really take it, and stick it out." At the very least, the decision to stay would build her character, Kalyn thought. And if her sponsor was right, the stronger her character grew, the better she would do in the business. Kalyn decided to give her company one more chance. It turned out to be one of the best decisions she ever made in her life.

A STORYTELLER

Kalyn was a storyteller. She would build rapport with prospects and draw them into the business by sharing vignettes of her personal experience in MLM. "Your story is the most powerful recruiting tool you have," says Kalyn.

It is also the easiest to use. Telling your story is as natural as eating or breathing. Kalyn usually told hers in a few brief sentences. It was the story of a woman who spent her entire life searching for financial freedom. She had worked many jobs, from being an artist's model to doing makeup in Hollywood. She had started businesses, running her own modeling agency in Los Angeles, at one point, and a flotation tank center in Arizona, at another. But only network marketing had given Kalyn what she wanted: residual income. And only her current company, Neways, Inc., had provided the products, the compensation plan, and the support that Kalyn needed to make MLM work.

> "Your story is the most powerful recruiting tool you have."

HEALTH-CONSCIOUS

Kalyn and her husband, Douglas, were acutely health-conscious. They ate organic food, dabbled in vegetarianism, and supplied their home with all-natural cleansers and personal care products. Before Neways, Kalyn had distributed for a network marketing firm that sold herbal supplements. Its focus on natural medicine meshed perfectly with Kalyn's interests. When a friend tried to lure her into a company called Neways, Inc., Kalyn wouldn't listen. She was perfectly happy where she was.

But the friend persisted. If Kalyn wasn't interested in the opportunity, he said, how about the products? "Do you know that there are potentially harmful ingredients in the personal care products that you use and put on your children everyday?" he asked. Kalyn bristled. "No there aren't," she insisted. "I get all my shampoo and facial stuff at health food stores." With a knowing smile, the man handed her a list of chemicals that were known to be harmful to the body. He invited her to check that list against the ingredients displayed on her product labels at home.

THE DOUBLE PITCH

Kalyn did as he suggested. She was shocked to find that most of her shampoos, skin creams, and other personal products contained at least some of the offending substances. "I threw out about $500 worth of products," she says. "I was livid at the fact that I was shopping at health food stores and not getting safe ingredients." Neways, on the other hand, guaranteed that its products were free of poisons and irritants.

"Whenever I pitch the opportunity, I always pitch the product," says Kalyn. "And whenever I pitch the product, I always pitch the opportunity." Either one may entice your prospect more, at a given time, and you never know which it will be. In Kalyn's case, the product hooked her first. Long before she was ready to give up her other company, she was captivated by Neways' product line, which included everything from all-natural moisturizers, hairsprays, and cosmetics to ecologically sound oil and fuel additives for your car.

A POWERFUL STORY

At first, Kalyn tried to serve two masters. She used and sold the Neways products, but continued recruiting for her other company. In time, though, Kalyn realized that the Neways story had greater power. All Kalyn had to do was relate her experience of coming home and finding her bathroom filled with poisonous substances, and her prospects were riveted. She then handed them the list of harmful ingredients and let nature take its course.

The products were an easy sell, but what about the opportunity? Kalyn and her husband visited Neways' company headquarters in Salem, Utah, one day, and were impressed by the integrity of the people. The comp plan appealed to Kalyn—a hybrid between a unilevel and a "soft" breakaway that offered generous back-end commissions from the deep levels, while still allowing part-timers to earn good money on their upper levels. "We went home and decided to go full time with Neways," says Kalyn. "And we never looked back."

SECOND THOUGHTS

Never, that is, until the business began to stagnate three years later. After sharing her frustrations with her sponsor, Kalyn pondered his words for days. *Whatever company you're in,* he had said, *you take yourself with you.* So if it wasn't the company's fault, Kalyn asked herself, then what was she doing wrong?

Kalyn discussed the problem with another Neways distributor one day. "I want to become successful in network marketing while I'm still vertical!" she told him. But it was hard. Kalyn just couldn't seem to get the kind of duplication she needed. It was easy to sign people up, but hard to motivate them into building a downline. Kalyn felt that she was trying to drag people, kicking and screaming, across the finish line.

THIRSTY HORSES

"I guess you can lead a horse to water, but you can't make him drink," her friend commented. That simple statement stopped Kalyn in her tracks. *Of course,* she told herself. *That's the problem. What I need is thirstier horses!*

Instead of trying to motivate her downline to do better, Kalyn realized, she should be going out and prospecting people who were already motivated, people with a track record of success in network marketing. Having a few more leaders in her organization was bound to spur growth, Kalyn decided. "My mind opened up to the possibility that there really were thirstier horses out there," she says. The only question was how to bring them in. For that, Kalyn fell back upon a simple but highly effective technique that had served her well in the past.

The Big Break

Kalyn had long been a believer in the power of goal-setting. Years before, she had found a husband by successfully employing the same sort of visualization techniques commonly used by sports teams and corporate executives. Her experiment proved so successful that she later wrote about it in a book called *Marrying Smart.*

Kalyn had decided at the age of thirty-two that she wanted to be married. She set about pursuing that goal in business-like fashion. First, she drew up a list of all the qualities she wanted in a husband and began visualizing him, in her imagination. Next, she began telling everyone her goal. Just admitting to people what she wanted caused a dramatic change in Kalyn's demeanor. Self-consciousness faded, and her life became focused around her mission. People around her also began seeing Kalyn in a new light. Friends and associates enlisted in her crusade, going out of their way to set Kalyn up with men whom they regarded as likely candidates.

FOCUSING RITUALS

Whether you view prayer as the supplication of a higher power or merely as a technique of focusing one's mental energies, there can be little doubt that it works. Kalyn prayed for the attainment of her goal, not only in conventional terms, but also through specific rituals that lent focus and intensity to her quest.

A business associate had told Kalyn about a Native American ritual in which you write prayers on a piece of paper, then burn the paper, letting the smoke blow to the four corners of the earth. Kalyn followed the man's prescription, reading her prayer aloud three times a day, three days in a row, then burning the paper on the third day. Amazingly, she met Douglas—the man destined to be her husband—on the very next day. Kalyn did not realize the significance of their meeting at first. The two did not even begin dating for many months. Only later, when Kalyn looked back over her diary, did the coincidence of their first meeting become apparent.

THE TREASURE MAP

Readers may judge for themselves how to interpret Kalyn's success. For Kalyn, it confirmed her belief that prayer, visualization, and goal-setting were potent tools for attaining one's objectives. She applied these same methods to her network marketing business. Within a week after Kalyn decided that she needed "thirstier horses" in her downline, she found her old ambition beginning to return. "I started setting goals again," says Kalyn. "Big goals."

One of the methods Kalyn used was a visualization exercise known as a "treasure map." Kalyn went through magazines, cutting out images that evoked her deepest desires and pasting them into a collage. Her treasure map featured photos of a large house, a new car, a million-dollar bill, a trip to Disneyland for her children, and much more. Kalyn hung it on the wall and looked at it every day. The very act of putting the collage together helped crystallize Kalyn's goals in her mind. It was not long before her renewed commitment bore unexpected fruit in her business.

PREPAREDNESS

Opportunities arise constantly. Yet only a few are wise enough to recognize them, and fewer still prepared to take advantage of those breaks. "Unless you are prepared to profit by your chance," wrote turn-of-the-century motivator Orison Swett Marden, "the opportunity will only make you ridiculous. A great occasion is valuable to you just in proportion as you have educated yourself to make use of it."

There was more to Kalyn's methodology than simply praying for good luck. A lucky break would have been useless to her, had she not spent years patiently schooling herself in the ABCs of downline-building. Among the skills Kalyn had acquired was the ability to tell the right story, to fit any given prospecting situation. An opportunity would soon present itself for Kalyn to use that skill to its fullest. Thanks to years of diligent effort and persistence, Kalyn would be ready.

> Opportunities arise constantly. Yet only a few are wise enough to recognize them, and fewer still prepared to take advantage of those breaks.

CHATROOM PROSPECTING

Over the years, Kalyn had evolved an online prospecting strategy that relied heavily on the America Online MLM chatrooms. Chatrooms allow people of similar interests to congregate together and trade written messages in real time. Kalyn would strike up relationships in the chatroom, then put her new prospects on her Buddy List—an AOL feature that alerts you each time one of your "buddies" logs onto AOL. Once your buddy is online, you can send him an Instant Message (IM). A box appears on his screen, with your message, and he can respond, in real time, by writing a message beneath it. The conversation can go on as long as you like.

"You keep bugging them with IMs," says Kalyn. "You ask whether they've looked at your Web site yet, or checked your autoresponder." The hard part is moving your prospect from an online relationship to a more personal one, on the phone. "Once you've got their phone number," says Kalyn, "then you can employ all the traditional methods, such as three-way and conference calls."

INSIDE INTELLIGENCE

"The secret of business," said billionaire shipping tycoon Aristotle Onassis, "is to know something that nobody else knows." Opportunity came to Kalyn in the form of inside information regarding one of Neways' chief competitors. This company had achieved great success with a growth hormone product that was widely believed to have rejuvenating effects. Kalyn had seen other MLM companies strike gold after introducing alternative health products that later caught on with the mass market.

"It was the hottest-selling MLM product of the year," says Kalyn. "It was this year's colloidal minerals or pycnogenal." In January 1999, Neways came out with a competing growth hormone product called Biogevity for less than half the price. In her chatroom prospecting, Kalyn tried to recruit heavy hitters from the competing company. "We had more product in the bottle and a higher dosage," she says. "It was just all around a better deal. But they didn't believe me."

SURGICAL STRIKE

By chance, Kalyn learned from inside sources that the competing company was about to go bankrupt. The information was detailed, accurate, and completely reliable. She even knew the exact day on which the announcement would be made. "It was Thursday night," Kalyn remembers, "and I knew that the company was going down the next day."

Kalyn moved decisively. She went on the Internet and searched for Web sites put up by distributors from the competing company. Twelve of the sites listed phone numbers. The next morning, Kalyn called all twelve people on her list. They had already received the bad news. Most were angry and morose. But Kalyn cut through their defenses with a surgical strike—a highly specific exercise in selective storytelling.

THE RIGHT STORY, AT THE RIGHT TIME

The key to good storytelling is knowing how much of your story to tell—and which part of it—in a given situation. Kalyn knew that her twelve prospects did not want to hear a pep talk about all the wonderful things MLM had done for her. All were accomplished networkers, for one thing, and knew the industry well. Also, many of them were not feeling kindly disposed toward MLM at that particular moment.

"I heard what happened to your company," Kalyn told one woman. "How are you feeling?"

"I feel like _____," her prospect replied, using a crude expression. "I feel like I've been totally betrayed."

"I know how you feel," Kalyn said. "I know how it feels to be betrayed by your company. I've been there." That was as much as Kalyn wanted to say at that moment, but her little story said enough. It conveyed both compassion and hope—compassion for the prospect's plight and hope that she could bounce back from disaster, just as Kalyn had done. "I might have something that would be of interest to you," Kalyn continued. Her story had done its job. The woman agreed to hear Kalyn's pitch and subsequently joined her downline.

INSTANT RAPPORT

Kalyn used essentially the same story for all the prospects she contacted that morning. The approach built instant rapport. But more important, it established Kalyn as a person who had been around the industry for awhile and who knew the score. "People aren't as naive today about picking their sponsors," she says. "They want a sponsor who has been through it a bit, and we definitely have been through it."

In the old days, it was understood that whoever introduced you to the opportunity had the right to sponsor you.

But people today shop for sponsors as carefully as they shop for companies. Kalyn recalls a man who posted a notice on Neways's message board on AOL, saying that he was looking for a sponsor. "It was very uncomfortable for our online community," says Kalyn, "because we were all pitching against each other. We had a big discussion about it and requested prospects not to do that anymore."

PARETO'S LAW

Network marketing downlines function according to Pareto's Law: Twenty percent of the people do 80 percent of the work. Those 20 percent are the business builders, the leaders, the heavy hitters—people who are willing to do what it takes to duplicate your efforts and find others willing to duplicate theirs. If your business is to succeed, you must recruit leaders. For that reason, Kalyn advises suspending the "sift and sort" rule when it comes to luring big fish into your net.

> If your business is to succeed, you must recruit leaders.

With most prospects, Kalyn wastes no time. If they do not seem interested, she politely but firmly cuts off the conversation and moves on. But with potential leaders, Kalyn changes her tactics. A heavy hitter from another company is a prize worth waiting for. You have a chance to net his entire downline into your organization, in one fell swoop. In such cases, Kalyn spares no effort. She will pursue her quarry relentlessly, waiting months, even years for him to change his mind. "Persistence is 90 percent of the game," she says.

CATCH A BIG FISH

One of the prospects Kalyn pitched from the bankrupt company seemed interested in Neways. Yet he would not join Kalyn's frontline. The man had such a good relationship with his upline that the only way he would go into a new company was if his sponsor went in first, and sponsored him in. That way, he would have the same sponsor in Neways as he did in the old company. It was an unusual request. But the story got stranger. When Kalyn contacted the man's sponsor, he, too, made the same request, regarding *his* upline. Kalyn tracked up five levels in the organization, getting the same story at each level. "The whole team wanted to stay together in the exact positions they were in," she marvels.

That kind of loyalty was a testament to the leadership at the top. At the apex of that downline, Kalyn realized, was a prize catch. He turned out to be a successful entrepreneur who had sold his construction business just weeks before, to go full time in network marketing. The sudden failure of his MLM company was a devastating blow. But the man hadn't learned of it right away. When the company went bust, he was on a ski trip in Aspen, Colorado. No one could reach him for days. Nevertheless, by the time Kalyn got through to the man on his cell phone, his downline had already left messages, pleading for him to go with Neways. "I don't even have a choice on this one," he told Kalyn. "My downline is forcing me into it. Here's my social security number. Sign me up."

THE RUB

By focusing on key players, Kalyn got more bang for her buck. "I only personally brought in five people on my front-line," she says. "But they brought in everybody else. It just started to snowball." Three weeks later, Kalyn had created five new legs in her organization, brought in hundreds of people, and more than tripled her previous income. "This is the kind of thing that people pray for," says Kalyn. "This is what network marketing promises but rarely delivers, because people don't stick with it long enough to find the people who will really make you wealthy."

Kalyn believes that success is inevitable if you just keep prospecting. You may have to prospect two thousand people before you find the big fish who will put you over the top—or it may only be fifty people. "For every person, the number is different," she says. "And you don't know what your number will be until you've achieved the success. That's the rub." But those networkers who have prepared themselves, through years of patient effort, will be ready to take advantage of the big break when it comes.

A BETTER STORY

Now Kalyn has an even better story to tell. It's the tale of how she turned her business around simply by telling her story, over and over again, year after year, until finally she told it to the right people. Kalyn's new success has spread through her downline, to the old legs as well as the new ones. Her organization has been energized by the power of Kalyn's new story.

As for Kalyn herself, she is well on her way to achieving the goals pasted up on her treasure map. The trip to Disneyland is a fait accompli. She and Douglas qualified for a free car bonus from Neways. And they are shopping now for a new house. "We were doing okay before," she says. "After four and a half years as full-time networkers, we were self-sufficient and supporting ourselves on Neways income. But it wasn't the big bucks." Now a new frontier has opened for Kalyn. She knows that the MLM dream can happen for her, too. Her organization is growing faster all the time, and Kalyn has no idea how much further the duplication will take her. But she sees little point in speculating. Kalyn just keeps on telling her story, day after day, and waiting for the next big break.

PART EIGHT WAVE 4

Keep It Simple

CHAPTER 30

Belly-to-Belly

"There is a phenomenon I call 'Wave 3 Mania' sweeping our industry, in response to all this technology," comments Chuck Huckaby, president of the MLM consultancy Profit Now, in the November/December 1997 issue of *The Network Trainer*. "Suddenly the opportunity meeting is passé and everyone wants a turnkey Wave 3 recruiting system." In the process, Huckaby says, people may be losing track of network marketing's key advantage—its face-to-face, belly-to-belly methodology.

Huckaby says he is as much a fan of the Wave 3 Revolution as anyone, but he sees a downside, too. "Though we are hundreds of times more efficient than in the old days, we are likewise much less likely to develop any personal contact with new distributors." Huckaby points out that an old-fashioned networker might spend twenty hours and $200 recruiting a new distributor, while a Wave 3 networker might spend only five hours and $50. The old-style prospector worked harder and spent more money, but he also gave more time to his recruits.

"There was a lot of drudgery in the old days," says Huckaby. "You had to stockpile product, deliver it to distributors, pay distributors out of your bonus check, and the only way to recruit, for the most part, was at opportunity meetings in a big hotel or in someone's house. But . . . it was . . . a routine that demands lots of personal contact with your distributors."

THE GLUE

Wave 3 Mania threatens to turn MLM into a "relationless business," Huckaby warns. This could hurt network marketers in many ways. Using automated prospecting methods, such as e-mail, Web pages, and fax-on-demand, Huckaby says, "People are ending up with '10,000-person downlines' who order one time and then are never heard from again. That's not building residual income."

Network marketing works best when you keep it simple, says Huckaby, working face-to-face and belly-to-belly with people on a daily basis. "The only glue that will hold together a network for very long is friendship, loyalty, and relationship," he says. For that reason, Huckaby predicts that Wave 4 will see a return to face-to-face networking, used in conjunction with technological aids such as the Internet.

> Network marketing works best when you keep it simple . . .

STICKS AND STONES

"Einstein said that World War III would be fought with nuclear weapons, but World War IV would be fought with sticks and stones," Huckaby told me recently. "That applies to MLM, too. Wave 4 will take us back to sticks and stones. People will have to get down in the trenches and find real customers somewhere."

I agree. Turnkey systems cannot replace elbow grease. They automate repetitive drudgework and free up more time for distributors. But if you want to build a strong downline, that time must be re-channeled into productive areas, such as face-to-face selling and training. "Reinvest some of your saved time and money back into the relationship," Huckaby urges.

INFORMATION OVERLOAD

Many of these insights were foreshadowed in *Wave 3*. That book contained a chapter entitled "Wave 4 and Beyond," in which I predicted that flesh-and-blood networkers would be an indispensable component of the new interactive marketplace. *Wave 3* was written in 1993 and 1994, before the Internet became big. Yet corporate America was already buzzing about the "information superhighway" in the form of interactive television.

In that chapter I quoted Wayne McIlvaine, former marketing director for McCann-Erickson advertising agency. After retirement, McIlvaine had become a marketing consultant for large corporations, such as General Foods, Campbell's Soup, Phillip Morris, and Nabisco. He also became a staunch advocate of network marketing.

"Network marketing is the wave of the future," he told me. "Major corporations are already having to embrace the fact that they will no longer have four TV networks to advertise on but a hundred. They're looking at the fact that they can buy six hours a day of television time to do educational selling, instead of 30 to 60 seconds. . . . Therein lies the great opportunity for network marketing. Because it may be difficult for people to find out how to access all this information without help from a network marketer."

THE INTERACTIVE PARADOX

What McIlvaine meant was that the sheer number of products and services advertised through interactive media would only confuse and dismay shoppers. Consumers would suffer from information overload. The more choices they faced, the less likely they were to make good choices. On the supplier end, companies marketing products through interactive media would have a more difficult time grabbing consumers' attention. Their message would get lost in the sauce. Herein lies the paradox of twenty-first-century marketing.

More than ever, we need human beings to guide us through the bewildering jungle of digitized come-ons, showing us how to access information and where to find the best deals. Where McIlvaine spoke of one hundred TV stations, now we have millions of Web sites on the Internet. The problem only compounds with each passing year.

BACK TO BASICS

In the Wave 4 era, networker marketers will be safari guides, leading customers through the digital wilderness in search of their quarry. The time networkers manage to save through turnkey systems will be reinvested in their businesses. They will spend more time building lasting relationships with customers and recruits.

As we will see in the next chapter, the most technologically advanced MLM companies are already giving rise to a new breed of hands-on networker. In many respects, they are going back to the MLM basics—working belly-to-belly and face-to-face with customers and recruits—providing exactly the sort of human touch that people need and crave in a digital society. "People will end up looking for relationships," says Huckaby, "where they feel they can trust people's ethics, get personal mentoring in developing business skills, and simply work in an organization with people they like and respect."

CHAPTER 31

The Human Touch

With the September 1999 roll-out of Quixtar.com, Amway's e-commerce Web site, the Amway Corporation has become an overnight giant on the Internet. Amway has long invested its massive financial resources in making sure that its distributors have the latest Wave 4 systems. Yet all the bells and whistles have not changed the basics of the business. Belly-to-belly interaction remains the backbone of a successful Amway distributorship. Even in the midst of high-tech ferment, it is the human touch that builds and maintains downlines.

Joe and Doris Shaw epitomize the face-to-face approach that makes network marketing work in the Wave 4 era. They keep it simple. Joe and Doris make friends and help those friends succeed in Amway. Retirees in their sixties, Joe and Doris draw from their lifelong experience in building and maintaining relationships. They recruit and train prospects with the same gentle concern with which they raised their six children. High-tech systems may underlie their business, but Joe and Doris put their faith in a warm smile and a caring attitude. Like millions of other network marketers, they bring a human touch to the digital marketplace.

BE YOURSELF

A retired schoolteacher, Joe Shaw entered the business with no sales experience. Yet he soon found that he could run a successful retailing operation just by being himself. One of Joe's sons was a paramedic who lived full time at an ambulance base. After selling cleaning supplies to his son's ambulance company, Joe became their regular supplier. It occurred to him that he could canvass other businesses in the area the same way. "I was already running to the four corners of the county anyway," says Joe, "so I figured I'd just fill in the gaps in between, along the highway."

Joe began stopping in at the businesses he passed. After introducing himself to the owner or manager, he would say, "I have a business supply route, and I have chosen the Amway products, because it's a good company, with good products, and a money-back guarantee." Reactions would vary.

> Even in the midst of high-tech ferment, it is the human touch that builds and maintains downlines.

Some people would assume that Joe was trying to recruit them into the Amway business. In such cases, Joe would reassure them. "I'm not here to recruit you," he would say. "I'm here to sell you products. I come around twice a month. If I'm here when you need the products, I've got a sale."

LOW PRESSURE

Low pressure is the key to Joe's approach. He places no obligation on the prospect. Before leaving, Joe politely asks whether the prospect would mind if he stops back the next time he makes his rounds. Most agree. He then gets the prospect's name, address, and phone number, and leaves behind an Amway catalog and a free container of E2171 antibacterial soap.

"The soap removes smells," says Joe. "It will take away onion smells, garlic smells, gasoline and diesel fuel smells, all in one washing." Cleaning and maintenance are tasks all small businesses have in common. In most cases, Joe's prospects won't be able to resist using the soap during the two weeks before they see him again. "That way," says Joe, "we have something to talk about when I come back."

A FRIENDLY FACE

Joe feels no pressure to close a sale and places none on his prospects. He knows that if he keeps coming back on a regular basis, eventually he will show up just at the moment that a prospect needs something. "Most salespeople want to make their sale on the first stop, but most buyers don't buy until the fifth stop," says Joe. "I just keep on building a relationship."

Joe seeks to become part of the prospect's routine. By showing up promptly every two weeks, he establishes in their minds that he is punctual and reliable. "The relationship gradually warms up," he says. "When they get to where they can count on me, they start buying. I'm the friendly face that appears every couple of weeks and fills their orders."

PERSONAL ACCOUNT MANAGER

Technically, the customers don't need Joe to place an order. Once they have an Amway catalog, they can order whatever they like by phone and have it delivered in two days. They use Joe's PIN number to place the order, so he gets paid every time even if he never sees the customer again. But Joe chooses to play the role of a personal account manager. His visits remind customers that it's time to order again. Joe answers questions and recommends products. His personal presence ensures that customers will not just toss the catalog aside and forget about it.

As a regular visitor, Joe can also evaluate his customers and decide when the time is right to pitch them on the Amway opportunity. His rule of thumb is to wait until they have placed $162 worth of orders—the price of an Amway starter kit. Joe points out to the customer that the same $162 he spent paying the retail price could have been used to get him started as an Amway distributor, buying the products at wholesale and making a profit selling them to others.

As always, Joe keeps the pressure low. "Some do it, some don't," says Joe. "About 23 percent join the business."

Find Your Groove

For Joe, the business route provides a method of working the business that is well suited to his personality. On his route, Joe can make his services available on a consistent basis, without imposing on people's time or patience. The hardest part of the job is done by the company. Amway takes the orders, ships them from the warehouse, and runs the commissions through its computerized accounting system. All Joe has to do is be himself.

"As a teacher, I could never leave the classroom," says Joe. "I was welded to that classroom for thirty-two years, seeing the same people every day. On my route, I can get out and drive around and talk to different people. It's kind of nice." But while he's relaxing and enjoying the fresh air, Joe is also building a serious business. He has over 175 regular customers on his route now.

Anywhere and Everywhere

"Not all distributors have to be retailers," says Doris, "and not all retailers have to be distributors." Doris has chosen to take a more aggressive approach to business-building. Before joining Amway, she had already created several successful enterprises, including an insurance business, a securities brokerage, an accounting firm, and a real estate agency with nearly $4 million worth of property under management. When one of their daughters pitched Joe and Doris on the Amway opportunity, it was Doris who immediately saw its potential for building residual income, and she who took the lead in building and running the business.

Her approach is simple. Doris pitches the business anywhere and everywhere, to whomever will listen. "I don't do any advertising," she says. "All my advertising is word-of-mouth." The small farming community of Edmore, Michigan, where the Shaws live, is hardly a hotbed of commercial activity. But between friends, family, and local business people, Doris has found no shortage of prospects. Nor does she confine her recruiting to locals. Doris tells of signing up one prospect after striking up a conversation on a long plane trip. The man returned home and started a new leg of Doris' downline—in Germany. "You have to get out of your comfort zone," she says, "both geographically and psychologically."

A HELPING HAND

Doris is in no danger of succumbing to "Wave 4 mania." Despite Amway's plethora of state-of-the-art support systems, Doris knows that her downline needs personal attention. Early on, she found that she was spending so much time coaching her recruits that it became more efficient to teach them all at once, in a regular class. Today, Doris offers an eight-day course that meets one weekend per month, for four months. Classes range from fifty to eighty people in size and cover goal-setting, prospecting, and strategies for qualifying for different commission levels in the Amway compensation plan. "We teach people how to be entrepreneurs," says Doris.

She also offers teleconferences every Wednesday night, featuring sales training and motivation. "We have about 180 locations that receive that teleconference," says Doris. Groups of people will gather at each location, to listen by speakerphone. "They can get together in their own homes, or with their upline or downline, and show the plan to new prospects."

HIGH TECH, HIGH TOUCH

As this book goes to press, Amway is in the process of unveiling Quixtar.com. The Shaws look forward to opening new markets in cyberspace. Yet they do not expect to sit back and let the Internet do all the work. "It's not going to be a cure-all," says Doris. "It won't be enough to just tell customers, 'We're on the Internet, this is my number, use it.' That approach won't get the results we're looking for."

Just as Joe's friendly face keeps his customers on the business route active, so the Shaws plan to supplement the high-tech interaction of Quixtar.com with some good, old-fashioned, "high-touch" intervention of their own. "The Internet can be very confusing," says Doris. "I'm going to do whatever I can to make it simpler for people. I'm going to talk to them and find out their needs, and show them how they can find what they want on Quixtar.com. I'm going to walk them through every function, so they feel comfortable using it."

UNLIKELY ROLE MODELS

The Shaws joined Amway in 1995. Their success has been meteoric. After only two years, they became Executive Diamonds—Amway's top commission level. By their third year in the business, they had tripled their pre-Amway household income. "It's made a big difference in our lives," says Doris. "The retirement plan we were doing didn't allow for a lot of travel. But now we go everywhere. We've been to Hawaii, Puerto Rico, St. Thomas, Aruba."

Doris seeks to share her success with others. "I want people to realize that this is not some big, hard thing. Other people can succeed, if they put in the same effort we did." The two senior citizens from Edmore, Michigan, hardly seem the typical role models for twenty-first-century enterprise. Yet it is people like them who provide the human touch that makes the interactive economy work.

PART NINE WAVE 4

Sift and Sort

CHAPTER 32

Disqualifying Prospects

Carla Mannes was excited. At last she had caught a really big fish—a supersalesman who had earned more than $150,000 a year as a stockbroker. Having lost his securities job, the man was reduced to selling propane for a gas company—a job that he hated, because it was a hard sell and kept him on the road away from his family. The man was young, energetic, and wide open for change. When Carla told him about her Shaklee opportunity, he immediately agreed to meet so they could discuss it further.

Unfortunately, disillusionment set in at their first meeting. Carla began, as always, by asking her prospect to state his goals. "I want to make $100,000 a year, within two years," he said. So Carla began explaining what it would take to meet that goal in the Shaklee plan. He would have to recruit and develop a minimum of ten business builders, Carla told him, each of whom would have to rise to the coordinator level—meaning that each would have a three-to-four-level organization and would be earning an average of $60,000. As Carla talked, she noticed that the man seemed uneasy about something. "This means I'm really going to have to get out there and work," he finally said unhappily. "I thought network marketing meant that I just had to find one or two good people, and they would build the organization for me."

ALARM BELLS

Carla had been in the business long enough to know trouble when she heard it. The man's words set every alarm bell in her head ringing. Despite appearances, he was not a good prospect. He saw network marketing as a gimmick, not a business. He was not willing to work at it. Carla's suspicions only deepened when she asked the man to draw up a warm list of personal and professional contacts. "I've got a list of one hundred people I know," he boasted. But when Carla tried to nail him down as to which of his prospects he would approach first, the man grew evasive. None of his prospects seemed right for MLM, he argued. In fact, the man was embarrassed to admit to any of his business contacts that he was involved in network marketing.

"I don't think this opportunity is for you," Carla finally told him. "I'm afraid you're going to get involved in this, and it's not going to be the kind of experience you want, because you're not willing to put the commitment into it." With that, she ended the interview. Carla had wasted an hour or so of her time, but that was nothing compared to the headaches she would have suffered had she gone ahead and signed the man up. Carla knew from experience that such people spend a lot of time complaining but little producing. The best thing to do was disqualify them right away. By identifying the problem at once, Carla was able to cut her losses and move on quickly to more promising prospects.

SIFTING AND SORTING

Accomplished networkers are masters of "sifting and sorting"— winnowing the good prospects from the bad and wasting as little time as possible with the latter. Carla's keen judgment in screening her prospects has been honed, through the years, by a unique set of work experiences. From earliest childhood, Carla was immersed in the MLM world. Her parents were big hitters in Shaklee. Today, Carla has taken over their business—but not before she spent years proving her mettle in the world of high-powered corporate sales.

"I grew up in network marketing," says Carla. "But I never really understood the impact it had on people's lives. Only after I'd been out on my own in the corporate world did I come to appreciate Shaklee." Today, Carla looks for people who have learned the same lesson she did. Her best prospects are those desperately hungry to escape the rat race, but also appreciative of the stability that comes from working with one of MLM's oldest, blue-chip companies.

> Accomplished networkers are masters of "sifting and sorting"—winnowing the good prospects from the bad and wasting as little time as possible with the latter.

AN MLM LIFE

With headquarters in San Francisco, Shaklee Corporation is one of a handful of network marketing firms whose life spans more than four decades. It was founded in 1956 by Dr. Forrest C. Shaklee, Sr., an early proponent of natural health. During the 1970s, Shaklee grew from $20 million to over $320 million in sales. It went public in 1973, was listed on the New York Stock Exchange in 1977, and in 1989 was purchased by the giant Yamanouchi Pharmaceutical Company of Japan. Today, Shaklee offers more than two hundred nutritional, personal care, and household products featuring natural ingredients. Its 1998 sales exceeded $750 million.

Carla's parents joined the company in the early '60s, and grew with it. They became multimillionaires and legends in the MLM field. Their reputation was such that it opened doors for Carla when she came of age. After college, Carla went to work as a publicist for an MLM firm in Salt Lake City. "It was amazing to me that people there had heard of my parents," says Carla. "I found that I was very marketable and people were open to hearing what I had to say, simply because of who my parents were. I was already a player and everybody knew me."

GOING IT ALONE

When that first company went out of business, Carla ended up working for a number of other network marketing firms as an employee. But Carla's sights were set far beyond MLM. She dreamed of making it big in the corporate world. "I wanted to be independent of my parents and independent of the network marketing industry," Carla recalls. "I thought it was very glamorous to work in corporate America. I wanted to chase that six-figure income and have a credible occupation. In many people's eyes, network marketing is just selling soap and pills. It doesn't have the glamour that comes from being part of a major corporation."

Carla attained her dream. She spent six years as a financial planner, investment advisor, and stockbroker for such major firms as American Express and Merrill Lynch. In some respects, Carla found that the financial services industry resembled network marketing. "There were similarities," she says. "The deeper you build your client base, the more assets you have, the more money you're paid. You build the business through referrals. Each client refers you to the next client." But there were differences, too. Carla was delighted to see admiration in people's eyes when she told them the names of the top-notch firms where she worked. "I finally got the pat on the back that I was looking for," she says.

CORPORATE DRONE

Yet Carla's American dream turned quickly into a nightmare. Her predicament struck home at the last company where she worked. "I made the six-figure income, but I never had time to enjoy it," she says. "The company owned me. I made 250 cold calls a week." Not only did the company take a hefty portion of Carla's sales, but its percentage grew along with her earnings. "The harder I worked, the more they took," she said. And if she ever left the company, Carla knew she would have to leave her clients behind. "I began to realize that it was insane to work so hard and have nothing to show for it, nothing that you can really call your own."

The awful truth of her situation sunk in one day when Carla got a call from a friend at the company. The friend told her that a mutual acquaintance of theirs, a broker who had worked thirty years for the firm, had just been let go. The company had tried to take some of his clients and give them to newer, younger brokers. When the man objected, he was dismissed. He and his son had built up a client base worth $400 million. "But when he walked out that door," says Carla, "he walked out with nothing. I couldn't believe it. I thought this was nuts." More to the point, Carla realized that what had happened to that man could just as easily happen to her. She resolved that she would not sit around and wait for the ax to fall.

33

Prescreening

The year 1997 was the toughest in Carla's life. Her father suffered a heart attack, forcing him to largely retire from his Shaklee business. Shortly afterward, Carla divorced her husband of fifteen years. With four children and a full-time career, life as a single mother looked grim. "I was so unhappy," says Carla. "I did not want to go to work for $70,000–$90,000 a year and never see my kids."

But the solution already lay in Carla's hands. Her father no longer had the energy to run his $30-million-per-year sales organization in Shaklee. Shortly after his heart attack, he had asked Carla to run it for him, for a small management fee. Carla could use the opportunity, he said, to start her own Shaklee downline and build a residual income of her own. It didn't take much to persuade her. Carla's marriage was already on the rocks, and she was deeply disillusioned with her job. Gone were the days when a spoiled young Carla could afford to look down her nose at network marketing. Life in the real world had given her a new perspective. After separating from her husband, Carla had lain in bed, depressed, for three months, unable to work. But now the pity party was over. The Shaklee opportunity was what she had, Carla realized, and it was time to make the best of it.

A Blue-Chip Company

Shaklee's blue-chip reputation would prove an important selling point in Carla's business. Many networkers avoid older companies, believing that their markets are saturated and their growth too slow. Mature companies do tend to grow more slowly than start-ups—at least when those start-ups succeed. But most start-ups fail within the first two years. Carla had had ample opportunity to see the other side of the fence during her days in Salt Lake City, working on the corporate end of MLM companies. Several of her employers had gone belly-up. And Carla had witnessed the bitterness and suffering they left behind.

"People would just jump in with their life savings," she recalls, "without really examining the company." Carla was shocked by the managerial disorder she saw in some of those corporate offices. "We're talking inventory problems, cash flow, financial controls. In comparison, Shaklee was run so professionally. In all the years my parents were involved, I never heard them say that their bonus check was late or was wrong." For these reasons, Carla found that some of her easiest recruits were people who had previously heard of Shaklee or who had had relatives involved with it. The company's track record proved a powerful ally in her prospecting.

PRODUCT PEOPLE

So did the products. "At least 95 percent of the time," says Carla, "the people who come up through the ranks and want to build the business are people who have had good success with the products." Carla learned early to target enthusiastic product users as potential business builders. "The best prospects for me are the ones who have been customers for three to six months, have gotten good results with the products, and have been sharing it with other people."

Carla tells of a woman in her downline named Ellen whose baby daughter had serious health problems. "She had gone from doctor to doctor," says Carla. "She'd been to the Mayo Clinic, to a children's hospital in Pittsburgh, and they couldn't figure out what was wrong with this child." At six months, the girl was still not crawling. She had a skin rash and a yeast-like infection coating her tongue. "By the time the child was a year old," says Carla, "she'd been on twenty-six rounds of medication. They'd put tubes in her ear twice. She was taking forty pills a day, but she was not getting better."

TESTIMONIAL POWER

A friend of Ellen's happened to be a Shaklee distributor in Carla's downline. The friend gave Ellen an audiotape by Dr. Linda Rodriguez, a pediatrician in Virginia Beach (also a Shaklee distributor) who treats many ailments naturally through a nutritional regimen based on Shaklee products. The mother contacted Dr. Rodriguez and described her daughter's symptoms. After being put on a special diet for candida, or yeast infection, the girl rapidly recovered. "Within three days, they could see their daughter turn around," says Carla.

What followed was a textbook case of testimonial marketing. Ellen's husband was a well-paid financial planner who supported her in style. Under ordinary circumstances, Ellen would never have considered getting involved in MLM. But she could not stop talking about her experience with Shaklee. Ellen shared her story with anyone who would listen. Before long, people started buying. "Within eighteen months, Ellen has gone from being a member buying $300 worth of Shaklee products a month for her family, to being a distributor moving $6,000 to $8,000 worth of volume per month," says Carla. "She's looking at making $50,000 this year."

WALK-INS

Unlike most MLMers, Carla chooses to work from a storefront. She maintains a 600-square-foot service center in Sioux Falls, South Dakota, from which she coordinates her Shaklee business and sells products at retail. "My Dad always had an office," says Carla. "He's never had the business in his home. I like it that way, too. At the end of the day, I can close the door, go home, and it's over."

Carla estimates that she moves about $10,000 worth of product from her retail store each month. The walk-ins provide an unusually fertile source of prospects. Virtually all are interested in the products, which means they fit Carla's number one criterion for a good recruit. But some are more susceptible to recruiting than others. Carla has developed a keen sense for separating the eager beavers from the drones.

SHAKLEE-IZATION

"When I sit down with someone who comes in the door, I never talk business," says Carla. "We talk product." The first step in Carla's prescreening process is to sell people on Shaklee's natural health philosophy and its products. Repeat customers who have had success with the products are encouraged to "Shaklee-ize" their homes—replace their existing brands of personal, household, and other products with Shaklee items.

Carla seldom presses the business on people right away. But as she builds a customer–supplier relationship, she watches for subtle cues that might provide an opening for a pitch. "If a customer asks for a discount," says Carla, "that's a good time to explain our program. We'll tell them that if they bring five people in and get these people to buy X number of products, then they can work on getting their bonus, which will pay for their products. People like the idea of getting their products for free."

ATTRITION

A certain percentage of customers disqualify themselves right off the bat. "Some people have had such a horrible experience with network marketing that they want nothing to do with it," says Carla. She doesn't push them. But neither does she write them off. People can change their minds, over time, as their financial circumstances change. And even the most closed-minded person might have an open-minded friend. "You never know who that person could bring to you, through a referral," says Carla. She strives to make sure that each and every customer has a good experience with the Shaklee products, so they keep coming back.

At the other end of the spectrum are people who come in asking about the business, but show little interest in the products. "We don't put much stock in those people," says Carla. "We don't write anyone off, but we don't spend a lot of time encouraging them to develop a business either."

EARLY WARNING SYSTEM

Once Carla has narrowed down her prospects to those who are both curious about the business and enthusiastic about the products, she moves in to close them. Carla sits her prospects down and explains the Shaklee compensation plan to them. Those who seem open are then put through a three-step goal-setting process. This serves as an early warning system, winnowing out the ambitious from the dabblers.

"I absolutely do not spend time with people who waste my time," says Carla. "You can't, because it drains you. So once I explain the plan to people, I ask them for three things before I'm willing to commit my time to them: a twenty-four-month time commitment: a written mission and vision statement; and a business plan."

CLEAR BENCHMARKS

The mission statement sets out the prospect's ultimate life goals. It tells Carla what he's about spiritually, what makes him get out of bed in the morning. The vision statement delineates his specific goals for the Shaklee business. How much money does the prospect want? How much free time does he want to be able to spend with his family? What sort of house, car, or dream vacation would he like to be able to afford? Finally, the business plan sets out a step-by-step program for attaining these goals, within the constraints of the Shaklee compensation plan. It enumerates exactly how many distributors the prospect will need to recruit and how much volume each will have to move, month by month, in order to fulfill the prospect's goals.

These written documents provide a quick test of the prospect's drive and sincerity. Carla finds that many people cannot even formulate clear goals. They literally don't know what they want. Such people generally turn out to be poor investments. "The ones without goals turn out to be the same ones who won't return your phone calls, who don't want to talk to people," she explains. "Their enthusiasm wanes immediately." Other prospects drop out when they realize how much work their business will require—a revelation that usually hits them while drawing up the business plan. "Once it's all down on paper, people are either really excited, or else they're overwhelmed and say, 'I can't do it,'" says Carla. "The latter are the people whom we absolutely just don't spend time with."

> The mission statement sets out the prospect's ultimate life goals.

A SOLID DOWNLINE

Through methodical sifting and sorting, Carla has built a downline composed of hardworking leaders and solid product users. She has managed to raise the income from her parents' group to about $35,000 per month—an increase of $10,000—in only two years. In her own business, which she works on the side, Carla has attained the rank of supervisor, making about $1,000 per month from her group of forty people.

When she first started with Shaklee, Carla sometimes found herself missing the glamour and prestige of corporate life. But no more. Now it is the corporate employees she meets who envy her. "Corporate America has lost its appeal," she says. "People are commuting more, making less money, and getting a lot less time at home." Carla, on the other hand, can structure her life as she pleases. While her business grows, she takes part in community activities and in her children's lives. Carla recently took her two oldest sons on a grand tour of Europe. "Network marketing has made an indelible mark on my life," she says. "The opportunities it affords me are amazing."

PART TEN

WAVE 4

Support
Your Downline

34

Compressing
Time

"I will never, ever have a boss, ever again," Evan Runde told himself. It was Sunday night. The following morning, Evan knew that he would be expected to report to work as usual. But Evan had other plans. The banking business had been good to him. By age thirty, Evan was making $100,000 a year, managing a $600-million region for a multibillion-dollar Maryland bank. But things had gone downhill ever since the bank had merged with another bank three months before.

In his old job, Evan was given carte blanche to run his portfolio as he saw fit. He wouldn't see his boss for two to three months at a time. The business flourished under this decentralized management. "Maryland was rocking and rolling, in the mid-'80s," says Evan. "Reagan was dumping money into the defense budget. It was wine, women, and song in the banking industry." But after the merger in 1990, the new managers cracked down. Evan lost his three assistants. His workload tripled. He was compelled to make daily progress reports. Evan's work week rose from fifty to eighty hours. He seldom saw his wife and two daughters. "One day, they dumped a four-foot stack of loan reports in my office for me to review," says Evan. "They were poorly written and poorly documented. It was obvious to me that there were millions of dollars of bad loans in the portfolio." Somehow, Evan was expected to straighten it all out. He decided that he had had enough. That weekend, Evan made up his mind to quit.

TIME FREEDOM

To Evan, the new management style at his bank felt like a betrayal. His new bosses treated him like a machine rather than a colleague. Instead of valuing his time, they loaded him down with busywork. Evan's experience at the bank taught him that time was a businessman's most precious asset. And the only way to take control of your time was to become your own boss.

Evan set out on a quest for self-sufficiency, but the road proved rockier than he had anticipated. He bought a TCBY franchise that went under in two years, leaving Evan with $200,000 in debt. He then got involved with a network marketing company whose heavy quotas kept Evan in the red, no matter how much product he moved. Evan threw in the towel five years later. "The biggest check I ever got was between four and five thousand dollars," he says, "and I had to spend three or four thousand dollars to generate it."

> . . . time was a businessman's most precious asset. And the only way to take control of your time was to become your own boss.

STAYING THE COURSE

Yet none of these setbacks dissuaded Evan from his goal. "We lost everything," he says. "But I stayed committed to being self-employed, no matter what." Evan's commitment ultimately led him to take a job that most grown men would have shunned—a paper route. "We took over a large newspaper distributorship," he says. "My wife did the administrative work and I delivered the papers at night in a van. I had gone from making six figures a year in the corporate world to being a paper boy."

Needless to say, Evan was wide open for alternatives. But when a friend approached Evan about a network marketing company called Life Plus, based in Batesville, Arkansas, he didn't want to hear it. "I had sworn off multilevel," he says. Even so, Evan agreed to try the products. Since 1994, he had suffered from lupus, an immune disorder that gave him bouts of depression, fatigue, sun sensitivity, and arthritis. "I was in my mid-thirties, but I had joints like an eighty-year-old," he says. "My hands got so bad, I couldn't button my shirt or tie my shoes in the morning." For two years, Evan had been treating his illness with nutritional supplements. Evan's friend claimed that the Life Plus products had helped his allergies enormously. "I figured if it impacted his immune system, it might help me," says Evan.

BEYOND WAVE 3

Life Plus was the brain child of pharmacist J. Robert Lemon. A natural health pioneer in the 1970s, Lemon tried to market some of his nutritional products through MLM. He founded a company called Multiway Associates in 1982. Yet sales were sluggish. The complex compensation plan, riddled with stiff monthly quotas, drove off many otherwise-enthusiastic product users. So in 1992 Lemon sat down with two partners to brainstorm a new approach to network marketing. The company they created, Life Plus, was destined to become a model for the Wave 4 Revolution.

The idea was to tear down all the psychological barriers that made MLM such a hard sell for many people. First of all, there would be no charge for becoming a member. Any customer could receive a wholesale discount just by signing up. There were no stiff monthly quotas required to maintain your discount. Nor was there any pressure to sell to friends and family. Life Plus's computerized drop-shipping program, well ahead of its time in 1992, allowed distributors to conduct their business entirely by phone. You simply recommended the product to people and gave them the company's 800 number, along with your PIN number. If they later recommended the product to others, you would get your commission from their recruits and customers automatically. Life Plus skyrocketed to 250,000 members and $60 million in annual sales in only two years. "It's beyond Wave 3," Lemon told *Success* magazine in June 1996. "This is a tidal wave."

MASSIVE ACTION

At first, Evan Runde refused to have anything to do with the Life Plus opportunity. But after a month on the products, he noticed significant improvement in his lupus symptoms. Intrigued by the product, Evan took a new look at the Life Plus business. "It blew my mind," he says. "My paradigm of the industry had been a lot of smoke, hype, and mirrors, with people buying $5,000 worth of stuff and schlepping it around trying to sell it to their friends and family and maybe, if they're lucky, sign up a couple of people to do the same." Evan realized that the Life Plus system was far more duplicatable than anything he had experienced before. "There was no sign up fee, no inventory," he says, "just a simple referral mechanism, using mail order. I looked at it and said, 'I can do this.'"

Evan teamed up with an old friend from his last MLM company, Todd Burrier. They entered Life Plus as partners. Desperate to regain his foothold on success, Evan committed himself to a "massive action" strategy—a one-time, round-the-clock prospecting blitz, designed to build the business as quickly as possible. "For six months, I was working eighteen hours a day, seven days a week," says Evan. "I still had my paper route, so I'd get off the phone at 1:30 in the morning, jump in my van, and go pick up a load of newspapers. I learned to get by on fifteen to twenty hours of sleep per week."

BOTTLENECK

Evan's business grew rapidly. In the first two and a half years, the partners signed up more than twenty thousand members and achieved a $40,000-per-month income, split 50/50 between them. Evan was elated, but he paid a price for his success. The time freedom Evan coveted still largely eluded him. Night after night, he found himself on the phone, repeating the same stories, the same sales pitch, over and over again, not only with his own prospects, but with those of his downline, in three-way calls.

Evan had become a bottleneck. The larger his downline grew, the more it required his personal attention. Not only was Evan's time being eaten up, but his distributors were being forced to wait in line for his help. In many ways, it reminded Evan of being back at the bank, staring at that four-foot stack of loan reports. "We realized that we had to find a way to compress time, both for ourselves and for our people," he recalls. "We had to put systems in place that would give us leverage as leaders and help our group be more efficient." In their effort to solve that problem, Todd and Evan would end up pioneering new methods of downline support that would push the envelope of Wave 4 innovation firmly into the next century.

CHAPTER 35

Auto-Support

For Evan, the last straw came one night when he was talking on the phone to one of his downline distributors. She was a real go-getter. Every night, after coming home from her job as a secretary, this woman would get on the phone from 7 to 11 P.M., building her downline. She had just called Evan after finishing her last call of the night. "Well," she sighed, after a few minutes, "I guess I'd better get going. I've still got fifteen audiotape packages to get out. It'll be another hour and a half before I get to bed."

It was 11 P.M. when she said that. Evan had trouble sleeping that night, thinking about that woman slaving away into the wee hours of the morning, stuffing envelopes. What a stupid waste of her time, he thought. It was exactly the sort of drudgery that people joined MLM to escape. With all the streamlining and automatization Life Plus had done, it bothered Evan that Stone Age methods such as this would still drain the productivity from his organization. As he pondered the problem, Evan reflected on all the other bottlenecks that he and Todd had identified in the business. He resolved, then and there, to do something about them.

CENTRALIZED DRUDGERY

The key, Evan realized, was to centralize as much of the drudgework as possible. He and Todd spent the next six months developing systems to insulate their people from repetitive, time-consuming tasks. In the process, they freed up much of their own time as well.

Their most ambitious innovation was a fulfillment center, designed to free people from having to stuff their own information packages. A distributor who found a likely prospect could now fill in a brief order form and fax it to the center. Within twenty-four hours, the center would dispatch an info kit, complete with audiotape, direct to the prospect. Aside from saving time and effort, the fulfillment center helped distributors distance themselves from the sales process—an important attraction for people shy about selling to their warm market. "Now you can call people you know and say, 'I just heard the most incredible tape about health and nutrition, and I'm going to have this company send you a copy,'" says Evan. "It makes you a third party to the transaction, which is a little more comfortable for new people."

THE GAP LINES

Another innovation the two partners brought online was a menu of eighteen prerecorded messages, accessible by 800 number and covering such topics as the products, the company, and Evan's personal success story. This eased a tremendous bottleneck of people waiting in line to have Evan or Todd speak personally to their prospects.

The idea came to Evan one night when he was on the phone with a prospect, explaining the Fast Track business building program, a sort of business-in-a-box in the form of a $300 start-up package complete with products and training materials. When Evan was done, the prospect exclaimed, "I wish I'd recorded that! You explained it so succinctly." Evan realized that he had polished his pitch from repeating the same spiel five or six times a day, month after month.

"Gee, why don't I just record it?" Evan asked himself. Now his spiels are available to any prospect at the touch of a telephone keypad. Evan calls the system GAP, for Grab a Pen. "If I'm talking to you about the business," Evan explains, "I can say, 'Hey, before we spend a whole lot of time here, let's see if this is something you're really interested in. Grab a pen and let me give you these two numbers.'" Only the serious prospects will bother calling back after they hear the recordings. "It's a great sifting tool," says Evan. "It enables people to sift through a large number of prospects and only spend time with those who have a high level of interest."

PHONE FRIGHT

The GAP line helps in other ways as well. Evan recalls a seventy-six-year-old woman in his downline who was doing well in the business. She had gotten good results with the products, and her personal testimony helped sign up many members. Moreover, the woman was incredibly outgoing. "She was willing to go out and stand at a busy intersection at 6:30 in the morning and walk up to cars and hand people flyers," says Evan. There was only one problem. The woman froze whenever she had to prospect people on the phone.

"Very often people are afraid of the phone, especially when they're new, because they don't know what to say," Evan explains. "The way to get over that fear is to practice. But people's fear often keeps them from taking action." After the GAP lines were introduced, this woman's business went through the roof. "All of a sudden, she was talking to fifteen to twenty people a day," says Evan. "She didn't worry about what she was supposed to say anymore. All she had to do was build a little rapport and refer them to the GAP numbers." Her sales volume doubled in a short time.

SAVING TIME

Evan's people can also access information via Internet or fax-on-demand. A Web site offers a twenty-minute click-through presentation of the Life Plus opportunity, along with profiles of key leaders, company and product information, a directory of who's who in the corporation, with contact info, and training information on the various lead generation and business building systems available to Evan's downline. Much of the same data can be retrieved automatically via fax-on-demand, simply by phoning an 800 number.

All of these systems are designed to achieve a common goal—saving time. In the old days, Evan explains, the first thing you would do is order some product, which might take four or five days to arrive. After using the products and listening to a conference call, you might decide to buy one hundred audiotapes to promote the business. By the time you received those tapes, packaged them, and mailed them out, a month might have passed with little or no action in your business. Evan's new system, however, lets you get started the first day, sending in tape requests to the fulfillment center and referring people to the Web site, fax-on-demand service, or GAP lines. "It's all about time compression," says Evan.

ENHANCED LEADERSHIP

"The more tools and systems we put in place," says Evan, "the less important the leaders become to the day-to-day activities. That doesn't mean that the systems replace leadership. It means they enhance it." Nowadays, for example, Evan finds that he spends a lot less time doing repetitive phone pitches and a lot more time training his top achievers.

> "We're giving part-timers the support they need so they can have some success in a relatively short period of time."

But the real beneficiaries, he believes, are the rank-and-file networkers in his downline, the vast majority of whom work the business part-time. "Nowadays, with more and more couples, both the husband and wife are working," says Evan. "They have less time than ever. When they get home, they're burnt out. They're getting home at six, seven, eight o'clock at night and they're not as likely to pick up the phone and grind it out for three hours, as they might have been back in the '70s and '80s." Evan's system offers the sort of time compression these couples need to make the business realistic. "We're giving part-timers the support they need so they can have some success in a relatively short period of time."

MYTH-BUSTING

The ultimate test of any business system is the bottom line. Here, Todd and Evan's innovations have proved their mettle many times over. Six months after they were installed, sales had grown 30 percent, as compared to 15 to 20 percent in the previous six months. "We've been growing like crazy," says Evan. "And we can see our people becoming more self-sufficient."

Evan sees his system as part of an industry-wide movement. As the Wave 4 Revolution takes form, companies are groping, day by day, to solve MLM's most persistent problem: how to make the business work for the part-timer. Evan believes that Life Plus has solved many of the big questions, with its streamlined comp plan and drop-shipping program. But his auto-support systems are going even further. "There's a myth in this industry that if you just make a warm list of a hundred people, the money's going to come pouring in," he says. "Well, it won't. Most networkers will have to talk to thousands of people before they can build a significant business. The companies that will really capture the next wave in this industry are the ones that can develop turnkey systems to help part-timers sift through as many prospects as quickly as possible."

PART ELEVEN

WAVE 4

Wave 5 and Beyond

CHAPTER 36

The E-Commerce Frontier

The first electronic money transfer in history was performed by the Wells Fargo stagecoach company, via telegraph, in 1864. On the rugged American frontier, where armed bandits such as Black Bart routinely commandeered cash boxes from passing stagecoaches, the telegraph allowed Wells Fargo to move money safely between its far-flung offices. The service caught on with the public, and many Wells Fargo agents doubled as telegraphers, to help meet the rising demand for transactions over the "singing wires."

Those wires are still singing as the twenty-first century dawns. But now they're often made of fiber-optic cable, and every bank, brokerage, stock market, corporation, and commodities exchange around the globe passes vast sums of money through them each day. At the turn of the millennium, electronic commerce—otherwise known as e-commerce—has revealed itself as the next great economic frontier. No one knows how big this market will eventually grow or how rapidly it will expand. But early signs suggest a monster in the making. In 1998, about 17 million Americans did $7 billion worth of shopping on the Internet. Some experts predict that by 2002, those numbers will more than triple, with at least 58 million people doing up to $41 billion worth of shopping online. Network marketers are already taking a lead role in the pending e-commerce explosion.

THE INTERACTIVE NIGHTMARE

My 1994 book *Wave 3* contained a chapter entitled "Wave 4 and Beyond." In that chapter, I tried to envision how network marketing would fit into a world where shopping was done almost exclusively through interactive media. "Imagine it's the year A.D. 2010," I wrote. "You do all your shopping from the telescreen. . . . Turn on your telescreen and move your cursor to the 'grocery' icon. Suddenly, you're strolling through a supermarket as vast as the Hanging Gardens of Babylon. Aisles of products stretch to every horizon. From each shelf, animated images of genetically engineered 'groceries' dance, cavort, and call you by name."

No one knows how big this market will eventually grow or how rapidly it will expand.

My point, in the chapter, was that electronic shopping might turn out to be as much nightmare as dream. The sheer number of products and the amount of information available on each one would greatly complicate the shopping experience, I predicted. No doubt, each "virtual" product would be equipped by its suppliers with a barrage of bells and whistles, designed to make it stand out from the rest. The result would be a maddening cacophony of advertising messages.

ELECTRONIC OVERLOAD

"A sealed package of irradiated hydroponic beans flashes strobe lights into your retina, " I wrote in *Wave 3,* "while a strange, hypnotic voice whispers, 'Buy me, buy me,' in perfect synchronization to your brain's theta-wave frequency. . . .

Over in the produce section, a crate of overgrown cucumbers cracks Jimmy Durante-style one-liners: 'I'm not your nose! I'm a genetically altered cucumber! Hot-cha-cha-cha-cha!' You blush as you pass a shelf of ripe tomatoes undulating obscenely and whispering explicit sexual come-ons into your ear.

"Each product has its own unique style. But they're all after the same prize. They want you to click your cursor over them. Be careful! The moment you click, you'll be under their control. Your screen will explode into a phantasmagoria of interactive programs, focusing on that particular product. Prompts for 'customer testimonials,' 'complaint and litigation history,' 'nutritional information'—even 'celebrity endorsements'—will parade across your field of vision in dazzling color, accompanied by flashing lights and rhythmic white noise designed to neutralize psychological resistance. In short, shopping in the year 2010 will be a nightmare."

THE CUSTOMER SERVICE CRISIS

Behind my tongue-in-cheek vision was the expression of a real problem—how to make the interactive shopping environment genuinely user-friendly. As the twenty-first century dawns, industry leaders are beginning to realize that customer service will be the litmus test distinguishing tomorrow's e-commerce empires from today's fly-by-nights. Customer complaints are rising even faster than sales. "Right now, customer service on the Web is really atrocious," says Jupiter Communications analyst Ken Allard, quoted in a February 20, 1999 article in the *Louisville Courier-Journal*.

Jupiter Communications visited more than 100 online shopping sites, sending in customer inquiries by e-mail. Many sites did not respond at all, and 42 percent took more than five days to answer. No wonder 33 to 66 percent of e-commerce customers terminate their purchases before the transactions are complete, according to the June 28, 1999 *New York Times*. Without a live person to answer questions or solve problems, the will to buy can fade in an instant.

THE FUTURE IS NOW

Web merchants are now scrambling to add a personal touch to their e-shopping sites with chatrooms and Internet telephony services. Chris McCann, senior vice president of 1-800-Flowers has described that company's Internet telephony program as "training wheels for new users"—a way of coaching shoppers through their first experiences on the site, until they become confident enough to use it on their own. It's a great idea. But the best method of introducing new customers to a Web site is doubtless the one I suggested back in 1994: network marketing. As this book goes to press, late-breaking events have borne out my prediction. They illustrate just how accurately I envisioned the e-commerce environment, and the role that MLMers would play in humanizing it.

On March 3, 1999, Amway and Microsoft Corporation announced that they were teaming up to offer what may turn out to be the largest retail Web site on the Internet: Quixtar.com. Scheduled to begin operations in September 1999, Quixtar will feature more than ten thousand different products and services, according to Amway sources. In addition to its own branded products, Quixtar is expected to offer a representative sampling of the existing Amway wares, which may include everything from Adidas sneakers and Panasonic sound systems to Amway-brand SA8 cleaning products and Artistry cosmetics.

VIRTUAL AISLES AND SHELVES

Amway is maintaining top secrecy regarding details of the Quixtar Web site prior to its roll-out. But some hints about its format have leaked out, suggesting just how accurately I imagined the interactive mall of the future, back in 1994.

Stephen McCarty, managing consultant on the Quixtar project for Microsoft, told *Network Marketing Lifestyles* magazine (*NML*) in the June 1999 issue that one of the scenarios being considered is to give Quixtar shoppers the illusion that they are browsing through an immense virtual mall, "perhaps even offering the visual experience of traveling down store aisles and 'clicking' items from shelves into a shopping basket," writes reporter Coy Barefoot in *NML*.

A NEW PARADIGM

"The really exciting thing about Quixtar, and one reason it's so important," says Bridget Fahrland, associate director of interactive marketing for Fry Multimedia (which is helping to design Quixtar), in *NML*, "is that it already has a huge following of loyal customers; so it's got a jump on all the other sites even before the launch. . . . That's a brand-new paradigm for e-commerce."

Since e-commerce exploded onto the Wall Street radar screen in 1998, its chief obstacle has been attracting and keeping customers. Even Amazon.com is still running millions of dollars in the red, despite the success of its affiliate recruiting program (see chapter 11) and lavish funding from Wall Street investors. Quixtar will be the first major e-commerce roll-out to enter the marketplace with a sizable customer base already in place—the three million Amway representatives worldwide. NML reports that, three months before Quixtar's launch, over 200,000 people had already registered at an Amway Web site promoting Quixtar, to request updates on the new site.

THE MAGIC BULLET

What really makes Quixtar different, however, is the High Touch factor—the ability of new customers to get personal service and assistance from the Quixtar representative who introduced them to the Web site. "The problem with online malls," says MLM Internet consultant Rod Cook, "has always been that they're too big and confusing. You might have a hundred different businesses in a mall. People have to be familiar with it in order to use it. They have to know what's there and how to get it."

Network marketing—as exemplified by Quixtar—may well provide the magic bullet that will finally make e-commerce universally accessible. "The power of the human voice has been our most powerful tool since we came out of the caves," says Cook. "The Internet will not change that. The most successful online businesses will be those that use the telephone in conjunction with the Internet. Network marketing is perfectly designed to fill that gap."

CHAPTER 37

Widening the Gateway

As this book goes to press, nearly 50 percent of all U.S. households have computers. An estimated 159 million people use the Internet worldwide—62 million in the United States alone, according to International Data Corporation. Those figures will be hopelessly obsolete in just a few years. Current estimates are that Internet use is increasing by one-third each year. Network marketing plays a significant role in that growth. More and more MLM companies are helping to widen the gateway to cyberspace by offering Internet access to their customers.

Even the most stubborn technophobe finds it hard to resist the blandishments of MLM's legions of word-of-mouth cyber-evangelists. No trick is overlooked, no leverage point left unprobed in the ceaseless quest to wire the unwired. Network marketers offer steep discounts for ISP service, tempting premiums, money-back guarantees, and lots of personal hand-holding as customers stumble through the early stages of Internet literacy. If that doesn't work, they offer cold, hard cash—the chance to earn money in an Internet-based MLM opportunity. The result of all this sales and recruiting activity is a fortuitous synergy—good for the Internet, good for network marketing.

THE MLM-INTERNET ALLIANCE

The happy results of this MLM-Internet alliance can be seen most clearly in the rejuvenation of Nu Skin Enterprises, Inc., based in Provo, Utah. Founded in 1984 by twenty-four-year-old Blake Roney and a group of friends, Nu Skin became one of network marketing's legendary success stories. By 1991, its annual revenues had reached $500 million. But as the company's domestic sales peaked, recruiting slowed. Growth continued overseas, but the perception spread that Nu Skin's market was saturated, at least in the United States. Ambitious networkers began moving on to newer, flashier opportunities. Some industry observers wrote off Nu Skin was yet another one-hit wonder—an MLM company that lacked the wherewithal to keep growing beyond its first surge of momentum.

> The result of all this sales and recruiting activity is a fortuitous synergy—good for the Internet, good for network marketing.

But Roney and his management team had other plans. They embarked on an ambitious course of diversification, going far beyond Nu Skin's traditional personal care product line. In 1992, they rolled out a nutritional division called IDN. Six years later, IDN acquired Pharmanex, Inc., a leading manufacturer of natural health supplements. Nu Skin had already unveiled Big Planet the year before, a high-tech subsidiary offering Internet access, Web hosting, long-distance service, consumer electronics, and other goods and services related to the wired economy. Whatever else the skeptics wished to say about Nu Skin, they could no longer call it "saturated." The company had reinvented itself, producing two new brand names that represented two entirely new MLM opportunities.

INFINITE MOMENTUM

Ron Wiggins left his job as a successful shoe salesman when he realized that his personal income was growing at a fraction of the rate of his overall sales. "I felt used," he says. "I was breaking records every year. My company had five hundred stores across the United States, and I took our store to number one. But it wasn't reflected in my paycheck."

In 1991, Ron and his wife Cris both joined Nu Skin. It was slow going at first. "We had missed the biggest growth curve with Nu Skin," he says. But the IDN division rolled out the following year. Ron and Cris jumped in with both feet. "It gave us a chance to get in on the ground floor of a major growth curve," he says. Ron managed to go full time within twelve months of joining Nu Skin. "I replaced my $40,000 income in the first year," he says. Six months later, the Wiggins' combined income was sufficient to enable both to go full time in Nu Skin.

RIDE THE WAVE

For the next six years, Ron and Cris worked the Nu Skin and IDN businesses successfully. But in 1997, an opportunity came along that was so big, they were ultimately persuaded to drop their other businesses to pursue it. That year, Nu Skin announced the launch of Big Planet. "We saw a debt-free, $2 billion company, Nu Skin, positioning itself to take advantage of the largest worldwide economic trend of all time," says Ron, "the convergence of the Internet, e-commerce, and telecommunications."

In addition to its other services, Big Planet offered an online store (at www.bigplanet.com) featuring everything from clothes, books, and flowers to jewelry, sporting goods, and computer hardware. Moreover, the company had made strategic alliances with some of the top names in the high-tech field. It sold prepaid paging products for SkyTel Communications, for instance, and contracted with IBM to sell its online computer and Internet training program, Learning University. "The next frontier in the world is high speed communications and Big Planet is poised to take advantage of that frontier," said Big Planet president Richard King at the company launch. He also predicted: "The opportunity associated with Big Planet could easily become the single largest network marketing opportunity ever."

"IF I CAN DO IT, YOU CAN DO IT"

Big Planet offers a High Touch approach for making the Internet accessible to the masses. Subscribers to its Internet service have access to twenty-four-hour technical assistance by phone. And the Big Planet representative who signs you up is also available to walk you through any problems.

Ron Wiggins was himself a computer neophyte when he joined Big Planet in April 1998. "Technology was my biggest obstacle," he says. "I had never been on a computer before I joined Big Planet, and I was intimidated. I got a computer just three weeks before, and someone had to show me the buttons for pointing and clicking. It took a few days, but it was a victory. Now I couldn't live without it." When Ron recruits other technophobes into the Big Planet network, he tells them, "If I can do it, you can do it." Ron and Cris rose to the top commission level in Big Planet within three months. They now devote their full-time effort to it. "It's given us a new freedom," says Ron. "We're at the birth phase of one of the biggest trends ever. Attendance at our weekly meetings and trainings has tripled since our Nu Skin days."

A SELF-HYPING BUSINESS

Ken and Kathy Klages have also tripled their business since switching to Big Planet. "We were able to move quickly through the ranks," says Ken, a former engineering manager for Chevron, "because this business sells itself. The Internet and e-commerce are so hot that everybody's already interested. It's self-hyping." One of Ken's favorite products is the iPhone, a $300 device produced by a Silicon Valley firm called InfoGear Technology Corporation. It is a telephone with a small screen, allowing users to log onto the Internet, send e-mail, and conduct e-commerce transactions without having to use a computer.

"InfoGear tried to sell the iPhone in stores," says Ken, "but they only sold about nine hundred units in nine months. The retailers didn't know where to put it. They threw it in the phone department, because it looks like a phone. But if it's not plugged in and people don't know what it is, they just think it's an overpriced telephone." What was missing was the High Touch factor—a human being to explain and demonstrate the device. InfoGear recognized the problem and, in October 1998, announced a deal to distribute its iPhones through Big Planet's MLM network. "As a new device, the iPhone is best appreciated when the customer gets to see, touch, and use the phone while having it explained to them," says InfoGear CEO Ed Cluss. "Big Planet's independent representatives have the training and ability to make this happen."

BREAKING DOWN BARRIERS

"We sold a thousand iPhones in the first day," says Ken, "more than were sold in nine months through traditional stores." Ken gave an iPhone to his mother for Christmas. A confirmed technophobe, she had never attempted to use a computer before. But in no time, Ken's mother was calling him up in great excitement to brag that she was trading e-mail with her friends. "My mom could have looked at Yahoo! commercials on television for the rest of her life and it never would have made her go out and get on the Internet," says Ken. "But because I sent her this device and told her how to use it, she is on the Internet almost every day."

The experience of Ken and Kathy Klages mirrors, in microcosm, the wider phenomenon of Inter-Networking—the fusion of MLM and cyberspace. As their business grows, the world becomes ever more interconnected. And prospects who might have resisted a more traditional network marketing opportunity are signing up in droves to take part in the taming of the cyber-frontier. "In our business, we're finding that hundreds of people who said no to Nu Skin are now saying yes to Big Planet," says Ken.

CHAPTER 38

The Cyberswarm

In chapter 11, we discussed the exploding market for Internet affiliate programs. These mini-businesses allow people to make money simply by installing links on their Web sites that take customers to third-party businesses, such as Amazon.com, where they can place e-commerce orders. Affiliates earn commissions on any sales made by customers who find the e-commerce sites through their links.

Already, affiliate programs have become the hottest topic in the e-commerce world. Any aspiring e-merchant can spread his links, virus-like, across the Internet, through the individual efforts of thousands—even millions—of self-interested affiliates. And the e-merchant doesn't have to pay those affiliates a cent until after they make a sale. By the standards of ordinary retailers, the affiliate system seems to provide tremendous leverage. But imagine how much greater the leverage would be if you added a multilevel compensation structure to the package—allowing affiliates to earn commissions not only from customers they refer, but also from people referred by their referrals, and so on. MLM consultant Rod Cook calls it "multi-affiliate marketing." He predicts that this system will revolutionize e-commerce in the years ahead.

ONE-CLICK PROSPECTING

Already, the first multi-affiliate programs are coming online. If you go to www.buyMLMtools.com, for instance, you'll find an affiliate program selling MLM-related books and tapes through a two-tiered commission structure. Once you install the link on your Web site, the program automatically builds a downline for you, with virtually no intervention on your part.

Let's say a customer comes to your site and clicks on your buyMLMtools.com link. He is whisked to the buyMLMtools.com Web site—which might be the corporate home page itself, or else a mirror image of the corporate page, customized for you, with your name, logo, or other individual information appearing alongside that of the parent company. The customer then proceeds to shop for network marketing books and tapes. You are automatically credited with a commission for any product he buys. And if he decides to become a buyMLMtools.com affiliate himself, he is added to your downline.

COOKIE POWER

Suppose your customer decides to return to the buyMLMtools.com site at a later date, this time without going through your link. You still get your commission from any purchase he makes. That's because, when the customer first visited your home page, the buyMLMtools.com server deposited a "cookie" onto his hard drive—a tiny data-tag that identified him as your customer.

As long as that cookie remains on his computer, every purchase he makes through buyMLMtools.com will be credited to you, whether he goes through your site or not. As this book goes to press, buyMLMtools.com—like most existing multiaffiliate programs—allows affiliates to draw commissions from only one level of recruits. But Rod Cook and other multiaffiliate pioneers are even now designing systems for their clients that will offer multiple levels of commissions, just as in traditional MLM opportunities.

BEYOND THE COMPANY

What effect will these developments have on the way network marketing is done? If the Wave 3 and Wave 4 innovations liberated people from the grind of repetitive labor, the multi-affiliate revolution may eventually free them from bondage to the company itself. "It will cause network marketing to grow, but not as we know it today," says Rod. "There will be less dependence on local meetings. The compensation plans will be very simple, with no cost to join in many cases. People will be more focused on product."

> As the barriers to leaving and entering a company come down, people will find it easier to distribute for many different companies at once.

As the barriers to leaving and entering a company come down, people will find it easier to distribute for many different companies at once. Just as people today can choose from over a thousand different affiliate opportunities at Web sites such as www.associate-it.com, so networkers of the future will construct personal e-commerce sites from scores of different multi-affiliate links.

THE GIFT OF FLIGHT

In the future, network marketers will fly through cyberspace with the freedom of flocking birds. They will band together when it suits them, and part company when opportunity calls them elsewhere. They will organize themselves not in corporations, but in cyberswarms—networks of entrepreneurs with ties to many different companies, who band together informally and temporarily around a common goal, coordinating their efforts through telecommunications.

In the multi-affiliate environment to come, the cyberswarm will reign supreme. Virtually anyone will be able to sell directly through his Web site, using sophisticated e-commerce functions. Every race, creed, interest group, and subculture will prowl the Internet in search of opportunity.

Swarms, sub-swarms, and mini-swarms will overlap and cross-promote a bewildering variety of goods and services.

CYBER-LEADER

George C. Fraser is leading a cyberswarm. Through his virtual store, Frasernet.com, George reaches out to fellow black Americans and to people of African descent all over the world. He promotes networking and sells his own books and tapes dealing with black empowerment, as well as products and services offered by other African Americans. Unlike an ordinary cyber-mall, George's store is not confined to a single Web site. It sells through a variety of Web-based MLM opportunities, such as the e-commerce department store Ahsum.com and Matah.com—a site specializing in goods and services produced by and for people of African descent.

George's vision is bigger than any particular company. "I serve entirely different customer bases through my different downlines," says George. "Matah is for very serious African-centered people who are committed to recycling black dollars within their community. Ahsum.com is a more general market. But I'm building downlines in both." In effect, Matah.com and Ahsum.com serve as affiliates of George's Frasernet.com, while at the same time George serves as a distributor for both organizations. The companies gain the benefit of the George Fraser name—widely known in the black community as an author, networker, and motivator—while George gains the benefit of their e-commerce capability and MLM compensation structure.

GLOBAL NETWORKER

George has long since established himself as the preeminent guru of black networking. His popular book *Success Runs in Our Race* calls on African Americans to build an "Underground Railroad of networking professionals," based upon "tribal unity," and dedicated to uplifting the race. His *SuccessGuides,* available through George's Cleveland-based

SuccessSource, Inc., offer city-by-city directories of tens of thousands of black movers and shakers, ripe for networking. "African Americans generate nearly five hundred billion dollars in income each year," he writes. "You and I represent the tenth largest economy in the industrialized world. And we can build on that. . . . We've got to connect and work together—because we have no choice! We can't expect others to do for us that which we will not do for ourselves."

In George's view, multi-affiliate marketing offers the best hope he has seen for realizing his vision. "Network marketing is the wave of the future for the small investor and the budding entrepreneur, and black people need to be a part of it," he says. "The convergence of MLM and e-commerce gives us global reach. In a given year, 20 percent of my Frasernet.com e-commerce sales come from Africa or people of African descent in the Caribbean and South America. In the past, I could never have dreamed of doing even 2 percent of my business from those parts of the world. It would not have been cost effective."

TRIBAL DOWNLINES

Tribal groupings have always been central to the MLM world. Because network marketers recruit within their personal spheres of influence, they tend to prospect people who are like themselves. Downlines, and even whole companies, often focus their recruiting on specific ethnic, religious, political, or other sharply defined subcultures. Thus we find MLM companies whose downlines are composed primarily of Mormons, born-again Christians, New Age vegetarians, or Republicans.

After a lifetime of teaching in public schools, Joe Shaw was weary of the left-of-center views that prevailed among his fellow teachers. Joining Amway gave him a new sense of community, through the company's emphasis on God, home, and country. "It was a real good fit for me," says Joe. "They were my kind of people. Teachers are mostly Bill Clinton types. Amway people are Ronald Reagan types."

SELF-SELECTION

The age of the cyberswarm offers opportunities for tribaliza-
tion that go far beyond traditional categories of ethnicity,
faith, and political creed. Quixtar.com, for instance—along
with a handful of other companies—is pioneering a high-tech
self-selection tool called the CD-ROM business card that
helps networkers determine which prospects belong to the
growing tribe of computer-savvy
technophiles. The "business
card" is actually a mini- ature
CD, no more than 3½ inches
wide, that fits on the inner circle
of a standard CD-ROM tray
drive and contains a multimedia
presentation of a product or
business opportunity. Quixtar
representatives hand them out as
prospecting tools.

> The age of the cyberswarm offers opportunities for tribalization that go far beyond traditional categories of ethnicity, faith, and political creed.

"It's a sorting device," explains Stuart Johnson, whose
company Video Plus, based in
Lake Dallas, Texas, produces
CD-ROM business cards for
MLM firms. "Because the business card itself is a computer-
based technology, anyone who accepts the card and actually
goes home and uses it has already demonstrated that he owns
a computer, that he is open to technology, and that he is probably a good prospect for an online business like Quixtar."

WHITHER WAVE 5?

In *Wave 3,* I wrote, "Ten or fifteen years from now . . . network marketing will be so pervasive in society, it won't even
qualify any longer as a separate and distinct industry. It will
be a standard tool used by every industry." The multi-
affiliate revolution promises to fulfill this prediction in a

shorter time than I realized. Armed with modular, inter-changeable affiliate links, cyberswarmers will hurtle through the digital marketplace, targeting splinter markets and sub-cultures at will. The MLM function will have become so perfectly automated that many cyberswarmers will hardly be aware that they are using network marketing at all.

When the day comes that MLM ceases to exist as a rec-ognizable entity, it will have grown beyond any possible lim-its or controversy. It will no longer be debated in financial journals, weighed in the minds of skeptical prospects, or ex-tolled in self-help business books such as this one. It will have become an extension of human consciousness itself, an instrument of our will, an unconscious tool of our instinct to succeed, explore, and band together with like-minded people. It will have entered the Wave 5 era.

PART TWELVE $W\!AV\!E\ 4$

Toward a
New Millennium

CHAPTER 39

Titan of 'Tude

"Why do the media ignore the Wave 3 Revolution?" I asked in my 1994 book *Wave 3*. At the time, it was a question very much on every networker's mind. "Intentionally or not," I wrote, "the media have tended to ignore positive news about network marketing. Successful companies like Amway and Mary Kay Cosmetics are often written about in mainstream business articles, but seldom referred to as network-marketing or MLM companies. Those forbidden phrases mainly crop up in negative stories, about companies that are being sued or investigated."

At the time I wrote these words, they were indisputably true. But the six years that have passed since then have rendered them obsolete. The phrase "network marketing" has long since entered the lexicon of mainstream business writers, from *The Wall Street Journal* to *Business Week,* and it is no longer a code word for "pyramid scheme." Even more important, the industry has taken control of its own fate by spawning its own media outlets, such as *Network Marketing Lifestyles,* a glossy consumer magazine launched in April 1999 (for which yours truly is a regular columnist).

If the traditional tension between MLM and mass media now seems a quaint relic of the past, a large part of the credit must go to a single man. He is John Milton Fogg, MLM's original "Titan of 'Tude."

THE NEW MEDIA

Among cyberjournalists, the expression "Titan of 'Tude" needs no explanation. But some readers may require a briefing. The phrase was coined by *Newsweek* in January 1999, to describe the maverick journalists of the New Media. Weary of being spoon-fed their news by major networks, people have been turning en masse to Web sites, cable TV, and talk radio, in search of news and opinions that have not been prescreened, censored, massaged, and filtered through the strainer of conventional thinking. Millions per day log onto such sites as The Drudge Report, NewsMax.com, and WorldNetDaily.com for the latest news behind the news.

Conventional journalists don't bother to hide their dismay at this invasion of their turf. "Old structures of authority and influence are breaking down. . . ." lamented Jonathan Alter in that now-famous January 18, 1999, issue of *Newsweek*. "The old media food chain . . . has been shattered." With unabashed nostalgia, Alter looked back on a time when "order" prevailed in the newsroom, when "Journalists and those who influenced them served as gatekeepers, deciding what people could know." But while it clearly pained him to do so, Alter grudgingly acknowledged that the "Titans of 'Tude" were here to stay. "Tom Brokaw, Peter Jennings, and Dan Rather still have millions of viewers and plenty of stature," Alter wrote, "but they must share center stage with a scruffier bunch . . ."

MLM GURU

When I first started writing about MLM, back in 1990, the "gatekeepers" were firmly in control—especially when it came to the subject of network marketing. Bad news about the industry was blown out of proportion. Good news was relentlessly censored. It was a lonely time to be covering the MLM beat.

But fortunately, I had a guide on my journey. Shortly after my first column on MLM appeared in *Success* magazine, I received a call from one John Milton Fogg. At the time, he was editor of a newsletter called *MLM Success* (later renamed *Upline*). John became my MLM guru. I phoned him frequently for advice. His monologues on the history, economics, and personalities of network marketing engrossed me for hours. John was a visionary. He saw network marketing not for what it was, but for what it was destined to become. It was during those long conversations that many of the ideas began to percolate in my mind that were later to congeal in the *Wave 3* and *Wave 4* series of books.

A Hidden Talent

John came into network marketing through the back door. Graduating from the Philadelphia College of Art in 1969, with a bachelor's degree in photography, John viewed himself as an artist. Nothing could have been further from his plans than to involve himself in MLM. But fate took a hand in John's life. After immersing himself in the hippie counterculture of Boston, Philadelphia, and New York City from 1969 to 1970, John retreated to a macrobiotic commune in New England to recuperate physically and spiritually. His connections in the macrobiotic world led to a job with a start-up health food company called Erewhon. John worked his way up from hoisting cartons on the loading dock to becoming the company's director of marketing.

It was there that John discovered he had a hidden talent. "I studied books on advertising and learned how to write," he says, "because we couldn't afford to pay anyone to do it." John's ad copy was elegant and energetic. But most important, it moved product. In the years ahead, John struck out on his own, writing freelance ad copy for the burgeoning natural food industry. He might have settled into a comfortable and lucrative routine as a key player in that fast-growing business. But one day a friend introduced John to a dried algae product sold by a company called Cell Tech in Klamath Falls, Oregon. Before he knew it, John had been recruited into his first network marketing opportunity.

UNDUPLICATABLE

"I made up a list of 165 people," says John, "and then I wrote a dynamite direct response letter and sent it to them." The response rate was phenomenal—132 people wrote back. But John suddenly realized that he didn't know what to do with those 132 recruits, now that he had them. "What I was doing was not duplicatable," he says. "I was a professional copywriter so I knew how to write letters. But the only people who could have duplicated that approach were other professional copywriters." John's business languished, despite the high response rate.

Though his downline faltered, John's writing did not. He produced a newsletter during his first week in the business. The second week, he wrote two. Before John's first month in Cell Tech was out, he was writing four newsletters per week, and his fellow distributors were eating them up. "I loved doing it," he says. "I realized that it was more fun and allowed me to make more of a contribution to the industry than if I became a heavy hitter."

A VOICE FOR THE INDUSTRY

John was fascinated by the MLM concept. "I'd worked for a lot of corporations as a marketing consultant," he says, "but I'd never seen any other business that allowed people to be paid a royalty income, commensurate with their efforts, as an independent contractor." Though he dabbled with other network marketing opportunities, John soon realized that his talents were best suited to writing about the industry, not participating in it. "In a sense, I didn't think one company was big enough for me," he recalls. "I wanted to have an impact on the whole industry."

And he did. John started *Upline* (then called *MLM Success*) in 1989. It quickly grew into a distinctive and powerful voice for the industry. When I began writing about MLM in the early '90s, I plowed through issue after issue of John's newsletter, drinking in ideas. It was in its pages that I first learned about economist Paul Zane Pilzer, who predicted that cutting distribution costs would be the next frontier of global business; Michael Gerber and his concepts of the E-Myth and the Turnkey Revolution; Faith Popcorn and her prophecy of the end of shopping. Though these concepts form integral threads in the tapestry of ideas that I now call *Wave 4*, it was John Fogg, not I, who first wove them together.

ROCK-STAR STATUS

My friend Duncan Anderson once wrote in *Success* magazine that John had achieved "near rock-star status" in the network marketing industry. If this is an exaggeration, it is only a slight one. As a ghostwriter and behind-the-scenes editor, John has made his mark on many of the bestselling titles in MLM. He estimates that his own bestsellers—that is, those that actually bear his name, such as *The Greatest Networker in the World* and its sequel, *Conversations with the Greatest Networker in the World*—have sold more than a million copies worldwide.

John speaks at MLM seminars and conventions around the world. Network marketers pay up to $2,000 apiece to participate in his mentor program, gaining access to John's coaching (and to that of other industry stars in John's network) through voice mail, teleconferences, and small group conferences—all arranged through MLM University in Lauderdale-by-the-Sea, Florida. John's Web site at www.greatestnetworker.com has become a hub of MLM activity on the Internet. And *Network Marketing Lifestyles* magazine, which John co-founded has become a bully pulpit for the most prominent leaders in the industry.

THE HIGH TOUCH FUTURE

Those of us who made our names lauding the MLM industry, in defiance of the media blackout, owe a debt of gratitude to John Fogg. As MLM's original Titan of 'Tude, it was John who showed us the way. For that reason, we listen closely when he speaks. And John is speaking very boldly today, as the Wave 4 Revolution gets underway. He speaks of a high-tech future in which network marketing will touch every life on this planet.

"Technology is going to liberate us from all the repetitive, mundane tasks that people have to deal with," he predicts. "But with all the high tech, we're going to need high touch, too. Human beings crave being in touch with each other. We're going to order products and get factual information through the Internet. But service will come from real people. In the twenty-first century, network marketing will marry high tech with high touch."

John sees that marriage proliferating through every industry, as each person finds the right microniche to suit his needs and interests. "Imagine a world where everyone makes money, simply by recommending products to friends and family," he says. "It could be cars, tennis rackets, wine, computers, Mont Blanc pens, the latest hit movie. It may sound wacky, but I can foresee a time when everyone on this planet could be affiliated, in some way, with a network marketing company." Considering the usual reliability of the source, it may not be such a wacky thought after all.

> He speaks of a high-tech future in which network marketing will touch every life on this planet.

CHAPTER 40

The Tidal Wave

Blood was running in the streets. Angry mobs toppled cars, smashed windows, siezed hostages, and stormed government offices. Violence raged through several cities across China. When it ended, ten people lay dead and more than a hundred injured. Was this a scene from the Boxer Rebellion? Chairman Mao's Cultural Revolution? The massacre at Tienanmen Square? No. It was the Chinese people's reaction to an April 1998 government ban on network marketing and all other forms of direct selling.

"It's necessary to stop the operation of pyramid sales," said Wang Zhongfu, director of China's State Administration for Industry and Commerce, "since it has begun to hurt social stability and economic development."

A NEW ERA

The crisis aroused little interest in the foreign press. But for millions of Chinese, the ban threatened their deepest hopes and dreams. "So what else is new?" the cynics may ask. Network marketers and government regulators have been locking horns in every corner of the globe for fifty years. Somewhere, at some time, most successful MLM companies have been condemned as "pyramid schemes." Jaded veterans of the industry could easily dismiss the Chinese ban as but one more example—albeit an extreme one—of network marketing's familiar regulatory woes.

But something was different this time. Unknown to China's Marxist rulers, a new era had dawned in network marketing, an age of unprecedented power for the industry. Chinese officials would discover, in just a few weeks, that they had picked a fight they could never hope to win. They had stumbled directly into the path of an onrushing tsunami.

NO MORE CINDERELLA

That tidal wave was the Wave 4 Revolution. Network marketing firms were no longer willing to play Cinderella to their older and richer Fortune 500 stepsisters. Whether in China or America, MLM companies were now demanding the same respect from governments and media that transnational giants such as Exxon/Mobil, Ford Motor, or Procter & Gamble ordinarily receive. And when the MLMers failed to get what they wanted, they now had the means to fight back.

Driving MLM's new power were the unstoppable economic forces previously described in this book. There was the spread of the Internet, the end of shopping, the splintering of mass media, the disintegration of large firms, and the death of jobs. There was the growing hunger of the masses for liberty, coupled with the unique ability of network marketing to provide that precious commodity. Finally, there was a rising awareness, from Washington to Wall Street, that America's future depended, in large measure, on this bold new experiment that we call network marketing.

AN UNEXPECTED ENDORSEMENT

"You strengthen our country and our economy," said the president of the United States, "not just by striving for your own success, but by offering opportunity to others. . . ." The president spoke in a videotaped statement specially prepared for sales representatives of Direct Selling Association member companies. "I've followed your industry's growth for years now . . . ," he continued. "Your industry gives people a chance, after all, to make the most of their own lives and, to me, that's the heart of the American Dream."

In his speech, the president did not use the term "network marketing," but his meaning was clear. Not only do the vast majority of DSA member companies use MLM compensation plans, but the president praised their sales reps specifically "for offering opportunity to others"—a clear reference to the practice of MLM recruitment and sponsorship. Who was this president? Was it Ronald Reagan, waxing eloquent on the glories of free enterprise? Was it George Bush speaking at an Amway convention? Neither. It was William Jefferson Clinton.

BLOWING WITH THE WIND

Few presidents have vetted their public pronouncements more cautiously than Bill Clinton. Few have tested the wind more thoroughly, before speaking out on any issue. What Clinton really thinks about MLM we may never know. But the fact that he would offer his personal endorsement of the industry speaks volumes about the direction in which he perceives the political and corporate winds to be blowing.

> In the new millennium, MLM will no longer be the exclusive preserve of entrepreneurial mavericks.

In short, those winds appear to be blowing in network marketing's favor. The industry has gone mainstream. Fortune 500 executives no longer envy MLM from afar. Now they jockey unabashedly for the choicest claims in the network marketing gold rush.

In the new millennium, MLM will no longer be the exclusive preserve of entrepreneurial mavericks. Through distribution deals, strategic alliances, mergers, and acquisitions, network marketing sales forces are even now being integrated into the global strategies of the largest and most powerful corporations. Not bad for an industry that was nearly abolished by the Federal Trade Commission only twenty years ago.

SIGN OF THE TIMES

The industry's defenders have argued for years that network marketing was an idea whose time had come. But in the Wave 4 era, MLM will no longer require defenders. The massive power of its corporate clientele will be the only calling card it will need. In the Chinese crisis of 1998, we gained a glimpse of the power MLM would wield in the future: No sooner had the Chinese outlawed direct selling than they began to feel its backlash.

"It is a serious matter," said U.S. Trade Representative Charlene Barshefsky at a news conference in Beijing, only three days after the ban was announced, "when a government simply bans the activities of legitimate, indeed legitimately invested, companies." Speaking on behalf of American corporations such as Amway, Avon, and Mary Kay Cosmetics, Barshefsky continued, "These companies have invested over $120 million in China and provide income to over two million Chinese. Obviously, the goal here is to re-establish these companies' operations as soon as possible."

CORPORATE SOLIDARITY

In a remarkable show of solidarity, major corporations from a host of different industries rallied against the ban. "We got support not only from direct selling companies, but from the insurance industry, consumer products companies, electronics companies, even airlines," says Richard Holwill, Amway's director of international affairs. "This was demonstrative of their recognition that, in a terribly complicated market like China, direct selling is essential to long-term economic health." In short, these companies recognized that an attack on direct selling was an attack on all legitimate businesses in China.

"The ban could spark a U.S.–China trade dispute on the eve of President Clinton's state visit in June," warned *Business Week* magazine. Direct Selling Association president Neil Offen discussed the ban in a personal meeting with the president, who made the issue one of five priority items on the agenda for his June 1998 China visit.

UNSTOPPABLE

By the time the U.S. delegation arrived, the Chinese had already repealed most of the ban. China subsequently agreed, in April 1999, to lift the remaining restrictions no later than January 1, 2003. Sensitive to the delicacy of international relations, the parties involved on both sides are close-mouthed regarding MLM's exact legal status during the interim. But Chin-ning Chu, president of Asian Marketing Consultants Inc. of Antioch, California, confirms that network marketing has quietly resumed in China, with the government's tacit approval.

Only twenty years ago, our government questioned the very right of this industry to exist. But today, the world's greatest superpower champions network marketing across the globe. Driven by technology, stimulated by the corporate drive for new markets, and energized by man's natural yearning for liberty, this gentle ripple we call network marketing has grown to a storm surge, an irresistible maelstrom of freedom and enterprise that I call "Wave 4." In the years ahead, the Wave 4 Revolution will shake our economy to its roots. It will leave this world a freer and more prosperous place. And it will transform network marketing into one of the most potent business forces of the new millennium.

GLOSSARY OF
NETWORK MARKETING TERMS

Achievement Level: A rank or title that is achieved by moving a certain amount of product per month and/or recruiting a certain number of distributors who themselves have attained a certain designated achievement level. As you progress to higher achievement levels, you are awarded a higher rate of commissions (or are allowed to draw earnings from a greater number of generations).

Affiliate Program: An Internet business, such as Amazon.com, that allows people to become affiliates simply by providing a link on their Web sites to a corporate home page, and pays affiliates a commission on all sales made through that link.

Autoresponder: A Web site feature that e-mails information automatically to anyone who clicks on the responder. Network marketers use it to send prospecting and training information.

Back End: The later, more mature, stages of a network marketing downline, after it has grown down several levels or generations. The term is most often used to distinguish between different times of pay plans. A plan that pays more on the "back end" is one that pays the highest commissions on the deepest levels or in the later stages of the plan.

Benefits: A catch-all term covering any and all compensation earned from a network marketing distributorship, including commissions, bonuses, overrides, special perks, and premiums.

Binary: A type of compensation plan that limits your frontline to two people and pays out weekly on one of the two legs of your organization. (See chapter 19 for a full explanation.)

Breakage: Sales volume generated by you or your downline for which you receive no compensation. Put another way, breakage is the difference between what your company promises to pay and what it really pays. MLM companies compete to offer the highest payout (defined as the percentage of the company's total sales paid out to distributors in commissions). But a company that offers a 75 percent payout may, in reality, pay only 50 percent. The 25 percent difference is breakage. It is built into the compensation plan in the form of subtle stipulations that lower your commissions, raise your qualifications, charge you penalties, or disqualify portions of your sales volume under certain circumstances.

Breakaway: An abbreviation for "stairstep/breakaway," one of the four major types of compensation plan. It can also refer to a distributor in your downline who has met certain minimum monthly qualifications and has consequently "broken away" from your group. Once a distributor has broken away from your group, you can no longer count his sales volume as part of your own monthly volume (for purposes of meeting your monthly quotas). However, you are entitled to draw a commission (called a royalty or override) from your breakaway's total organizational volume, rather than just on the volume of those portions of his group that happen to fall within your normal pay range.

Breakaway Leg: The organization or downline of a breakaway distributor.

Bonus Pool: A special fund set aside by a network marketing company, from its profits, and distributed as a special incentive to qualified sales leaders.

Bonus Volume: See BV.

Business Briefing: An alternate term for opportunity meeting.

Business Builder: A distributor who is actively prospecting, as opposed to one who is simply buying product at wholesale for personal use.

Buy-Back Policy: The money-back guarantee offered by all reputable MLM companies to distributors. Generally, companies will pay 70 to 100 percent of the wholesale price on any product that a distributor purchases, but then decides to return, for whatever reason.

BV (Bonus Volume): An alternate expression for point volume (PV) or business volume (BV). It is a value used by MLM companies to calculate overrides and commissions, based upon the wholesale price of the items for which overrides and commissions are being paid. Generally, but not always, the BV is lower than the wholesale price of the items in question. For instance, if you sell $100 worth of product at wholesale, for a 5 percent commission, the 5 percent will be calculated not from the $100 price of the product, but from the $80 BV of the product. The purpose of bonus volume is to enable companies to make money on less profitable items. If a company offering a 50 percent payout sells a container of fuel additive for $20 that costs $10 to manufacture, the company makes no profit. Rather than jack up the price, many companies will simply assign a lower BV to the product, thus paying out lower commissions on it.

Circle of Influence: The people who are closest to you and who constitute your warm market. Also, those who might be easily influenced by you because of your reputation in a particular profession or community.

Cold Market: Prospects outside your circle of friends, family, and associates.

Commission: The percentage you earn from the sales volume of your organization.

Commissionable Volume: An alternate term for bonus volume.

Compressed Plan: A pay plan that stacks or "compresses" the bulk of its commissions on the front end, that is, in the first three levels. To qualify as "compressed," a plan should pay out at least 40 percent on wholesale dollars, on the first three levels.

Compression: When a distributor quits or is terminated, his downline moves up one level, thus filling the empty space he left, and "compressing" the company's downline by one level.

Consumables: Products, such as skin creams and herbal supplements, that are consumed on a regular basis and must be periodically replaced, thus ensuring repeat business for the network marketers who are selling them.

Depth: The number of levels in your MLM organization.

Direct Selling: A form of selling whereby independent representatives, working on commission, sell face-to-face outside of an established retail location. Network marketers are generally considered to be direct sellers, though there are other types of direct sellers who work on straight commission and are not MLMers. Note that MLM distributors who work out of storefronts would not be considered direct sellers, because they sell in an established retail location.

Distributor: A person who contracts independently to sell products or services for an MLM company.

Downline: All the people recruited as distributors into a network marketing company constitute that company's downline. Your downline consists of everyone whom you recruit, who is recruited by your recruits, and so on.

Drop-Shipping: The practice of shipping product directly to customers from the company warehouse, rather than through an independent distributor. Customers generally place orders through an 800 number or a Web site.

Duplicatability: The extent to which an MLM opportunity can be easily mastered by new recruits.

Duplication: The process of replicating business builders in your downline.

E-mail Blasting: Broadcasting unsolicited e-mail to prospects, inviting them to join an MLM opportunity. See also spamming.

Encumbered Volume: Sales that cannot be counted as part of your group volume and therefore do not contribute toward your monthly quota for a particular achievement level. In many plans, the sales volume from a particular leg of your group will become encumbered the moment that leg breaks away.

Fax-on-Demand: A service that automatically faxes information to people who call a designated phone number. Network marketers use it to send prospecting and training information.

Front End: The upper levels or earliest stages of a compensation plan.

Frontline: The group of distributors whom you directly recruit and sponsor, and who are placed on the first level of your organization.

Frontloading (Front-End Loading): The practice of strong-arming distributors into stockpiling more product than they can realistically sell, by imposing excessive entrance requirements or monthly quotas.

Generation: A leg of your organization, headed by a breakaway distributor or—in a non-breakaway plan—headed by a distributor who has met some other executive qualification in the compensation plan.

Generational Bonus: A feature of some stairstep/breakaway plans that allows you to make money from people many levels below your ordinary pay range. In breakaways, for instance, it is a percentage of the generational volume of one of your breakaways. If you're in a six-level plan, and your breakaway is on your sixth level, you may collect a bonus on purchases up to twelve levels deep.

Generational Volume: The monthly sales produced by a particular generation or generational leg.

Ground Floor: The earliest stage of an MLM company start-up, right at or just after the official launch date.

GSV (Group Sales Volume): The monthly sales volume of your personal group.

(GV) Group Volume: The total volume of wholesale purchases made by your personal group in a given month.

Heavy Hitter: A top sales leader in an MLM company.

Home Meeting: An opportunity meeting held in a distributor's home, sometimes with the aid of a satellite conference or teleconference.

Hotel Meeting: An opportunity meeting held in a rented hotel conference room.

Infinite Bonus: A feature that theoretically creates infinite depth in a pay plan.

Infinite Depth: A feature of some compensation plans allowing distributors to draw earnings from deeper levels, below their ordinary pay range. The depth is not literally "infinite," since you earn less money the deeper you go, and various forms of breakage usually limit the depth to just a few levels. But some plans go as deep as 20–30 levels

Leader: A top achiever in an MLM downline.

Leg: A downline within your downline, usually headed by one of your frontline distributors.

Level: The vertical position of a distributor in your organization. If you recruit someone, he is enrolled on your first level. His recruits will be on your second level, and the recruits of his recruits on your third level.

Lukewarm Market: Prospects who are neither in your warm market nor your cold market, but somewhere in between. Can refer to people whom you have spoken to once or twice or people referred to you by others in your warm market.

Marketing Plan: An alternate term for compensation plan or pay plan.

Massive Action: A sustained, one-time barrage of prospecting activity.

Matrix: A comp plan that limits the number of people on your frontline, usually to two or three. For a full explanation, see chapter 19.

Max Out: A comp plan is said to be maxed out when you have put enough people in place, moving a sufficiently high level of monthly volume, to qualify you for the maximum level of commissions available in the plan.

MLM/Multilevel Marketing: Generally, an alternate term for network marketing. It can also be used to distinguish those particular network marketing plans that permit distributors to draw income from more than one level.

Momentum: The phase of a network marketing company's growth when sales and recruiting begin to grow at an exponential rate.

Monthly Volume Requirements: An alternate term for qualifications.

Multi-Affiliate Program: An affiliate program that allows affiliates to recruit other affiliates and to be paid multilevel commissions on sales of their recruits.

Network Marketing: Any form of selling that allows independent distributors to recruit other independent distributors and to draw a commission from the sales of those recruits.

Opportunity: The chance to join a network marketing distributorship, or another term for the distributorship itself.

Opportunity Meeting: A recruiting rally or business briefing held by MLM distributors for the purpose of presenting the opportunity to prospects.

Organization: That portion of your downline from which you are allowed to draw overrides and commissions. It includes all distributors placed on levels that fall within your pay range. In stairstep/breakaway plans, it would also include your breakaway legs.

OV (Organizational Volume): Monthly sales volume generated by your organization, through product purchases from the company.

Overrides: The monthly commission you receive from your breakaway legs.

Payout: The percentage of a company's total revenue that it pays out to distributors, in the form of overrides, commissions, and bonuses.

Pay Plan: An alternate term for compensation plan.

Pay Range: All levels of your downline from which your comp plan allows you to draw overrides and commissions.

Personal Group: All distributors in your pay range, whom you have personally sponsored, but who have not broken away.

PIN Number: A special code assigned to each distributor in an MLM company. When customers order from the company, they give the PIN number of the distributor who introduced them to the products. That way, distributors receive a commission from their customers' purchases, even if they take no part in the transaction.

Pre-Launch: The period just before an MLM company's official launch.

Prospect: A potential customer or recruit.

Prospecting: The process of seeking customers or recruits for your MLM business.

PSV (Personal Sales Volume): The volume of product that you personally sell in a given month.

PV (Personal Volume): The volume of product that you buy at wholesale from the company in a given month.

PV (Point Volume): An alternate term for bonus volume.

Pyramid Scheme: An illegal business that makes money by charging enrollment or membership fees, or by front-loading recruits into buying product they don't need. The rule of thumb is that if the last person in can't make money, it's a pyramid scheme. People who join early make money by getting a percentage of the fees from people who join after them, or by frontloading their recruits. But the last person in gets no fees or commissions, because there are no more recruits. In a legitimate MLM company, the last person in can always make money by buying product at wholesale and selling it to customers for a retail profit. A legitimate company has real customers buying and using its products. In a pyramid scheme, products are just a gimmick for frontloading, or an excuse to collect entrance or training fees.

Qualifications: Monthly quotas that distributors are required to meet, in order to qualify for a given achievement level. Quotas are usually set in terms of group and personal volume. Occasionally, there are recruiting quotas, requiring that you bring a certain number of people onto your frontline each month.

Qualified Executive: An alternate term for a breakaway distributor.

Qualifiers: A form of breakage. These are conditions in a comp plan that make it harder for distributors to meet their monthly quotas. One example would be a rule stating that the amount of commissions you can draw from your lowest levels is dependent on the number of qualified executives in your frontline.

Recruit: A prospect who has agreed to join your downline, or (if used as a verb) the act of prospecting someone to become a distributor.

Renewal Fee: A yearly membership fee paid to an MLM company, in order to maintain your status as a distributor. Fees must be small, since it is against the law for an MLM company to "sell" distributorships for profit.

Retail Profit: The spread between the wholesale price you pay for product, and the retail price at which you sell it to your customers. Nowadays, MLM distributors rarely take physical possession of the products they sell at retail, since customers buy direct from the company. But company computers still award a retail profit to distributors when customers use their PIN number to order.

Roll-Up: A feature in some plans stipulating that if you fail to qualify for commissions in a given month, because you did not meet your quota, you are declared inactive, and will receive no commissions from your downline that month. All the commissions you would otherwise have received "roll up"—i.e., are paid—to the next active distributor above you in the hierarchy.

Royalty: An alternate term for override.

Satellite Conference: A televised training session, business briefing, or recruiting rally broadcast by a network marketing company via closed-circuit satellite network. Distributors can watch the broadcast from home, invite prospects over to watch it, and can sometimes engage in live interactions with the conference participants by telephone.

Saturation: The theoretical point at which a network marketing company runs out of potential customers and recruits, and stops growing.

Scrutiny Phase: The phase of a successful company's growth, usually after it goes into momentum, when it is most likely to come under the scrutiny of journalists and government regulators. Only the strongest companies survive this phase.

Sifting and Sorting: The practice of quickly identifying the most promising prospects and focusing your recruiting efforts on them, while ignoring the rest.

Spamming: The practice of making unsolicited electronic pitches for your MLM opportunity on the Internet, usually through e-mail blasting but also through posts on message boards.

Sponsor: A distributor in an MLM company who recruits and trains another distributor. Used as a verb, it means to recruit and train another distributor.

Stairstep: An alternate term for an achievement level, or for a stairstep/breakaway compensation plan.

Stairstep/Breakaway: A type of compensation plan that requires distributors to meet monthly volume quotas, in order to qualify for an ascending series of achievement levels, or "stairsteps." When a distributor reaches a certain level, he "breaks away" from his sponsor's group. (See chapter 19 for a full explanation.)

Stockpiling: The practice of buying and hoarding more product than you can possibly sell, usually in an attempt to meet excessive monthly quotas, to qualify for commissions.

Teleconference: A recruiting rally or business briefing that is broadcast by telephone. Prospects are told to phone in at a certain time to hear the event. Distributors can also invite prospects to their homes and have them listen to the event on a speakerphone.

Three-Way Call: A prospecting technique that allows distributors to build a downline while training recruits. When a raw recruit wants to pitch a new prospect over the phone, he will patch his sponsor into the call. The sponsor gives the pitch while the recruit listens and learns. Three-way recruiting can also be done in person.

Transfer Buying: The practice of switching from one brand of a product to another. Network marketers usually prefer to sell products that lend themselves to transfer buying, in other words, that replace products the potential customer is already in the habit of using. The theory is that it is easier to get a customer to switch brands of a familiar product than to get him to use a completely new product.

Two-Level Plan: Another name for the compressed plan, derived from the fact that many compressed plans stack the bulk of their commissions (though not all their commissions) on the first two levels.

Unencumbered Volume: All sales volume from your organization that is counted toward your group volume and can be used to qualify for an achievement level. (See "Encumbered Volume.")

Unilevel: A type of compensation plan in which you must qualify for achievement levels, but in which people in your downline cannot break away.

Upline: All of the people above you in a network marketing organization. Also, an alternate term for sponsor.

Warm List: A list of personal contacts drawn up by new recruits that constitutes their warm market.

Warm Market: All potential prospects for your business whom you personally know, either because they are family members, friends, or business associates.

Wave 1: The "underground" phase of network marketing's evolution, roughly from 1945 to 1979, when the industry's legal status was murky and ambiguous. Wave 1 ended with the Federal Trade Commission's 1979 ruling that Amway—and, by extension, network marketing in general—was a legitimate business, not a pyramid scheme.

Wave 2: The "proliferation" phase of network marketing's evolution, roughly from 1980 to 1989. During this phase, the number of MLM start-ups skyrocketed, due to the advent of PC technology.

Wave 3: The "mass market" phase of network marketing's evolution, roughly from 1990 to 1999. Wave 3 saw the introduction of managerial and technological innovations, such as voice-mail and e-mail broadcasts, drop-shipping, teleconferences, three-way phone calls, satellite TV, and fax-on-demand, which made it easier for ordinary people to succeed as distributors.

Wave 4: The "universal" phase of network marketing's evolution, beginning roughly in the year 2000. During this phase, Internet technology, easier comp plans, and other extensions and outgrowths of the Wave 3 Revolution are beginning to bear fruit, resulting in the universal acceptance of MLM as an integral part of corporate America.

Wholesale Buyer: A person who enrolls as a distributor in order to obtain a wholesale discount but does not seek to build a business.

Wholesale Profit: The spread between the wholesale price you pay for product, and the higher wholesale price at which you sell it to your distributors. It is an old-fashioned concept, however, since MLM distributors rarely sell products at wholesale to their downlines anymore. Nowadays, network marketers receive a straight commission when people in their organization use their PIN numbers to order product direct from the company.

Width: The number of people in a distributor's frontline, or the number of people allowed in a distributor's frontline by the rules of the compensation plan.

INDEX